A PUBLIC FAITH

MICHAEL CROMARTIE is the vice president of the Ethics and Public Policy Center and director of its Evangelical Studies project. He is the editor of ten books including *Caesar's Coin Revisited, Creation at Risk, Disciples and Democracy, No Longer Exiles, Peace Betrayed?*, and *A Preserving Grace*.

A PUBLIC FAITH
Evangelicals and Civic Engagement

EDITED BY
Michael Cromartie

ESSAYS BY
*Nigel M. de S. Cameron, David Orgon Coolidge,
Michael Emerson, John C. Green, Allen D. Hertzke,
Mark J. Rozell, Jeffrey Satinover, Kurt Schaefer,
Amy L. Sherman, David Sikkink, Clyde Wilcox,
W. Bradford Wilcox, Rhys H. Williams and
R. Stephen Warner, John Wilson*

ROWMAN & LITTLEFIELD PUBLISHERS, INC.
Lanham • Boulder • New York • Oxford
ETHICS AND PUBLIC POLICY CENTER

9108541

ROWMAN & LITTLEFIELD PUBLISHERS, INC.

Published in the United States of America
by Rowman & Littlefield Publishers, Inc.
A Member of the Rowman & Littlefield Publishing Group
4501 Forbes Boulevard, Suite 200, Lanham, Maryland 20706
www.rowmanlittlefield.com

PO Box 317
Oxford
OX2 9RU, UK

Copublished with the
ETHICS AND PUBLIC POLICY CENTER
1015 Fifteenth Street NW, Washington, D.C., 20005
www.eppc.org

British Library Cataloguing in Publication Information Available

Library of Congress Cataloging-in-Publication Data

A public faith : evangelicals and civic engagement / edited by Michael
Cromartie.
        p. cm.
Includes bibliographical references and index.
   ISBN 0-7425-3100-7 (cloth : alk. paper)—ISBN 0-7425-3101-5 (pbk. :
alk. paper)
   1. Evangelicalism—United States—History. 2. Church and social problems—United
States. 3. United States—Church history. I. Cromartie, Michael.
   BR1642.U5P83 2003
   277.3'083—dc21

                                                    2003007440

Printed in the United States of America

⊖™ The paper used in this publication meets the minimum requirements of American
National Standard for Information Sciences—Permanence of Paper for Printed Library
Materials, ANSI/NISO Z39.48-1992.

In memory of

DAVID ORGON COOLIDGE
(1956–2002)

a seeker of justice and lover of mercy
who walked humbly with his God

Contents

Preface

Michael Cromartie

The electoral map of the 2000 presidential election showed a striking difference in the geographical location of voters for candidates Bush and Gore. In a two-color version, big blocks of red denoting states that went for Bush stretched across the heartland, while Gore's blue was concentrated along the East and West coasts. And the polarity extends far beyond politics. The heartlanders and the coastalites inhabit divergent social and religious worlds as well. The social critic David Brooks has observed that "we in the coastal metro Blue areas read more books and attend more plays than the people in the Red heartland . . . but don't ask us, please, what life in Red America is like. We don't know. We don't know who Tim LaHaye and Jerry B. Jenkins are, even though the novels they have co-written have sold about 40 million copies over the past few years. We don't know what James Dobson says on his radio program, which is listened to by millions. . . . We don't know what happens in megachurches on Wednesday evenings, and some of us couldn't tell you the difference between a fundamentalist and an evangelical, let alone describe what it means to be a Pentecostal" ("One Nation, Slightly Divisible," *The Atlantic Monthly,* December 2001).

The essays in this volume seek to shed light on the beliefs and values of conservative Protestants, who on the whole inhabit the American heartland. The authors address such topics as the family, homosexuality, bioethics, abortion, welfare reform, Charitable Choice, public schools, race relations, legal battles over same-sex marriage, international human rights, and the evolving influence of the Christian Right.

Many journalists and scholars believe all evangelicals fit nicely into a "Christian Right" frame of reference. As believers in fixed moral codes and a traditional understanding of the family, as strong opponents of abortion and homosexual practice, and as voters who overwhelmingly can be counted on to vote Republican, many evangelicals are indeed conservative in their views of theology, politics, and culture. But this "right wing" frame of reference does not explain the rapid and growing evangelical constituency concerned for international human rights, or the efforts to bridge the racial divide by such groups as the Southern Baptist Convention and Promise Keepers. Nor does it consider the growing charitable and social-relief enterprises of the evangelical world, or the worldwide prison-reform efforts of Charles Colson's Prison Fellowship ministry.

The attempt by evangelicals to shape domestic and foreign policy issues according to their own distinctive theological beliefs has generated impassioned public debate over the past three decades. The American public in general and the mass media in particular tend to think either that evangelical political influence is on the verge of total collapse (see, for instance, Paul Weyrich's comments after the Clinton impeachment hearings) or that it is about to take control of the entire political system (see, for instance, Bill Moyers's comments right after the 2002 election). The scholars in this volume strike a more reasonable note. They argue that evangelical influence in American civic and political life is significant but not to such a degree as to merit triumphalism from its adherents or alarm from its opponents.

These essays were first presented at a conference held in June 2001 at the Inn by the Sea in Cape Elizabeth, Maine. The conference was supported by a generous grant from the Pew Charitable Trusts; their support is greatly appreciated.

I would also like to thank two colleagues from the Ethics and Public Policy Center for their invaluable assistance. Senior editor Carol Griffith edited the conference papers with her usual superb skill. About fifteen years ago, a veteran reporter for *Time* who had worked with Carol at another magazine told me she was the finest editor he had ever met, and I gladly second his assessment. Laura Fabrycky's diligent assistance in organizing the conference and the papers, always with good cheer and high competence, is deeply appreciated.

This book is dedicated to the memory of David Orgon Coolidge, a beloved colleague and contributor to this volume. In his work as director of the Marriage Law project, Dave was a forceful, energetic, and effective champion of traditional marriage. He died from a brain tumor in March 2002. He is greatly missed.

Through its conferences and publications the Ethics and Public Policy Center strives to stimulate thoughtful discussions among political, religious, and cultural leaders. Our aim always is to foster a wiser moral and political debate across ideological barricades. We hope this book will encourage constructive thinking and fresh dialogue both within the evangelical community and among the wider communities concerned with the issues it addresses.

Correcting Misconceptions About Evangelicals and Civil Society

John Wilson

Revisionists typically announce themselves with a rapper's swagger, but for the most part the scholars who speak in this volume are exceedingly modest, even as they repeatedly demolish widely held assumptions about evangelical participation in civil society. They speak softly and carry a hard drive loaded with empirical research. John Green, for example, concludes that if all forms of civic engagement are taken into account, evangelicals compare favorably with mainline Protestants, black Protestants, and Catholics. But you would never guess from his low-key manner just how radically the evidence he presents contradicts the confident pronouncements of many leading participants in the civil-society conversation. Hence, to gain perspective on this inventory of evangelicals in civic life, we need to step back from the essays and look at the larger picture.

Conservative Protestants crop up again and again in the ongoing conversation about social capital, individualism, and community. They appear variously as fundamentalists, as evangelicals, and as zealots in the army of the Religious Right. They are usually talked *about* rather than talking. And principally they serve in two ways: first, as examples of a powerful threat to civil society or deliberative democracy or whatever the desirable state is to be called; and second, as apparent counterexamples to diagnoses of pervasive fragmentation and anomie in American society, counterexamples that the analyst will then proceed to reveal as flawed.

We can see how this plays out in the work of Stephen Macedo, Robert Putnam, and Robert Bellah, three influential voices in the civil-society debate.

John Wilson is the editor of *Books & Culture,* a bimonthly review that engages the contemporary world from a Christian perspective. Since 2000 he has edited the annual collection *The Best Christian Writing.*

1

The three share the sense of what Bellah and his co-authors call a "crisis of civic membership," but they frame this crisis in different ways, and the differences are significant for the way they see conservative Protestants.

THE AMBIGUOUS HANDSHAKE OF CIVIC LIBERALISM

Stephen Macedo's focus is political, though political in an expansive sense. In fact, he defines his program as "civic liberalism" because, while it "rests on a circumscribed range of public principles and reasons, . . . its implications are broader and deeper than the proponents of 'political liberalism' have typically allowed."[1] As he writes in *Diversity and Distrust: Civic Education in a Multicultural Democracy*, Macedo and his kindred spirits—most notably Amy Gutmann and Dennis Thompson in *Democracy and Disagreement*—are concerned with "the project of forming citizens in a liberal democracy."[2]

Where Macedo crucially differs from liberals of the past generation is in his frank admission of what this process of formation entails. Liberals have operated under the fiction that education in American civic identity is neutral with respect to the diverse values of American citizens. That fiction has been unmasked in two ways, Macedo suggests: first, by the increasing celebration of diversity for its own sake—under the banner of "multiculturalism," for instance—which leads inexorably to neglect of "shared liberal values and civic virtues"; and second, by the increasingly aggressive claims of fundamentalist Christians to win exemptions from certain demands of civic formation, as in the *Mozert* case, when a group of families in Hawkins County, Tennessee, wanted their children exempted from a reading program they found offensive to their religious values. (Macedo acknowledges that the *Mozert* families "asked school officials to allow their children to opt out of the reading program, and that program only, while remaining in the public schools. They agreed to cover the missed reading classes at home and have their children take the same statewide reading tests as other students." Nevertheless, Macedo finds their claims "weak" and insists that such exemptions must not be allowed.[3])

In short, while fundamentalists and the champions of "diversity" generally regard each other as enemies, both are guilty of undermining the common good—and the soft liberals who fail to see the consequences of a single-minded, uncritical devotion to the "freedom to choose among diverse ways of life" are exacerbating the problem.

This is the crisis as Macedo frames it. His solution is "a tough-minded version of liberalism," a "liberalism with spine" that is robustly confident of its virtues and thus frank to acknowledge its demands:

> Our civic project—which has a limited agenda and which is justified in terms of public values—nevertheless has broad and deep implications

for our lives as a whole, including all of our deepest moral and religious commitments. This statement seems paradoxical, but its truth is inescapable. The success and health of a liberal democratic constitutional order depend upon the religious beliefs and other deep moral convictions that citizens form and act upon. The success of our civic project relies upon a transformative project that includes the remaking of moral and religious communities.[4]

This paragraph from Macedo's preface bears careful rereading, particularly for its candor about the implications of his "civic project." Confronted by objections that public schools and civil institutions more generally are attempting to mold American values in ways that run counter to deeply held beliefs of religious conservatives, consensus liberals have typically pooh-poohed such fears. Religion, they suggest, occupies a separate sphere on which they have no designs. Not so, Macedo says. The success of civic liberalism *relies upon* nothing less than a project "that includes the remaking of moral and religious communities."

In case anyone has missed the significance of that ambition, Macedo drives it home again a few lines later: "Although this kind of liberal public justification"—that is, justification in terms of what Gutmann and Thompson call "mutually acceptable reasons"—"may not rest on a particular conception of religious truth, it must assume that whatever is true as a religious matter is consistent with and supportive of liberalism."[5] Civic liberalism is to be the arbiter of what "is true as a religious matter"; religious claims that are inconsistent with civic liberalism are untrue.

Having laid his cards on the table with admirable frankness and clarity, Macedo later hedges a bit. "The civic liberalism we have begun to explore," he writes, "offers a way of holding out a hand to religious believers and others who reject the comprehensive ideals sometimes associated with liberalism." He goes on to contrast civic liberalism with the totalizing "secular humanism" of John Dewey, who argued explicitly (and here Macedo is quoting Dewey) for "the subordination of churches to the state (sometimes falsely termed the *separation* of church and state)," with "state consciousness" ultimately assuming the role once reserved for religion.[6] So Macedo isn't proposing a totalitarian "state consciousness"? What a relief! Given the way civic liberalism cashes out, religious believers may be forgiven for wondering why, with friends like this, they need enemies.

Macedo's "transformative project" that includes the remaking of religious communities was also on view when he appeared on a panel at an Ethics and Public Policy Center forum in 2000. The subject was the case of the InterVarsity group at Tufts University that had excluded a member from a leadership role because she was a lesbian who openly rejected the group's understanding of biblical authority on homosexual practice.[7] In its initial judgment (which was under appeal at the time of the forum and was later reversed), the student committee with oversight of organizations at Tufts found this a violation of the university's non-discrimination policy and voted to "de-recognize" the Inter-Varsity group, in effect putting it out of business. Macedo agreed with the decision. Liberalism with a spine, remember?

A Corrective to Excesses

Do the writers in the present volume suggest some useful lines of re-sponse to Macedo and other scholars who promote some variant of civic liberalism? Emphatically, yes. Here are many examples from the thirteen chapters that follow.

1. David Coolidge's account of successful campaigns against same-sex mar-riage in Alaska, California, and Nebraska (chapter five) suggests that many evangelicals are well aware of the need to deploy "public reasons" rather than theological arguments in public-policy debates. Confirmation on that score can also be found in a source outside the essays: David French's book *A Sea-son for Justice: Defending the Rights of the Christian Home, Church, and School.* French, a lawyer who specializes in First Amendment religion-clause litigation, serves as counsel for InterVarsity Christian Fellowship's Religious Freedom Crisis Team. In recounting the ultimate success of the InterVarsity group at Tufts, French shows that it was precisely by appeal to public reasons—espe-cially the basic principle of reciprocity—that the student committee was per-suaded to overturn its original ruling.[8]

At the same time, Coolidge's essay also shows that the two approaches are not mutually exclusive, as Macedo wrongly argues. Consider Coolidge's ac-count of the Nebraska campaign against same-sex marriage, which ran on two separate tracks—one appealing directly to theological authority, the other self-consciously based on "public reasons." As John G. West, Jr., has shown in his indispensable book *The Politics of Revelation and Reason,* from the begin-nings of American democracy, evangelicals engaged in the business of civic life have appealed *both* to the principles of natural reason—Gutmann and Thompson's "mutually acceptable reasons"—and to the truths of Christian rev-elation.[9] West recounts a vivid case in point: the unjustly forgotten campaign against the removal of the Cherokees under the Jackson administration, a campaign inspired by the writings of the evangelical missionary Jeremiah Evarts. Choosing to emphasize one approach rather than the other is a matter of prudential judgment, and evangelicals will often disagree among themselves, as in the campaigns Coolidge describes.

2. David Sikkink's report on evangelicals and schooling (chapter 10) also poses a challenge to Macedo. Sikkink finds that, far from isolating evangelicals in "religious cocoons," Christian schools and home-schooling "provide a social

context that draws parents into networks marked by trust and solidarity, and sends them out into political and nonpolitical forms of civic life." Macedo's fears about the civic consequences of schooling that isn't governed exclusively by the norms of civic liberalism seem greatly exaggerated.

Much of Macedo's *Diversity and Distrust* concerns the role of public schools in civic formation, and so it is striking that he virtually ignores the growing home-schooling movement. The closest he comes to considering the subject is in the context of calls for public-school reform and the notion that parents should be able to decide what is best for their children. Macedo quotes Amy Gutmann in response:

> History suggests that without state provision or regulation of education, children will be taught neither mutual respect among persons nor rational deliberation among ways of life. To save their children from future pain, especially the pain of eternal damnation, parents have historically shielded their children from diverse associations, convinced them that all other ways of life are sinful, and implicitly fostered (if not explicitly taught them) disrespect for people who are different.[10]

To which Macedo adds, "This may be slightly overstated, but it contains an important element of truth."

Without too much of a stretch, one could infer a judgment about home-schooling from this. And here we come to one of the most important ways in which the essays in this book provide a corrective to the excesses of the civil-society debate: the contrast between *ex cathedra* pronouncements and the patient research that underlies Sikkink's essay and indeed this volume as a whole. As Mitchell Stevens shows in *Kingdom of Children: Culture and Controversy in the Homeschooling Movement,* one need not be an evangelical or a fundamentalist or indeed a believer of any stripe to do justice to the realities of home-schooling—realities that aren't mapped by the tidy boundaries of Macedo's civic liberalism.

PUTNAM AND BELLAH: EVANGELICALS AND SOCIAL CAPITAL

Probably more than any other scholars, Robert Putnam and Robert Bellah have shaped the debate on civil society—Putnam with his celebrated 1995 article "Bowling Alone" and the massive book that followed five years later under the same title, plus many speeches and TV and radio appearances (he is a highly animated and witty presence onstage); Bellah with *Habits of the Heart,* co-written with four others and first published in 1985, and the follow-up volume *The Good Society,* published in 1991. Both Putnam and Bellah deplore a loss of social capital in America, and both consider the extent to which evangelicalism has mitigated that loss. But there are significant differences between them.

Putnam and "Bowling Alone"

Putnam's thesis doesn't need recounting here.[11] He has been criticized on matters large (such as the elasticity of the notion of "social capital") and small. Still, his book has had an enormous impact. What should be registered here for the benefit of readers who know the thesis but haven't slogged through the 400-plus pages of text (plus 90 pages of notes in tiny type) that make up *Bowling Alone* is Putnam's near-fanatical disinclination to let stand without challenge any trend, no matter how modest, that appears to contradict the megatrend he's tracking—that is, the loosening of social bonds and the decline of civic engagement over the past thirty or forty years. That makes his treatment of religion in America, and evangelicalism in particular, all the more significant.

"Churches and other religious organizations," Putnam writes, "have a unique importance in American civil society. America is one of the most religiously observant countries in the contemporary world." So far so good. Indeed, "faith communities in which people worship together are arguably the single most important repository of social capital in America." Moreover, "trends in civic engagement are closely tied to changing patterns of religious involvement."[12] But if, "measured by the yardstick of private beliefs, Americans' religious commitment has been reasonably stable over the last half century," doesn't this constitute a striking *exception* to the "bowling alone" megatrend?

No. Mark that slippery phrase "measured by the yardstick of private beliefs," and underscore "private." Putnam marshals evidence intended to show that, in fact, religious participation has declined significantly over the last three or four decades. (Much of this evidence will strike many observers of American religion as inconclusive at best, and in some cases clearly unpersuasive.) But what about conservative Protestants? On the distinction between evangelicals and fundamentalists, Putnam is confused. At one point he seems to suggest that evangelicals are simply lineal descendants of fundamentalists who have moved from the boondocks to the city. Elsewhere, in a note, he more or less throws up his hands, implying that the two terms are largely interchangeable. Whoever they are, he acknowledges, fundamentalists and evangelicals *have* experienced growth during this period when religious participation in general has sharply declined. Yet he quickly discounts the impact of this growth on social capital by quoting sociologist Robert Wuthnow: "whereas the mainline churches participated in progressive social betterment programs during the first half of the twentieth century, evangelical churches focused more on individual piety."[13]

But wait a minute. Wuthnow's comment refers to "the first half of the twentieth century," not to the period with which we are concerned, which is roughly from the 1960s to the present. Putnam's tendency to massage the evidence is painfully apparent here. Indeed, the closer one looks at his treatment of evangelicals, the more his unfamiliarity with the subject and his overreliance on a handful of secondary sources become clear. There's no animus in his account—not at all. He simply doesn't know the territory.

Another telling example comes in the concluding chapter, when Putnam discusses megachurches in connection with the prospects for "another Great Awakening":

> Megachurches, to take a single example, use contemporary marketing and entertainment techniques to craft an accessible religious experience for their typically suburban, middle-class market. . . . While their church services, by dint of size if nothing else, often seem impersonal and theologically bland, megachurch leaders are savvy social capitalists, organizing small group activities that build personal networks and mix religion and socializing (even bowling teams!). Meanwhile, in a different portion of the religious spectrum, . . . evangelical and fundamentalist churches (along with their counterparts among Jews and other religious traditions) constitute one of the most notable exceptions to the general decline in social capital that I have traced in this book.[14]

Surprisingly, evangelical and fundamentalist churches have here been promoted to the category of "notable exceptions," while in the chapter devoted to religious participation their apparently exceptional status was severely deconstructed. But more surprising is Putnam's assumption that "megachurch" and "evangelical" (or "megachurch" and "fundamentalist") are mutually exclusive terms. Is it possible that the author of *Bowling Alone* has never heard of Willow Creek and the Willow Creek Association, not to mention the many other evangelical megachurches? And why does he suppose that services in megachurches are "often . . . theologically bland"? In my experience, the opposite is more likely to be true.

The point of all this is not to belabor inaccuracies. Rather, it is to show that in one of the most influential contemporary treatments of social capital, there is a pervasive lack of grip on evangelicals. And so readers of *Bowling Alone* should be sent on to the present volume as a corrective.

Bellah and "Habits of the Heart"

Where Putnam's take on civil society is at once pragmatic and framed by unapologetically old-fashioned moral exhortation verging on the corny, Bellah's is finally religious. Bellah is one of the foremost sociologists of religion of the past half-century, a man of extraordinarily deep learning and subtle intelligence. Having rejected the Protestantism of his youth, first for a Marxist-tinged perspective and then for the vantage point of the free-agent sociologist who understands everyone else's beliefs but is not tied down himself, Bellah came in later years to a new appreciation of the transcendent, albeit in the guise of "symbolic realism."

Habits of the Heart thus helped to initiate the "return to religion" that has been one of the most striking developments in the academic world over the last fifteen years—a return in the sense that religious perspectives are allowed into conversations from which they had previously been excluded.[15] Bellah and his co-authors combined an insightful survey of the contemporary malaise that triggered the civil-society debate with occasionally vatic pronouncements that take in long reaches of history

In Bellah's telling, the rot set in at the very beginning of the American experiment, a kind of Original Sin whose consequences we are reaping today. The religious language that infuses the concluding peroration of *Habits of the Heart* can be unsettling for readers for whom such language has a specific content:

> We will need to remember that we did not create ourselves, that we owe what we are to the communities that formed us, and to what Paul Tillich called "the structure of grace in history" that made such communities possible. . . .
>
> We have imagined ourselves a special creation, set apart from other humans. In the late twentieth century, we see that our poverty is as absolute as that of the poorest of nations. We have attempted to deny the human condition in our quest for power after power. It would be well for us to rejoin the human race, to accept our essential poverty as a gift, and to share our material wealth with those in need.[16]

For many readers of *Habits of the Heart,* those words had a prophetic quality—a prophecy tragically fulfilled, perhaps, on September 11, 2001. But for others, Bellah's judgments sounded very much like the righteous rhetoric of the sixties—the denunciations of "Amerika"—recast in quasi-theological form: the total depravity of America. Is it true that most Americans of our time—sinners all, to be sure—imagine themselves "a special creation, set apart from other humans"? Can it rightly be said—even with poetic license—that we Americans need to "rejoin the human race"?

Evangelicals occupy a curious place in this account of America. On the one hand, they have not forgotten the language of sin and grace that Bellah respects, the language he has appropriated for his overarching vision. And Bellah is fair-minded enough to grant them a considerable measure of respect. So, for instance, when *Habits of the Heart* considers the congregation of Pastor Larry Beckett (who describes his church as "independent, conservative, and evangelical, and as neither liberal nor fundamentalist"), Bellah acknowledges that this congregation "is a warm and loving one. . . . the whole community has the feeling of a family. . . . members practice the virtues of their biblical ethic, learning to put the needs of others before their own. For Larry Beckett and the members of his congregation, biblical Christianity provides an alternative to the utilitarian individualist values of this world." This would seem to be a stunning affirmation of a powerful countertrend to all that Bellah deplores. But judgment falls swiftly, beginning in the next sentence:

> But that alternative, appealing precisely because it is "real clear," does not go very far in helping them understand their connection to the world or the society in which they live. . . . To "follow the Scriptures and the words of Jesus" provides a clear, but narrow, morality centered on family and personal life. . . . But outside the sphere of personal morality, the evangelical church has little to say about wider social commitments. Indeed, the sect draws together those who have found a personal relationship to Christ into a special loving community, and while it urgently seeks to have everyone make the same commitment, it separates its members off from attachment to the wider society. Morality becomes personal, not social; private, not public.[17]

A few pages later, after another critique of "religious conservatives" in the same vein, Bellah contrasts their narrow, privatized, literalist Christianity with the historic role of the mainline churches in American society. With far less excuse than Putnam, because he knows the territory better, Bellah has reproduced the clichés trotted out by all those who simply don't like evangelicals very much, for whatever reason. After all the fieldwork, all the interviews that went into *Habits of the Heart,* this is the result. You can't see what you don't want to see.

But for those who have eyes to see, there's plenty of evidence to the contrary, and much can be found in *A Public Faith*. Essay after essay in this volume refutes the notion that "the evangelical church has little to say about wider social commitments," that it offers only a "narrow morality centered on family and personal life." For starters, Bellah and his co-authors should read Amy Sherman on evangelicals and Charitable Choice, Allen Hertzke on evangelicals and international engagement, and Rhys Williams and Stephen Warner on urban evangelicalism. Later they might turn to Ram Cnaan's brilliant new book *The Invisible Caring Hand: American Congregations and the Provision of Welfare,* which should prompt Putnam and Bellah alike to revise their understanding of conservative Protestants and civic engagement.

Williams and Warner, it should be said, offer a superb model for future research. Unencumbered by previously formed conclusions, they look with curious eyes at urban youth ministries in Chicago and find all sorts of interesting things—not least, the surprising combination they observed in a number of Latino-based youth programs: strongly conservative theology and sharply drawn moral boundaries with a socially liberal outlook and inclusion across racial-ethnic-class boundaries. And like other contributors to this volume, they show that "outsiders" as well as "insiders" can perceptively report on what is really going on among evangelicals; indeed, *both* perspectives are essential. These essays are representative, on a small scale, of a growing number of first-rate ethnographies of conservative Protestants, including books such as Mitchell Stevens's *Kingdom of Children*, the study of home-schoolers (both religious and non-) mentioned above, and Susan Friend Harding's *The Book of Jerry Falwell: Fundamentalist Language and Politics*.

The alternative to half-baked characterizations of evangelicals and civic engagement is not, of course, some form of evangelical triumphalism, and nothing in the essays that follow underwrites a triumphalist attitude. Several writers offer sharp reminders of evangelical failures, as when Brad Wilcox, surveying resistance and accommodation to "family modernization," notes that conservative Protestant divorce rates are slightly higher than the national average. Nevertheless, taken together with Cnaan's book and a good deal more emerging scholarship, these essays decisively correct the misconceptions about evangelicals that have been given currency in the civil-society debate.

CHAPTER ONE

Evangelical Protestants and Civic Engagement: An Overview

John C. Green

Evangelical Protestants are at the center of the debate over the role of religion in the civic arena. One reason for their visibility on this question is, of course, the size and vitality of the evangelical community, but another is the recent re-engagement of evangelicals in civic affairs, from social services to electioneering. Numerous observers continue to be surprised by this engagement, and many are uncomfortable with it, in principle or in fact.[1] Although much of the commentary on it comes from outside the evangelical community, there is no shortage of discussion among evangelicals themselves.[2] This debate over the role evangelicals should play in civic affairs is part of a broader set of questions involving religion and the reconstruction of civil society.[3]

Some empirical questions present themselves. What are the actual attitudes of evangelicals toward civic engagement? How actively engaged is the evangelical community in the civic arena? And how do evangelicals compare in this regard with members of other religious traditions? This essay will offer some preliminary answers to these questions. A special set of surveys reveals that evangelicals are open to a broad scope of civic engagement by religious people, probably more so than a generation ago. They are engaged in a wide variety of areas, forms, and venues of civic affairs. And though they often lag behind other religious traditions in specific ways, these differences are often quite small. Overall, evangelicals nearly match mainline Protestants, Catholics, and black Protestants in level of faith-based engagement.

John C. Green is director of the Ray C. Bliss Institute of Applied Politics at the University of Akron. His research interests include American political parties, campaign finance, and religion and politics. He is co-author of *The Bully Pulpit: The Politics of Protestant Clergy* (1997) and *Religion and the Culture Wars: Dispatches From the Front* (1996).

Like other religious traditions, evangelical Protestants are characterized by distinctive religious beliefs. Although the exact details have varied somewhat within the tradition and over time, the core religious values include a belief in Jesus Christ as the only means of salvation, a high view of scriptural authority, belief in the need for individual conversion, and an imperative to proselytize.[4] These core values have given evangelicalism a highly individualistic cast (compared with other Christian traditions), including a stress on voluntary participation in religious and communal life. Such individualism has produced an extraordinary social energy, sometimes directed toward private life and the personal salvation of believers, and at other times directed toward public life and the political goals of the faithful.[5]

The Continuum of Civic Engagement

Evangelicals have always had diverse views on how their faith should be applied to civic life, and the full range is visible in the current debate over their civic engagement.[6] The continuum of such approaches would begin with religious people *having no public role* in solving social problems and end with religious people *seeking political solutions* to social problems. Two intermediate steps are worth noting because of their relevance to evangelicals: *helping individual fellow believers* solve their personal problems, and *helping individual non-believers* solve theirs. These four options build upon one another. All presume a significant social presence of churches and other religious institutions, and each step widens the scope of civic engagement by religious people.

At one end of this continuum, some evangelicals have seen their faith as almost entirely a private matter. A strong emphasis on personal piety combined with a dispensational theology (the belief that God deals with mankind in distinctive ways during various time periods or "dispensations") led some evangelicals to eschew contact with the broader society, and to remain aloof from politics.[7] Sometimes even the basic duties of citizenship were regarded as suspect. Here a focus on each individual's relationship with God preempts all forms of social involvement save church activity narrowly defined. Perhaps the best example of this tendency was among fundamentalists, who argued for a strict separation of the faithful from a "world" that was so corrupt as to be beyond redemption by human agency.[8] This separatist outlook influenced the approach of many evangelicals to civic affairs roughly from the mid-1920s until after World War II.[9] Although strong proponents of a strict separatism are rare today, it is still part of the debate over evangelical civic engagement.

The next step along the continuum of civic engagement, helping fellow believers solve their personal problems, has always been common among evangelicals.[10] Here the essentially private nature of the faith is understood to have social consequences through the agency of individual believers. The converted are more likely to behave in a socially desirable fashion, turning away from sin and toward productive endeavors. Therefore churches and other religious institutions have an important indirect social impact: the redemption of individuals is in part the redemption of society.[11] From this perspective, civic engagement is properly limited to generating believers and encouraging them to live according to their beliefs. Broader social engagement, and particularly political action, is viewed with great skepticism, although the faithful are often encouraged to meet the minimum duties of citizenship.[12] Today advocates of a strong and distinctive evangelical subculture tend to hold some version of this position.[13]

The third step along the continuum of civic engagement, helping nonbelievers as well as believers solve their personal problems, has always been popular in some segments of the evangelical community and has become more so in the last generation.[14] Here faith is understood to have both a private and a public character: believers are expected to seek converts and also to practice love and mercy toward their neighbors. From this perspective, the faithful are required to reach out beyond their own communities and minister to the needy, helping them solve their personal problems.[15] Civic engagement thus extends to participating in nongovernmental social programs, and building the organizations that can provide them. Such organizations contribute to a vital "third sector" of society and can "mediate" between the government and the individual.[16] This perspective often includes an expanded view of Christian citizenship but is skeptical of extensive involvement in politics. Today advocates of a distinctive evangelical presence in civil society tend to hold some version of this position.[17]

The other end of the continuum of civic engagement, political involvement to solve social problems, is newly popular among some evangelicals. This perspective was common in the nineteenth and early twentieth centuries, disappeared, and then dramatically reappeared in the 1970s.[18] The best-known agent of this reappearance is the Christian Right, but many more moderate and liberal evangelicals share this perspective.[19] Here the faithful have a responsibility to advocate for religious values in the political process, whether those values are part of traditional morality, social justice, or some combination of the two. A key assumption is that some social problems cannot be solved by religious or nongovernmental efforts alone and require governmental intervention.[20] Evangelical voices should therefore join with other religious and secular advocates in debating public policy.[21] Needless to say, there is also disagreement over the substantive ends of politics: although most evangelicals are politically conservative, the community is hardly a political monolith.[22]

Although evangelicals have arrived at these four perspectives with reference to their special religious values, none of the four is unique to evangelicals. Other religious traditions have debated these same options, often with a com-

parable range of results.[23] To give just one example: some Protestant modern-
ists have argued that faith is essentially a matter of private conscience, with no
appropriate role in public affairs, while others have claimed that the essence
of faith is right relationships with other people, and therefore faith requires a
comprehensive involvement in politics.[24] Thus, religious people from different
faith backgrounds may arrive at the same view of civic engagement for different reasons.

Implicit in this continuum are disagreements over the forms, areas, and
venues for civic engagement by the faithful. In this regard, religious activity
within churches is a matter of some controversy: should public worship be
considered a form of private activity, a precursor to civic engagement, or a
form of such engagement in its own right? Some analysts argue that the presence in society of churches is itself a critical form of social capital, but others
claim that religious activity within churches tends to preclude broader civic
engagement by absorbing the time and resources of believers. There is more
agreement over the value of social programs sponsored by religious organizations, and some scholars also think that religious activity has a spill-over effect
on secular social programs. In addition, some disagreement exists over the
areas in which religious people should be involved, ranging from working
with traditional charities to registering voters.[25] And even among those who
strongly advocate political involvement by the faithful, there are disputes over
its appropriate goals. Should the political goals of religious people be narrow,
stressing the expression of special values or the solution to specific problems?
Or should the goals be broader, encompassing the transformation of society?[26]

The Surveys

Some answers to these questions are to be found in two surveys conducted
at the University of Akron on behalf of the Ethics and Public Policy Center and
sponsored by a grant from the Pew Charitable Trusts. One was a mail survey of
evangelical elites—a wide variety of leaders of evangelical institutions (both
church and parachurch) as well as prominent journalists, intellectuals, and
public figures closely associated with evangelicalism. This survey, conducted
in the summer and fall of 2000, produced 356 usable responses, for a return
rate of 51 percent. There appears to be no systematic bias in the responses in
terms of region, gender, or type of leader surveyed.

The other was a telephone survey of the American public in the spring of
2000 that included a random sample of 4,004 adult Americans plus a 1,000-
person over-sample of white southern adults. The initial cooperation rate was
46 percent. These respondents were re-surveyed immediately after the 2000
presidential election; this effort produced 2,925 post-election interviews. The
two samples were then combined and weighted on the basis of demographic
data from the 2000 U.S. Census, producing 6,000 weighted pre-election cases

and 3,000 weighted post-election cases. Although the surveys of the evangelical elites and the public differed in many respects, they also asked a number of identical questions.

Attitudes Toward Civic Engagement

A good place to begin is with the continuum of approaches to civic engagement outlined above. The first item in Table 1 reports which of the four approaches the evangelical elites and public felt best represented their own position. The first column reveals that the elites tended to favor a broad scope of engagement. For example, only 1 percent agreed that religion was a private matter, and less than one-fifth felt that religious people should focus on helping their co-religionists solve their own problems. Thus four-fifths of evangelical elites affirmed a role for religious people beyond the confines of their own communities. However, the elites were evenly divided on the scope of public engagement: some two-fifths believed that religious people should help indi-

---

TABLE 1

ATTITUDES TOWARD CIVIC ENGAGEMENT:
EVANGELICAL ELITES AND PUBLIC

	Evangelical Elites	Evangelical Public
Religious people should:		
Not try to solve social problems—religion is a private matter	1 %	12 %
Help co-religionists solve their own problem	19	38
Help other individuals solve their own problems	39	34
Engage in politics to solve social problems	41	16
Religious people should:		
Separate to avoid evil	2	8
Engage to fight evil	98	92
If enough people are brought to Christ, social ills will take care of themselves:		
Agree	51	73
Neutral	9	12
Disagree	40	15
Religious people's political goals should be:		
None—stay out of politics	14	15
To proclaim special values	19	19
To solve specific problems	18	39
To transform society	49	27

SOURCE: 2000 Survey of Evangelical Elites, University of Akron; Third National Survey of Religion and Politics, University of Akron, 2000.

viduals beyond their religious communities solve their own problems, and another two-fifths supported political activity to solve social problems.

Although we do not have comparable survey data from the past, today's evangelical elites seem to be more supportive of political involvement than their counterparts of a generation ago, and there may also be an increase in support for helping individuals in the society at large.[27]

However, the individualistic cast of evangelicalism is still evident in these results, with six of ten elites choosing non-political options. As one might expect, many of the elites had complex and sophisticated views of these issues. For example, one respondent chose all four options, but for different purposes: a private role for religion in spiritual matters; help for fellow believers regarding personal behavior; help for non-believers on the grounds of charity; and political activity on questions of social order.

What about the evangelical public? The second column in Table 1 shows less support for civic engagement there than among the evangelical elites. Approximately one-eighth of the evangelical public regarded religion as a private matter, and nearly two-fifths chose helping co-religionists solve their own problems—more than twice the proportion among the elites. So on balance just one-half of the evangelical public advocated civic engagement beyond the confines of their religious community. Unlike the elites, the evangelical public showed a strong bias against political involvement, with about one-third choosing to help other individuals solve their own problems, and only about one-sixth favoring political involvement. These numbers may also reflect increased support for a broader scope of civic engagement than in the past, but the evangelical public is still strongly individualistic in its approach to civic engagement.

The next two items in Table 1 amplify these findings. First, when asked if religious people should "separate from the world to avoid evil" or "engage in the world to fight evil," just 2 percent of the elites chose the separatist option. The evangelical public had nearly the same response, with just 8 percent holding the separatist view. Even self-identified fundamentalists among the evangelical elites and masses strongly rejected separatism. Hence, the influence of separatist views in the debate over evangelical civic engagement is now largely academic.[28]

However, the next item again reveals the continuing potency of evangelical individualism. When asked if they agreed or disagreed with the statement "if enough people are brought to Christ, social ills will take care of themselves," just over one-half of the elites agreed with this statement, with two-fifths disagreeing. The evangelical public was less divided, with almost three-quarters agreeing with the statement and only about one-sixth disagreeing. If evangelicals are no longer separatists, then they still regard conversion as efficacious in solving social problems, and this view is especially strong in the public.

The final item in Table 1 addresses the goals of political activity, asking about the breadth of goals religious people should pursue if they engage in politics. About one-sixth of evangelical elites and public were strongly opposed to any political activity by religious people. Almost one-fifth of each group believed that religious people should focus on "proclaiming their special values" in the public square. Nearly one-fifth of the elites chose solving specific problems, a position expressed by almost two-fifths of the public— roughly twice the proportion. In contrast, nearly one-half of the elites favored transforming society, while only a little more than one-quarter of the evangelical public opted for such broad political goals.

Thus evangelical elites not only were disposed toward a broader scope of civic engagement, and especially political involvement, but also tended to favor broad political goals. By comparison, the evangelical public was less inclined toward civic engagement, with only a minority opting for political involvement or broad political goals.

How do evangelicals compare with members of other religious traditions in America? Table 2 (page 18) compares the evangelical public with black Protestants, mainline Protestants, and Roman Catholics on these questions; the results for the entire sample, including non-Christians and secular respondents, are listed in the final column as a point of reference. First, note that more mainline Protestants and Catholics claimed religion as a private matter than evangelicals; mainliners and Catholics were also less likely to support political involvement of religious people. However, roughly the same proportion of evangelicals, mainliners, and Catholics chose helping co-religionists solve their personal problems, and exactly the same proportion opted for helping other individuals solve their own problems. The modal evangelical response to this question, then, was the same as that of mainliners and Catholics.

Black Protestants represented an exception to these patterns. Nearly one-third chose political involvement over the other options. Surely this reflects the greater politicization of the black church.[29] But note that more than one-half of black Protestants also chose helping co-religionists or other individuals solve their own problems, and black Protestants showed the largest support for separatism. In addition, black Protestants matched evangelicals in agreeing that conversion would remedy social ills, a position accepted by only about one-half—and rejected by nearly one-third—of mainline Protestants and Catholics. Overall, these patterns reveal both historic differences among the major Christian traditions and the individualistic character of the American public writ large.

There were also clear differences in the political goals supported by the major religious traditions. One-sixth of evangelicals, compared to slightly more than the one-tenth of black Protestants, believed religious people should stay out of politics. In contrast, nearly one-third of mainliners and Catholics opposed political

TABLE 2

ATTITUDES TOWARD CIVIC ENGAGEMENT:
EVANGELICALS AND OTHER RELIGIOUS GROUPS

	Evangelical Protestant	Black Protestant	Mainline Protestant	Roman Catholic	Entire Sample
Religious people should:					
Not try to solve problems— religion is a private matter	12 %	11 %	15 %	19 %	14 %
Help co-religionists solve their own problems	38	27	40	37	30
Help other individuals solve their own problems	34	31	34	34	37
Engage in politics to solve social problems	16	31	11	10	17
Religious people should:					
Separate to avoid evil	8	13	8	9	12
Engage to fight evil	92	87	92	91	88
If enough people are brought to Christ, social ills will take care of themselves:					
Agree	73	75	50	46	60
Neutral	12	12	19	22	16
Disagree	15	13	31	32	24
Religious people's political goals should be:					
None—stay out of politics	15	11	32	32	27
To proclaim special values	19	12	11	14	15
To solve specific problems	39	40	42	40	38
To transform society	27	37	15	14	20
Religion is important to political thinking:					
Important	60	64	37	34	42
Of some importance	21	17	26	27	22
Less important	19	19	37	39	36
High engagement of religion in civic affairs	53	61	43	41	42

SOURCE: Third National Survey of Religion and Politics, University of Akron, 2000.

involvement by religious people, more than twice the proportion of evangelicals and roughly three times that of black Protestants. At the other end of the scale, about one-quarter of evangelicals and more than one-third of black Protestants adopted the broad goal of transforming society, a position taken by less than one-sixth of mainliners and Catholics. There was, however, some agreement across these large religious traditions on the value of narrow political goals: some two-fifths of each group agreed with political involvement to solve specific problems. The least popular goal of proclaiming special values got somewhat more support from evangelicals than in the other traditions.

The next-to-last item in Table 2 is the respondents' report of the relevance of their faith to their political thinking. This question is not directly related to civic engagement; since religious views might lead one to stay out of politics altogether,[30] but it does help to put the patterns in Table 2 in context. Some three-fifths of evangelicals and black Protestants claimed that their faith was important to their political thinking, and only about one-fifth claimed it was of little importance. In this they contrast sharply with mainline Protestants and Catholics, where less than two-fifths claimed their religion was important to their political thinking and about an equal proportion reported it was not. This suggests that much of the opposition to political involvement of religious people by these two large religious traditions may result from secular outlooks rather than religious opposition to civic engagement.[31]

The final entry in Table 2—"High engagement of religion in civic affairs"— offers a summary of these findings: the percentage of each group that scored above the mean on a simple additive index of these attitudes toward civic engagement among religious people.[32] Nor surprisingly, black Protestants came in first, with some three-fifths scoring high on the index. Evangelicals were second, with just over one-half, substantially ahead of mainline Protestants and Catholics at about two-fifths.

Taken together, Tables 1 and 2 reveal significant support for a broad scope for civic engagement among evangelical elites. The evangelical public is somewhat less inclined to this point of view, well behind black Protestants but ahead of mainliners and Catholics. In all these respects, there is considerable skepticism toward political involvement by religious people, and the most support for helping individuals solve their personal problems.

Levels of Religious Engagement

All these attitudes toward civic engagement presume a significant social presence of churches and other religious institutions. Otherwise these questions would be moot. Thus it is worthwhile to review the level of religious engagement for the evangelical public. (We did not put the same question on religious activity to the evangelical elites because previous research had indicated that it was uniformly high.[33]) Table 3 (page 20) shows the level of reported activity for ten measures of religious engagement by the evangelical public and by members of other religious traditions.

We begin with the frequency of prayer outside of worship, a very common religious behavior. Prayer is, of course, a form of private religiosity, but it can

TABLE 3
ENGAGEMENT IN RELIGIOUS ACTIVITIES:
EVANGELICALS AND OTHER RELIGIOUS GROUPS

	Evangelical Protestant	Black Protestant	Mainline Protestant	Roman Catholic	Entire Sample
Pray outside of church at least once a day	8 %	85 %	60 %	58 %	61 %
Formal member of local congregation	71	79	58	68	52
Attend worship once a week or more	57	60	35	44	41
Participate in activities at church once a week or more	55	65	40	40	43
Give 5% or more of annual income to religious groups	49	60	30	23	33
Particpate in a small group once a month or more	45	50	29	20	32
Support missions	39	29	24	25	25
Hold church leadership role	24	33	19	10	20
Support religious media	18	22	8	8	11
Volunteer for programs outside of congregation	16	18	10	10	12
High engagement in church activities	65	77	44	44	47

SOURCE: Third National Survey of Religion and Politics, University of Akron, 2000.

also have important social consequences. After all, praying for other people, including public officials, can be considered a form of civic engagement for those who regard intercessory prayer as efficacious. A clear majority of all the groups in Table 3 reports praying at least once a day. Black Protestants were the most prayerful (85 percent), followed closely by evangelicals (80 percent), with mainline Protestants (60 percent) and Catholics (58 percent) markedly less so. With a few minor exceptions, this pattern holds for the rest of Table 3, and is consistent with previous research.[34]

The next three items assess participation in local congregations. Some seven out of ten evangelicals claimed formal membership in a congregation; almost three-fifths reported attending worship once a week or more, and more than one-half participated in at least one church activity a week beyond worship.

While these self-reports must be viewed with some skepticism, evangelicals and black Protestants claimed substantially more religious engagement than mainline Protestants or Catholics. This pattern extended to participating in small groups (45 percent for evangelicals), serving as church leader (24 percent), and volunteering for programs outside of church (16 percent). Finally, evangelicals report more financial support for their church (49 percent gave 5 percent or more of annual family income), missions (39 percent contributed), and religious media (18 percent contributed). Only on contributing to missions did evangelicals exceed black Protestants in religious engagement.

The last entry in Table 3 summarizes religious engagement by reporting the percentage of each group above the mean on an additive index of ten religious activities.[35] Black Protestants reported the most engagement (77 percent), followed by evangelicals (65 percent), and then mainline Protestants and Catholics (each with 44 percent).

Civic Priorities: Evangelical Elites and Public

Next the survey measured the priority that evangelical elites gave to various kinds of social programs sponsored by religious and/or secular agencies and then compared their views with the reported activities of the evangelical public. Table 4 (page 22) lists the results for fourteen areas of activity: the first column gives the percentage of the evangelical elites who claimed such activities should be given "top priority," and the second column gives the rank order, from one to fourteen. The third and fourth columns list the reported activity of the evangelical public in each of these areas and then the rank order of this activity.

The evangelical elites gave the highest priority to pregnancy programs, especially crisis counseling (77 percent); many saw this as an alternative to abortion. Traditional charities came next (76 percent), including emergency feeding programs and income assistance. (Although these results are not given in Table 4, the evangelical elites assigned a similar priority to prison ministries, racial reconciliation efforts, and opposing religious persecution abroad.[36]) Programs to support families (71 percent), drug and alcohol rehabilitation programs (69 percent), and international famine relief (also 69 percent) rounded out the top five areas.

The second five areas were given top priority by more than one-half of the elites: programs for the elderly (65 percent), Christian schools (64 percent), programs for youth (58 percent), other education programs, such as literacy efforts (also 58 percent), and programs associated with homosexuality (counseling, AIDS awareness) (56 percent). Although not listed in Table 4, litigation efforts on behalf of religious causes (57 percent) and supporting Christian men's and women's groups (56 percent) ranked with these activities as well.

Interestingly, most direct political activities ranked low in Table 4, with less than one-half of the evangelical elites assigning them top priority—a finding

TABLE 4

RECOMMENDED PRIORITIES AND REPORTED ACTIVITIES:
EVANGELICAL ELITES AND EVANGELICAL PUBLIC

| | ELITES | | PUBLIC | |
	Recommended Priorities	Rank	Reported Activities	Rank
Pregnancy programs	77 %	1	23 %	10
Traditional charities	76	2	62	1
Family programs	71	3	31	6
Rehabilitation programs	69	4	29	7
International famine relief	69	5	18	12
Elderly programs	65	6	40	4
Christian schools	64	7	10	13
Youth programs	58	8	48	3
Education programs	58	9	25	8
Homosexuality programs	56	10	9	14
Electoral activities	46	11	24	9
Political action groups	36	12	20	11
Environmental programs	34	13	49	2
Lobbying activities	35	14	36	5

SOURCE: 2000 Survey of Evangelical Elites, University of Akron; Third National Survey of Religion and Politics, University of Akron, 2000.

consistent with the approaches to civic engagement reported in Table 1. Electoral activities, such as voter registration and getting out the vote, came in first (46 percent), followed by support for political action groups (36 percent) and lobbying public officials (35 percent). Environmental programs were given the lowest priority by the evangelical elites (35 percent). Although not shown in Table 4, economic development programs also received relatively low priority (38 percent).

A comparison of the rank order of elite priorities (column 2) with the rank order of reported activities by the evangelical public (column 4) is fascinating. Traditional charities ranked near the top on both lists (second for elites, first for the public), and youth and elderly programs rank also ranked relatively high for both. However, there were some striking inconsistencies as well. Environmental programs ranked second in reported public activity and last in elite priority, a striking finding, and both pregnancy programs and international famine relief ranked much lower in reported public activity than in elite priority. As for political activity, the evangelical public's level of involvement in elections and political-action committees is quite similar to the priorities assigned by the elites. But in relative terms the public reports being more involved in contacting public officials than the elites recommend.

Of course, some such differences between elites and the public are to be expected. Some programs are easier for the evangelical public to participate in than others. In all traditions, moreover, the American laity regularly ignore some of the admonitions of their leaders. However, this tendency may be especially problematic among evangelicals because of their strong individualism. Perhaps the most useful way to interpret these data is that the evangelical public does not display the distinctive profile in civic engagement advocated by its leaders.

Engagement in Social Programs

Table 5 (page 24) describes the level of reported engagement in ten types of social programs (ranked from first to last) by the evangelical public and the other religious traditions. Respondents were asked whether they donated either time or money to support such programs, and whether the programs they supported operated in religious or secular venues. As with levels of religious engagement, such reports must be viewed with some skepticism. However, the likely overreporting of activity makes the patterns in Table 5 especially interesting.

One important pattern is worth noting at the outset: mainline Protestants reported the highest level of support in most areas, and when they were not first, they ranked second. This pattern is consistent with other evidence of the high levels of civic engagement among mainliners.[37] Indeed, these figures may understate the involvement by mainliners: as we saw in Table 3, among mainline Protestants there is a substantial minority with very low levels of religious commitment. Were such persons excluded from the analysis, the percentage supporting these social programs would increase.

Overall, the evangelical public claimed lower levels of activity compared to members of other religious traditions, and quite frequently ranked last or next to last, although not always by a large margin. Evangelicals and black Protestants were just as likely to support social programs in religious venues as mainline Protestants and Catholics, but less likely to participate in secular venues.

Interestingly, the rank order of reported activity by area was roughly the same across the religious traditions. Traditional charities ranked first, with evangelicals participating about as much as Catholics but less than mainline Protestants. However, here religious venues were more important for evangelicals and black Protestants, and secular venues were more important for mainliners and Catholics. Environmental programs ranked second, and secular venues were far more common than religious ones for all the groups. Here black Protestants were markedly less active. Youth, elderly, and family programs rounded out the top-five areas supported, with secular venues typically outpacing religious ones. The next five areas were, in order, programs for

TABLE 5
ENGAGEMENT IN SOCIAL PROGRAMS:
EVANGELICALS AND OTHER RELIGIOUS GROUPS

	Evangelical Protestant	Black Protestant	Mainline Protestant	Roman Catholic	Entire Sample
Traditional Charities	62%	59%	68 %	63 %	61%
Religious venue	32	34	32	28	27
Secular venue	30	25	36	35	34
Environmental Programs	49	38	60	56	52
Religious venue	6	8	7	6	6
Secular venue	43	30	53	50	46
Youth Programs	48	49	56	52	49
Religious venue	14	18	14	11	13
Secular venue	34	31	42	41	36
Elderly Programs	40	44	43	36	39
Religious venue	17	23	17	12	15
Secular venue	23	21	26	24	24
Family Programs	31	37	38	31	33
Religious venue	15	16	19	12	13
Secular venue	16	21	19	19	20
Rehabilitation Programs	29	29	34	27	29
Religious venue	14	12	19	10	12
Secular venue	15	17	15	17	17
Education Programs	25	43	30	30	31
Religious venue	7	15	8	7	8
Secular venue	18	28	22	23	23
Pregnancy Programs	23	24	22	20	22
Religious venue	15	10	12	8	10
Secular venue	8	14	10	12	12
International Programs	18	22	28	23	24
Religious venue	11	11	18	11	11
Secular venue	7	11	10	12	13
Homosexuality Programs	9	16	13	15	14
Religious venue	3	6	5	4	4
Secular venue	6	10	8	11	10
High Engagement					
Total	41	44	48	43	43
Religious venues	31	35	31	23	26
Secular venues	31	32	38	36	30

SOURCE: Third National Survey of Religion and Politics, University of Akron, 2000.

drug and alcohol rehabilitation, education, pregnancy support, international relief, and homosexuality. Exceptions to the overall pattern were: more support for education in secular venues among black Protestants, and a special emphasis on pregnancy programs in religious venues by evangelicals.

As before, the last entries in Table 5 summarize the results by reporting the percentage of each group above the mean on three additive indexes of the ten activity areas: total, religious, and secular.[38] The results present some modest surprises. In overall activity, mainline Protestants scored the highest, with 48 percent above the mean, compared to all the other groups at 43 percent. These differences were smaller than the other entries in Table 5 might suggest. This pattern reflects two related features in these data. First, many mainline Protestants engaged in just one type of activity, and second, the mainline advantage in activity was weaker among the most engaged citizens. There were also variations by venue: evangelicals tied mainline Protestants on high levels of activity in religious venues, and Catholics nearly tied mainliners on activity in secular venues. Thus the mainline Protestant advantage in this kind of civic engagement came from high levels of activity across the board.

Levels of Political Participation

What about political engagement? Table 6 (page 26) lists ten common kinds of political activity. As with our measures of religious and civic engagement, these self-reports must be viewed with some caution, since survey respondents regularly overstate their activity. The pattern of these reports was nevertheless instructive. (We did not ask the same questions of the evangelical elites, but there was strong evidence that as a group they were very active in politics.)

Presidential voting is by far the most common form of political participation in the country, and its heading the list of political activities is no surprise. In the 2000 election, mainline Protestants had the highest turnout (58 percent), while evangelicals, black Protestants, and Catholics all had a turnout of 50 percent. A similar pattern obtained for estimated congressional turnout in 2000. However, the fact that evangelicals matched the other major religious traditions in voter turnout in 2000 represents a gain in political involvement compared to the past. The 50 percent turnout among black Protestants was also noteworthy, and taken together, these figures help to explain the closeness of the 2000 election.

Another common form of political activity was talking politics with family, friends, and co-workers, an activity undertaken by about one-half of the population. Here evangelicals trailed slightly behind the other traditions. The remaining types of participation were much less common in all groups. A little more than one-third of evangelicals reported contacting a public official in the previous four years (since 1996).[39] Here evangelicals matched mainline Protestants and were ahead of the other groups. Less than one-third of evangelicals claimed to be an active member of an interest group, and about one-quarter reported making a campaign contribution of some kind in the previous four years. In both these cases, evangelicals trailed the other religious traditions by a small margin.

The final four types of political activity were the least common, and here evangelicals either ranked last or tied for last among the religious groups, but also by small margins. Less than one-fifth of evangelicals claimed to have followed the government closely in 2000 or to have attended a public political meeting in the last four years, while one-tenth reported working in a campaign and one in twenty participated in a demonstration during that period. The final entry in Table 6 once again summarizes the table by reporting the

TABLE 6
ENGAGEMENT IN POLITICAL ACTIVITIES:
EVANGELICALS AND OTHER RELIGIOUS GROUPS

	Evangelical Protestant	Black Protestant	Mainline Protestant	Roman Catholic	Entire Sample
Voted for President in 2000 election	50 %	50 %	58 %	50 %	51%
Talk politics several times a month or more	48	51	52	54	48
Voted for Congress in 2000 elections	43	43	49	43	42
Contacted public official in last four years	36	27	37	34	34
Active member of at least one political group	30	32	34	35	33
Made political contribution in last four years	24	27	27	25	24
Follow government "closely"	18	22	19	20	18
Attended public meeting in last four years	17	21	21	17	18
Worked in campaign in last four years	10	13	10	11	10
Participated in demonstration in last four years	5	11	6	6	8
High engagement in political activity	35	37	39	39	36

SOURCE: Third National Survey of Religion and Politics, University of Akron, 2000.

TABLE 7

LEVELS OF OVERALL ENGAGEMENT:
EVANGELICALS AND OTHER RELIGIOUS GROUPS

	Evangelical Protestant	Black Protestant	Mainline Protestant	Roman Catholic	Entire Sample
Full Engagement (high religious and secular)	25 %	30 %	22 %	20 %	20 %
High Faith-Based Engagement (high religious, low secular)	32	34	19	21	22
High Secular Engagement (low religious, high secular)	15	13	26	25	24
Low Engagement (low religious and secular)	28	23	33	33	34

SOURCE: Third National Survey of Religion and Politics, University of Akron, 2000.

percentage of each group above the mean on an additive index of the ten forms of political activity.[40] As with support for social programs, the edge among mainline Protestants declined among the most active citizens. Mainline Protestants were tied with Catholics for the highest score, at 39 percent, followed closely by black Protestants, at 37 percent, with evangelicals last at 35 percent. Of course, these differences are quite small. Although the patterns may reflect the special circumstances of the 2000 election, they also suggest that evangelicals have substantially caught up with the other major Christian traditions in terms of political activity.[41] By historical standards, this level of activity presents a significant change for evangelicals.

Overall Patterns of Engagement

How do all these measures of civic engagement fit together? Table 7 reports four categories of engagement based on a combining of several of the summary indexes reported in the previous tables.[42] The four categories are: *full engagement* (high levels of religious and secular activity); *high faith-based engagement* (high religious and low secular activity); *high secular engagement* (low religious and high secular activity); and *low engagement* (low on both).

One-quarter of the evangelical public was in the full-engagement category, showing high levels of religious and secular activity. This figures was lower than for black Protestants (30 percent), but higher than for Catholics (20 percent) and mainline Protestants (22 percent). In contrast, about one-third of evangelicals and black Protestants were in the high-faith-based category, figures substantially higher than for mainline Protestants and Catholics (about one-fifth each). Roughly one-sixth of evangelicals and black Protestants were in the high-secular category, less than the one-quarter of mainline Protestants and Catholics. Finally, all the groups had a substantial proportion in the low-engagement category: black Protestants had the smallest proportion here, 23 percent, followed by evangelicals at 28 percent, with mainliners and Catholics tied at 33 percent.

There are a number of ways to look at these figures. Perhaps the most striking finding was the small differences among the religious traditions in many of the categories. For evangelicals, this lack of difference in and of itself marks an important change from the past. The chief cause of the small evangelical advantage over mainline Protestants in both the full-engagement and low-engagement categories is their higher level of faith-based activity. Indeed, the relative importance of the full-engagement and high-religious-engagement categories among evangelicals and black Protestants suggests that religious engagement can be both a source of, and a substitute for, secular engagement. However, if the full-engagement and high-secular-engagement categories are added together—each representing persons active in public affairs—mainline Protestants (48 percent) and Catholics (45 percent) outpaced black Protestants (43 percent) and evangelicals (40 percent).

What explains the differences among these four summary categories of engagement? One key difference is cognitive support for civic engagement of religious people, as reported in Table 1. The full-engagement category was the most supportive of a broader scope of civic engagement; least supportive was the high-secular-engagement category, followed closely by the low-engagement category. Persons in these two categories were especially opposed to the involvement of religious people in politics. Interestingly, the high-faith-based-engagement category was nearly as supportive of a broad scope of civic engagement as the full-engagement category. These patterns held across all the religious traditions.

Another distinguishing feature was socio-economic status. In all the traditions, the full-engagement category had better educated, more affluent, and older people, and more men, than the high-faith-based category. People in the high-secular category also had high socio-economic status, while the low-engagement group had the lowest socio-economic status. Thus, persons in the high-faith-based category appear to lack the personal resources to become fully engaged in civic life, compared to their co-religionists, while persons in the low-engagement category suffered even more severely from such a resource deficit.[43] Religious beliefs also helped distinguish these categories, with the two more religious categories reporting more traditional positions on doctrinal matters than the two more secular categories. However, there was considerable political diversity within all these categories. For example, the full-engagement category contained both political conservatives and political liberals in all the religious traditions.[44]

Concluding Observations

What do these findings contribute to the debate over the role of religion in civic engagement, within and beyond the evangelical community? Three conclusions come to mind. First, *evangelicals are now open to a broad scope of civic engagement by religious people,* including political action. In all probability, such openness is significantly greater than it was a generation ago, and strong positions against civic engagement, such as separatism, have all but vanished. This openness is strongest among evangelical elites, a significant minority of whom favor political engagement over other forms of civic engagement, and also the broad political goal of transforming society. Although less interested in politics or broad political goals, the evangelical public is as open to civic engagement as mainline Protestants and Catholics, and shares with black Protestants a sense that faith is important to political thinking.

Second, *individualism is still an important feature of evangelicals' approach to civic engagement.* Most evangelicals still have a preference for helping individuals solve their own problems in one form or another, and still regard individual conversion as an efficacious means of solving social problems. This tendency is partly reflected in the high level of religious engagement of evangelicals and in their support for social programs in religious venues. The evangelical public often trails behind the other traditions in the level of engagement in secular activities, including support for social services and political action; but such differences are often small and are even less significant among the most involved individuals. Religious individualism has thus not prevented evangelicals from approaching the other major religious traditions in level and variety of civic engagement. Indeed, the pattern of engagement by the evangelical public is frequently less distinctive than the evangelical elites would like.

Third, when all these forms of civic engagement are taken into account, *evangelicals compare favorably to mainline Protestants and Catholics, and even to black Protestants.* Indeed, the proportion of the evangelical public that is fully engaged in public life is on a par with the proportion in other major traditions, and the proportion substantially disengaged is lower than for mainline Protestants and Catholics. Evangelicals' higher level of religious engagement makes up for their lack of high secular engagement compared to the other traditions.

The debate over the proper role of religious people in civic engagement will continue to be an important one, and nowhere more so than among evangelicals.

CHAPTER TWO

The Christian Right: Evolution, Expansion, Contraction

Mark J. Rozell

The modern Christian Right is a movement composed mainly of evangelical Protestant groups that seeks to influence U.S. politics in a conservative direction. To do this, leaders of the movement may choose either confrontation or accommodation. If they choose confrontation, on such issues as abortion, gay rights, and prayer in the public schools they will maintain the strict positions that their members favor. But this approach may fail to persuade elected political leaders, who are likely to favor compromises so as to maintain a broad base of voter support. If Christian Right leaders opt instead for accommodation, "softening" their positions and being pragmatic and open to compromise, they may lose the support of many of their members.

Ralph Reed formerly was the leading Christian Right proponent of a pragmatic approach to politics. Under his leadership, the Christian Coalition moderated its rhetoric and shifted its policy emphasis away from contentious social issues and toward economic issues. The organization backed Republicans of all ideological stripes, and Reed worked behind the scenes to win support for a more moderate GOP platform plank on abortion. Such pragmatism allowed the Christian Coalition and other movement organizations to grow and to become important players in GOP politics, winning control of many state and local party organizations.[1] Yet Reed's pragmatism angered some leaders and many movement activists, and created a deep division in the Christian Right.[2]

Reed left the Christian Coalition leadership in 1997, and it now appears that he had timed perfectly his leap off a sinking ship. For a variety of reasons,

Mark J. Rozell is professor and chair of the Department of Politics at The Catholic University of America, Washington, D.C. He is the co-author of *Second Coming: The New Christian Right in Virginia Politics*, co-editor of three other books on the Christian Right and U.S. elections, and also co-editor of the 2003 volume *The Christian Right in U.S. Politics: Marching Toward the Millennium*.

that once dominant Christian Right organization is in such a deep decline that it may not long survive. Some view its decline as a symbol of the impending doom of the broader movement. That conclusion is a mistake, as were predictions of the demise of the movement made in the late 1980s after the folding of Moral Majority. The movement has experienced its peaks and valleys politically, but it persists as a real influence in American politics. The future of the Christian Right—whether it expands, consolidates, or contracts—depends to a great extent on the internal debate about strategy and tactics, about confrontation versus accommodation.

In this essay I will examine the evolution, expansion, and current contraction of the Christian Right. I will emphasize its more recent political activity, especially its efforts in the 2000 elections.

NEW CHRISTIAN RIGHT: THE FIRST TWO DECADES

The modern Christian Right first mobilized in the United States in the mid- to late 1970s, inspired in part by local and state activity—a parents' uprising about textbooks in Kanawha County, West Virginia, a gay-rights referendum in Dade County, Florida, and a gambling referendum in Virginia.[3] Entrepreneurs used this activity to build political organizations: Robert Grant helped merge several anti-gay, anti-pornography, and pro-family groups in California into the **Christian Voice**, and Jerry Falwell launched his **Moral Majority** soon after he helped to defeat the 1978 gambling referendum in Virginia.

As described by Matthew Moen, the first phase of the Christian Right was characterized by moralistic language, emphasis on a narrow range of social issues, and extreme positions with no chance of policy success.[4] Leaders mobilized support through such phrases as "put God back into government" and "end the murder of the unborn." Such rhetoric mobilized the activist base, but it also made the Christian Right appear threatening to outsiders. Movement leaders focused their efforts on a few social issues, primarily abortion, gay rights, and prayer in schools. They called for such extreme measures as banning gays from teaching, quarantining people with AIDS, and eliminating abortion rights in all cases, including rape and incest (and in some cases, even threat to the life of the mother).

Earlier incarnations of the Christian Right had been active in the Democratic Party, but in the 1980s the Christian Right mobilized politically in the Republican Party. After Ronald Reagan's election to the presidency in 1980, Jerry Falwell became a leading figure on the national scene. Falwell said he had mobilized several million conservative Christian voters, and the size of the Republican landslide that year made his claim seemed almost credible.

The Christian Right achieved an important goal during the Reagan years when the president gave it legitimacy by addressing social issues, and Reagan viewed this as a sufficient payoff to the movement that had helped elect him.

He did not push its agenda. In speeches he would often include some reference to a position of the Christian Right—for example, a plea to "put God back into the classroom"—but then his administration would do little to advance such a goal. Reagan understood that the Christian Right agenda was too controversial, and that to focus on social issues would undermine support for his presidency and ultimately for his economic agenda and defense buildup.

It is telling that the most conservative president of the post–New Deal era avoided pushing the policy agenda of social conservatives. The Christian Right delivered votes and campaign energy to GOP candidates in the 1980s but got very little in return, in large part because of its controversial positions and the extreme and uncompromising rhetoric of its leaders.

The Decline

Christian Right organizations of the early 1980s were limited by their particularistic religious appeal. The Moral Majority membership was mostly confined to churches of the Baptist Bible Fellowship, Falwell's home denomination. The preachers who headed the state and county organizations invited their own congregations to participate but made Catholics and Pentecostals feel less welcome. Preaching that theirs was the only true religion, the leaders proved unable to build ecumenical political organizations. The Moral Majority was primarily a national direct-mail endeavor; it had few active state chapters and few county or other local organizations. Other movement groups were even less focused on organizing.

By the late 1980s, the Moral Majority was in deep financial trouble as Reagan's reelection and then George H. W. Bush's election, coupled with a series of televangelist scandals, substantially dried up contributions. As the Moral Majority faced bankruptcy, Pat Robertson launched a bid for the presidency. He lost badly, despite his spending of more than $36 million. By spring 1989 the Moral Majority had been disbanded, the Christian Voice had closed down its political-action committee and was being subsidized by the Rev. Sun Myung Moon, and Robertson was back on television hosting the "700 Club."

Scholars list several reasons for the failure of the first wave of the Christian Right: the extreme rhetoric and uncompromising stands on issues; the emphasis on mass mailing and on personality-driven national organizations rather than on effective grass-roots network; and the religious prejudice that made it impossible to build a broadly ecumenical political movement.[5] But the Robertson campaign, failure though it was, provided the seeds for the second flowering of the Christian Right in the 1990s.

The Resurgence

Robertson's campaign had brought a number of young, previously apolitical Pentecostal and charismatic Christians into politics, and at the end of the

1988 elections many of them held influential positions in state and local political parties. More importantly, Robertson converted the large contributor list from his campaign into the beginnings of a national grass-roots organization, the **Christian Coalition,** and hired .the savvy political tactician Ralph Reed as its executive director. Robertson had obviously learned some important lessons: that success in the political environment requires (a) a strong grass-roots presence and (b) a visible political leader who can speak the secular language of politics and work effectively with the media. The controversial religious broadcaster apparently realized that he himself had to keep a lower political profile.

The Christian Coalition built state, county, and local organizations across the country. Ralph Reed recruited state and local leaders with backgrounds in business, interest-group politics, or civic activity. This enabled the Coalition to build a truly ecumenical organization. Its national lobbying office has at various times included mainline Protestants, evangelicals, Catholics, and even a Jew, and many state and local chapters were similarly diverse.[6] The Christian Coalition activists may not agree on religious doctrine, but they can agree to work together in support of pro-life, conservative GOP candidates.

This second flowering of the Christian Right revealed a politically maturing movement that had learned from the past. Reed himself had once compared his political tactics to guerrilla warfare and had bragged that he ambushed opponents and left them in body bags; he later repented of such rhetoric and wrote to supporters that "phrases like 'religious war' and 'take over' play to a stereotype of evangelicals as intolerant." Reed urged followers to avoid threatening-sounding language: "We must adopt strategies of persuasion, not domination."[7] And so the Christian Right of the 1990s had a more moderate sound. The issue appeals were broader-based, going beyond the social agenda to include such things as the balanced budget and revision of tax rates. Movement leaders expressed a desire to work from as wide an ecumenical base as possible. They wanted to become part of the conservative mainstream, and they worked hard to form coalitions with other conservative groups to share membership lists, cosponsor candidate fundraisers, and back one another's candidates and issue stands. New organizations built impressive grass-roots networks.[8]

Christian Right leaders increasingly emphasized the necessity of compromise. A good example was the recognition by many in the movement that abortion rights were not likely to be struck down, nor would there be a consensus in favor of eliminating abortion. Therefore it made sense to work for restrictions—e.g., parental notification, mandatory waiting periods and counseling of those seeking abortions, no taxpayer funding for the procedure, and elimination of so-called partial-birth abortions. Such policies may somewhat reduce the number of abortions performed, and have the distinct advantage of being politically possible.

Without a doubt, accepting the necessity of compromise has been the most difficult assignment for the Christian Right. For many in the movement, to compromise on abortion or on any matter of religious doctrine is to make a deal with the devil. For example, more than a third of Christian Right activists in the Virginia GOP indicated in a survey that they thought compromise was not necessary for politics, and nearly half reported that there was only one true Christian position on most policy issues. Although many of the best-known and most successful leaders of the movement had learned that the agenda cannot be advanced without compromise, the most ideological activists clearly reject the idea that compromise is possible on moral issues.[9]

By the late 1990s the Christian Right found itself faced with a dilemma. To continue to pursue the pragmatic course of compromise and bargaining was to risk losing many of its most deeply committed members. Yet if the movement reverted to its more ideological roots, then it risked engendering a countermobilization among moderates and liberals, and once again being seen within the GOP as more of a liability than a benefit.

Pragmatism and Its Discontents

The Christian Coalition pursued almost purely partisan politics in the 1990s, endorsing Republican candidates regardless of their positions on key movement issues. The Coalition backed U.S. Senate candidates Paul Coverdale (Ga.) and Kay Bailey Hutchison (Tex.), though neither supported a ban on abortion. In the 1996 GOP nomination contest, Coalition leaders threw their support behind the nascent presidential campaign of Bob Dole, despite the presence in the race of movement favorites such as Patrick Buchanan, Alan Keyes, and Bob Dornan. Reed worked to soften the pro-life plank in the GOP platform, arguing that it cost the Republicans votes.

Reed's tactics were applauded by the media and by some moderate Republicans, who welcomed the electoral support of the Christian Coalition and were pleased to find the group lobbying for tax cuts and welfare reform. But within the Christian Right, Reed's tactics were not always popular. A number of movement leaders, most prominently James Dobson, criticized the new moderation and proclaimed that Reed did not speak for their issues. Cal Thomas wrote of his dismay that Dole would spend a week of the presidential campaign defending tobacco but would not make a speech denouncing abortion. Thomas wondered if it was time to abandon the GOP, and other leaders and activists echoed his concern.[10]

By the late 1990s Christian Right dismay with GOP politics ran very deep. And understandably so. The Christian Right had labored for the Republican Party since 1978, but it did not appear to have received much in return. Ronald Reagan rewarded his economic constituency and the defense hawks, yet gave the Christian Right only rhetoric. George H. W. Bush showed little interest in the social-issues agenda. Eight years of the Clinton presidency forced the Christian Right into a largely defensive posture.

The intensity of the cultural wars during the Clinton era had once again cast the Christian Right movement in a negative light, and the real limits of the movement's pragmatism had become apparent. After the disastrous GOP results in the 1998 elections, many blamed the Christian Right for convincing party leaders to adopt the politically suicidal strategy of focusing on Bill Clinton's personal character during the congressional campaigns. When Robertson suggested in 1999 that perhaps it made little sense to push for the president's removal because the Senate votes clearly were not there to accomplish this, he opened a major rift within the Christian Right between those who counseled pragmatism and the legions of supporters who deeply detested Clinton and, win or lose on the Senate floor, wanted to make a statement.

Having begun the 1990s defying predictions of its demise, the Christian Right had succeeded in entering the mainstream of U.S. politics and was able to claim some credit for Republican victories—a House of Representatives with a Republican majority for the first time in four decades, and the election of state and local candidates throughout the country. But by the end of the 1990s observers once again were speculating about the demise of the movement. Once again, however, the Christian Right defied those predictions.

THE 2000 ELECTIONS AND BEYOND

The early conventional wisdom regarding the Christian Right's role in the Republican presidential contest in 2000 did not mirror reality. Prior to the nomination battle between Texas governor George W. Bush and Arizona senator John McCain, observers were nearly uniform in their assessment that the Christian Right was a minimal player in the GOP nomination process. At most, many suggested, the movement would influence the vice presidential nomination and some party platform positions.

There were credible reasons for observers to believe that the Christian Right would not be a major player in the nomination process. First, it lacked a standard-bearer. Throughout 1999, then Missouri senator John Ashcroft—a Christian social conservative with a record of appealing to different constituencies—appeared to be running for the nomination and to be the movement's favored candidate. When he announced he would not seek the presidency, there was not an obvious candidate to unify the Christian Right and help the movement flex its muscle in the primaries.

Second, the Christian Coalition was in serious trouble. Its fund-raising and membership were in substantial decline. The organization was beset by infighting and by resignations of staff and of state and local chapter chairs, and some of its chapters either disappeared or continued to exist only on paper. *Fortune* magazine dropped the organization from its list of the top twenty-five Washington lobby groups. *National Review* featured an article about the Coalition entitled "Slouching Toward Irrelevance." Some scholars suggested that the organization's decline reflected the waning influence of the Christian Right.[11]

Third, in the absence of a standard-bearer for the Christian Right, numerous candidates tried to appeal to its members, thus splintering the movement. Each of the GOP hopefuls had a credible claim to the movement's support: Gary Bauer, Pat Buchanan, George W. Bush, Elizabeth Dole, Steve Forbes, Orin Hatch, John Kasich, Alan Keyes, John McCain, Dan Quayle, and Bob Smith. Uniquely among them, George W. Bush emphasized socially conservative views couched in the liberal rhetoric of compassion and tolerance. Many leading Christian Rightists, particularly Robertson and Reed, signed on early to back Bush as the most electable candidate. Yet their early support of Bush was not matched by grass-roots Christian Right enthusiasm. Many openly decried Bush's use of liberal language and his support from party elites as evidence that he was, like his father, an establishment figure more than a true movement conservative. Many derided his self-description as a "compassionate conservative."

The Republican Primary Campaign

Early on, the race appeared to be between the moderate-establishment wing of the GOP, supporting Bush, and the movement-conservative wing, which lacked a standard-bearer. That Robertson and Reed backed Bush was not of great consequence for the Christian Right; to many of its activists and some of its leaders, those two figures represented the pragmatist wing of the movement and seemed more interested in gaining access to power than in promoting a cause. Other prominent Christian Rightists backed other GOP candidates, most of whom dropped out of the campaign. Kasich, Quayle, Dole, and Hatch withdrew the earliest. Buchanan left the GOP to seek the Reform Party nomination; he remained in the race as the Reform candidate but could barely draw any attention. Both Forbes and Bauer stayed in the campaign through several primaries but also dropped out early. Keyes remained in the race even though he never had a chance of winning.

As the Republican race quickly became a bitter contest between Bush and McCain, the Christian Right took central stage in the drama and ultimately delivered victory to Bush. Amid predictions of the movement's political irrelevance in 2000, Christian Right activists became the kingmakers in the GOP contest.[12]

The New Hampshire open primary narrowed the GOP field. Bauer dropped out after getting 1 percent of the vote.[13] Forbes pulled a disappointing 13 percent and stayed in the campaign temporarily. Keyes got just 6 percent of the vote but seemed determined not to leave the race no matter how poorly he fared. McCain stunned the GOP establishment with a 49 to 30 percent victory over Bush.[14] But the exit polls showed a GOP fissure that would become problematic for McCain later on: whereas McCain did exceptionally well among independents, Democrats, and some Republicans, Bush showed his greatest strength among Christian social conservatives.[15] The social-conservative voting base in the New England states is quite small, and so the exit polls provided encouraging news for Bush as the campaign moved toward South Carolina.

Among those identified as Republican who voted in the New Hampshire GOP primary (53 percent), 41 percent chose Bush and 38 percent McCain. The Arizona senator won overwhelmingly among both independents (62 to 19 percent), who made up 41 percent of the voters, and Democrats (78 to 13 percent), who made up 4 percent. Liberals and moderates also overwhelmingly backed McCain, whereas he and Bush almost evenly split the conservative vote. Those who identified themselves as "very conservative" backed Bush 33 to 21 percent (with 24 percent choosing Keyes and 20 percent Forbes).

Bush won the Christian Right vote. Among "religious right" voters, he prevailed 36 to 26 percent over McCain (19 percent went for Keyes and 14 percent for Forbes). Yet these voters made up only 16 percent of the GOP primary electorate, suggesting that Bush had strong vote-getting potential in the more culturally conservative states outside the northeast. Bush also won among those voters who said they attend church more than once a week (10 percent of the voters) and those who said they oppose abortion in all circumstances (12 percent).

And so McCain had become the candidate of the moderate wing of the GOP and Bush the candidate of the Christian Right. Both were strongly pro-life, and it was almost impossible to detect any differences between them on social issues. Bush's gubernatorial record and McCain's eighteen-year voting record in Congress gave them equally valid claims to support from the Christian Right.

The Opposition to McCain

McCain had staked much of his presidential quest on his commitment to campaign finance reform. His campaign positions on this issue, supported by his earlier reform efforts as a senator, were anathema to interest groups such as the National Right to Life Committee and the Christian Coalition. These organizations, like many others, rely heavily on the use of "independent expenditures"—money spent for a communication urging election or defeat of a candidate, without consultation with the benefiting candidate's campaign—and McCain's favored reforms would force such groups to refocus their efforts. Consequently, both of these organizations geared up to oppose McCain's presidential quest, with Robertson leading the inaccurate charge that the Arizona senator was hostile to the pro-life agenda. Robertson's attacks at times were personal: he suggested that McCain lacked the temperament and emotional stability to be president. Focus on the Family director James Dobson criticized McCain's personal fitness as a moral leader because of the senator's earlier admitted adultery and then divorce.

The leaders of the nation's three most prominent social-conservative organizations, then, were united in their opposition to McCain. They put forth a major effort to stop his candidacy in South Carolina, backed by extensive independent spending efforts. Robertson in particular made numerous appearances on television news and commentary shows denouncing McCain and asserting that social conservatives would sit out the general election if the Arizona senator were nominated by the GOP.

The Christian Right in its all-out assault on McCain's campaign in South Carolina attacked his credibility as an advocate of the social-conservative cause on four counts: (1) his suggestion that the GOP should soften the language of the party's anti-abortion platform plank to make the party more inclusive; (2) his vote to allow fetal tissue research for combating Parkinson's disease; (3) his suggestion, later retracted, that he would not support a repeal of *Roe v. Wade*; (4) his statement that if his daughter became pregnant he would leave the abortion decision up to her.[16] These factors hardly justified the severe attacks on McCain, especially given his consistently pro-life voting record in Congress. The National Right to Life Committee in fact had consistently given McCain nearly 100 percent ratings for his votes in Congress, and the candidate consistently affirmed his pro-life stand in the campaign. Nonetheless the National Right to Life Committee led the attack on McCain with mass mailings, radio ads, and voter telephone calls throughout the state.[17]

The Christian Coalition was remarkably quiet in South Carolina—a reflection of the organization's weakened state rather than any decline in social-conservative voters in the GOP. Robertson was a highly visible spokesperson during the primary, targeting his energies against McCain. So while the National Right to Life Committee did the grass-roots campaigning, Robertson commanded attention on the national airwaves. The consistent message was that McCain was unacceptable to the Christian Right.

The Bob Jones Issue

The role of religion in the campaign took center stage when McCain attacked Bush's decision to speak at Bob Jones University—a fundamentalist institution that prohibited interracial dating and characterized Catholicism as "a satanic counterfeit," and whose founder had made disparaging comments about the Pope. McCain made Bush's visit to the university a campaign issue, blasting his opponent for failing to criticize the institution's overtly bigoted policies and failing to say anything about its anti-Catholicism. The attack hurt Bush's standing with Catholic voters, and he ultimately expressed regret for his appearance at the university. In a letter to Cardinal John O'Connor, Bush referred to his failure to address the university's anti-Catholic views as "a missed opportunity, causing needless offense, which I deeply regret." Bush admitted, "On reflection, I should have been more clear in disassociating myself from anti-Catholic sentiments and racial prejudice."[18]

McCain could not concede the Christian Right vote to Bush in South Carolina and hope to have any chance of winning. Once Bauer dropped out, the McCain camp lobbied heavily for the Christian Right leader's endorsement, and Bauer agreed to endorse McCain at a joint appearance at Furman University. First to introduce McCain was Rep. Lindsay Graham (R-S.C.) who seemed to suggest that McCain had been preserved by God to run for president when his plane was shot down in Vietnam: "John McCain was supposed to die, but he didn't. You're here [turning toward McCain] because God wants you to be here."[19]

Bauer's endorsement of McCain caused many Christian Right leaders to disavow him. Bauer's support also didn't matter: Bush won South Carolina 53-42 percent. The Christian Right carried the state for Bush. Among the 61 percent who said in exit polls that they were *not* members of the "religious right," McCain won 52-46 percent. Among the 34 percent religious-right voters, Bush won overwhelmingly—68-24 percent. Bush once again prevailed heavily among the voters who said that abortion should never be legal (67-19 percent), and he won among the 43 percent of the voters who chose either "moral values" or abortion as the most important issue in their voting decision.[20]

Two major factors boosted Bush's showing in South Carolina. First, his margin over McCain among religious-right voters went from a mere 10 percent in New Hampshire to 44 percent in South Carolina. Second, the percentage of socially conservative voters was substantially higher in the South Carolina primary than in New Hampshire. Most analysts have suggested that a loss in South Carolina would have ended Bush's candidacy. If that is so, the Christian Right vote surely could lay claim to having saved his presidential bid.

On to Michigan

With each candidate claiming one major state primary victory, the campaign focus now shifted to the crucial Michigan contest. That state has a heavy Catholic population, and the McCain campaign was counting on anger at Bush's Bob Jones University appearance to help the senator.

Once again, Christian Right and pro-life groups became involved. The powerful Michigan Right to Life Committee sent pro-Bush, anti-McCain mailings to 400,000 voters and followed up with phone calls. Robertson taped an anti-McCain phone message for social-conservative Michigan voters lambasting McCain's New Hampshire campaign manager, former GOP senator Warren Rudman, as "a vicious bigot" who once made disparaging comments about the Christian Right. Rudman indeed had a history of clashing with social conservatives. The taped calls became a national news story about the tactics of the Christian Right, and even the Bush campaign privately urged Robertson to tone down his rhetoric.

McCain's campaign targeted Catholic voters. The candidate himself denied knowledge of efforts by an independent group to conduct mass phone calls to Catholics to alert them to Bush's appearance at Bob Jones University. Eventually McCain admitted that he knew of the plan to target those voters, and he too came under criticism for playing the "religion card" too heavily in the campaign.

McCain won the Michigan open primary 51-43 percent. Much the same pattern held: McCain won independent and Democratic voters, and Bush won the Republican identifiers. Among the two-thirds of voters who were *not* members of the religious right, 60 percent went to McCain, 36 percent to Bush. Bush again overwhelmed McCain among religious-right voters, 66-25 percent. But his numbers declined among pro-life voters, suggesting that although he lost nothing in religious-right appeal, he lost some Catholic pro-life voters. Among pro-life voters, Bush won 54 percent; his numbers were strongest among those who said that abortion "never" should be legal (62 percent for Bush, 27 percent for McCain).[21]

McCain's strong showing in Michigan led to a round of analyses suggesting that he was clearly the strongest candidate for the GOP in the general election. In a record primary turnout in Michigan, 29 percent of the voters said they were casting their first Republican primary vote ever. Those voters went heavily to McCain. There was a substantial turnout of labor unionists, independent voters, and Democrats, all of whom favored McCain heavily. But these facts underscored a problem: McCain could not win the nomination by appealing to largely non-GOP voters. Most of the key states yet to come held "closed" primaries—open only to registered party members. The next major contest was in Virginia, home to the Christian Coalition and the former Moral Majority, and fertile ground for Christian Right candidates.

Although Virginia has an open primary, the state GOP instituted a requirement that all voters in the primary must sign a "loyalty oath" as a condition for voting. The oath was a nonbinding statement in which the signer affirmed that he or she would be loyal to the party and vote for its nominee in November. Not all voters understood the purpose of the oath, and many thought it was legally binding. The effect was to substantially lower participation among non-Republican-identifying voters. That was the goal of the state GOP leaders, all of whom backed Bush.

For months Bush had been spending heavily on mass mailings and television ads in Virginia, and McCain initially appeared not to be contesting the state. But once the polls showed that McCain had moved to within a single digit of Bush, the senator took a remarkable gamble that some likened to a

"Hail Mary" pass. The day before the February 29 primary, McCain went to Virginia Beach, the hometown of Pat Robertson, to make a speech laced with stinging criticism of both the Christian Coalition founder and Moral Majority founder Jerry Falwell. McCain, who affirmed his own religious faith several times in the speech, drew a clear distinction between the values of Christian social conservatives and the political tactics of certain Christian Right leaders. At the urging of Bauer, he also drew a distinction between a number of widely admired Christian Right leaders and the two in question, Robertson and Falwell. These distinctions were lost on the media and the electorate—especially on supporters of the Christian Right, who widely interpreted McCain's remarks as an attack on the involvement of people of faith in politics.[22] McCain also angered many social conservatives by equating Robertson and Falwell with Louis Farrakhan and Al Sharpton. His speech precipitated an emotionally charged national debate over the role of the Christian Right in the GOP: many social conservatives were outraged, while others saw an act of political courage.

McCain lost Virginia 53-44 percent, and once again the Christian Right had delivered the victory to Bush, voting 86 percent against McCain. Among the one in five voters who were self-described members of the religious right, 80 percent supported Bush and 14 percent McCain, while McCain prevailed 52-45 percent among the nearly four in five voters who said that they were *not* members of the religious right. McCain overwhelmingly won the pro-choice vote, and Bush overwhelmingly won the pro-life vote. McCain handily won the votes of Democrats and independents, and Bush won Republicans 69-29 percent.[23]

Super Tuesday

McCain's strategists thought they saw an opportunity in their candidate's attacks on Robertson and Falwell. Although the strategy hurt McCain in Virginia, the GOP contest soon turned to more progressive states with smaller Christian Right voting blocs, among them New York and California. Perhaps it was McCain's intention all along to try to look principled by denouncing the Christian Right leaders in their home state.

But there would not be an electoral payoff for McCain. His attacks sank his candidacy. After the Virginia loss a reporter asked McCain about his strong language against Robertson and Falwell, and McCain rhetorically replied: "You're supposed to tolerate evil in your party in the name of party unity?" He later backtracked from the comment, but the damage had been done. Commentators lambasted McCain for crossing the line of allowable criticism by calling his Christian Right opponents "evil." Bauer stopped defending him and issued a statement asking the senator to apologize for his "unwarranted, ill-advised, and divisive attacks on certain religious leaders."[24]

The Super Tuesday primaries took place one week after the Virginia primary. Among the crucial states were New York, California, Maryland, Georgia, Mississippi, and Ohio. Pro-life groups stepped up their attacks on McCain. The National Right to Life Committee alone spent over $200,000 on anti-McCain phone calls in the Super Tuesday states; voters were told that McCain was not a genuine pro-life advocate and that Bush had the stronger record on the social issues. "For the children's sake, please vote for George Bush," said the phone message.[25] In all, what the National Right to Life Committee spent to defeat McCain was extraordinary: over $500,000 in the primaries, more than half its total spending on all races in the 1998 election cycle and a figure about equal to the organization's total budget reported at the beginning of 2000.[26]

In the wake of his "evil" comment, McCain's standing among key religious constituencies began a precipitous decline. The senator had staked much of his effort on New York state, hoping to capitalize on the large Catholic vote, but a Zogby poll prior to the New York primary showed that a once substantial McCain lead among Catholics had disappeared. Many leading politically conservative Catholics rallied to Bush's defense. Deal Hudson, the editor and publisher of *Crisis*, called McCain a "demagogue" for portraying Bush as insensitive to Catholics. "He is creating a division among traditional allies, including religiously active Catholics and evangelical Christians," Deal said of McCain.[27]

Super Tuesday ended McCain's candidacy. Although he won several New England states with low Christian Right populations, he lost all the important contests. His attacks on Robertson and Falwell had backfired. A third of the voters in New York and Ohio said that McCain's comments had influenced their voting decisions, and those voters opposed him four to one. His negative rankings in the Super Tuesday exit polls were the highest of any point in his campaign. The Christian Right delivered the key votes to Bush in most of the states. For example, in Ohio McCain won the three in four voters who said they were *not* members of the religious right (52-44 percent), while among the one in four who *were* members, Bush won strongly (74-19 percent).[28]

In New York, only 15 percent of the voters were self-described members of the religious right; they backed Bush over McCain 62-28 percent, while the rest of the GOP vote was split evenly between Bush and McCain (47 percent each). Again, McCain took the pro-choice vote and Bush overwhelmingly won the pro-life vote. Half of New York voters were Catholic, and those voters favored Bush over McCain 52-43 percent, suggesting that there was indeed a backlash against McCain's efforts to link Bush with anti-Catholic bigotry. Bush easily carried the Protestant vote, and McCain won only one religious bloc: the Jewish vote.[29]

McCain suspended his candidacy after Super Tuesday and several weeks later gave Bush a tepid endorsement. He told Bush that he would not accept the vice presidential slot. Just in case, Robertson and other Christian Right leaders continued to push their argument that having McCain on the national ticket in any capacity would cause social-conservative voters to sit on their hands on election day. In late April, Robertson told the press, "To think that that man is one heartbeat away from the presidency would scare me to death!"[30] Ironically, at about the same time the Christian Coalition issued its annual scorecard of legislative votes and gave McCain a 91 percent positive score. The previous year his score had been 100 percent, a fact that was readily available during the GOP primary.[31]

THE GOP CONTEST: CHRISTIAN RIGHT KINGMAKERS

McCain had a long record as a conservative voter in Congress, and that included his votes on the social issues. Yet he was anathema to the conservative movement in 2000, especially the Christian Right. Social-conservative opposition cost him the nomination. Tables 1 and 2 make the case quite clearly that the Christian Right delivered Bush's nomination.

An ABC News poll in late February 2000 underscored the challenge McCain faced in running for the GOP nomination. Seven in ten Americans either believed that McCain was a liberal or a moderate, or could not place him ideologically.[32] Christian Right groups effectively distorted his record. McCain contributed to the Christian Right's unease with his support for moderating GOP platform language, with some of his own campaign rhetoric, and especially with his attacks on certain movement leaders. Exit-poll data from the primary states show that in every Republican contest, around a third of the voters ranked moral values as the most important matter facing the country, and among those voters Bush prevailed heavily.

TABLE 1

FIVE REPUBLICAN PRIMARIES:
VOTES OF RELIGIOUS RIGHT AND NON–RELIGIOUS RIGHT VOTERS

	New Hampshire	South Carolina	Michigan	Virginia	New York
% Religious Right	16	34	27	19	15
Bush-McCain%	**36**-26	**68**-24	**66**-25	**80**-14	**62**-28
% Non-RR	80	61	67	77	80
Bush-McCain%	28-**54**	46-**52**	36-**60**	45-**52**	**47-47**

SOURCE: Voter News Service, Republican primary exit polls, 2000.

TABLE 2

GOP PRIMARY VOTERS CITING MORAL VALUES AS CHIEF CONCERN:
VOTES FOR BUSH AND McCAIN

Percentage Citing Moral Values as Chief Concern	Voted for Bush	Voted for McCain	Bush Vote vs. McCain Vote
Arizona, 29	39%	53%	-14%
California, 35	56	33	+23
Colorado, 32	71	16	+55
Connecticut, 29	44	47	-3
Delaware, 27	58	23	+35
Georgia, 37	70	23	+47
Maine, 36	56	36	+20
Maryland, 36	58	30	+28
Massachusetts, 30	29	68	-39
Michigan, 29	51	40	+11
Missouri, 34	65	24	+41
New Hampshire, 28	32	47	-15
New York, 26	56	37	+19
Ohio, 34	63	29	+34
Rhode Island, 30	37	58	-21
South Carolina, 37	55	36	+19
Vermont, 31	40	54	-14
Virginia, 33	61	34	+27

SOURCES: Voter News Service, Republican primary exit polls, 2000, and John Kenneth White, *The Values Divide,* (Chatham House, 2003), 90.

A Pragmatic Choice?

What should scholars make of the role of the Christian Right in delivering the Republican nomination to Bush? The early decision to back Bush seems an act of pragmatism: Bush, the candidate of the establishment wing of the GOP, was widely hailed as the one with the best chance for uniting the party and for winning the general election. There were several more genuinely social-conservative candidates, but Robertson, Reed, and others jumped on the Bush bandwagon early, hoping to become players in the next GOP administration. To be sure, the Christian Right was not united early on in supporting Bush. Many of the other movement leaders gravitated to candidates such as Forbes who may also have appeared pragmatic choices.

The case for Christian Right pragmatism is less easily made with regard to the Bush-McCain race. All the polls suggested that McCain had a much stronger chance than Bush of winning the general election. One possible explanation is that once the Christian Right leaders had strongly backed Bush, they had to protect their own credibility and stay loyal to their candidate. Nobody anticipated McCain's strong challenge for the nomination. Yet the Christian Right leaders not only stood behind Bush but launched an extraordinary offensive against McCain. The severity of the response to McCain's candidacy would be understandable from the Christian Right perspective were he a moderate, pro-choice Republican. But his voting record in Congress and issue positions made him an almost ideal candidate for the Christian Right.

It is plausible that some Christian Right opposition to McCain was of a more personal than political nature. Dobson was candid about his view that past adultery, divorce, and a tolerant attitude toward gays made McCain unacceptable, no matter how "right" the senator was on the issues. Bush clearly was more comfortable than McCain at articulating "family values" issues and defending the Christian Right against its critics. Also, McCain, despite a conservative voting record, had never shown much interest in the intersection of religion and politics. By contrast, Bush spoke very openly of his faith and of his personal redemption after an undisciplined youth and early adulthood, and he made much of his own belief in the value of faith-based institutions for solving social problems. Furthermore, Bush projected a warm and likable personality, whereas McCain could at times appear self-righteous. Bush was eager to show that he listened to the views of different groups. McCain wore as a badge of honor his stubborn independence and his refusal to pander to group leaders.

Nonetheless, it is also difficult not to conclude that, more than any other reason for opposing McCain, Christian Right leaders perceived his emphasis on campaign finance reform as an assault on the political activities of their various interest-group organizations, and that their opposition had more to do with protecting their own power than with McCain's views on the social agenda. Yet they worked to mobilize their supporters by characterizing the senator as hostile to the pro-life agenda while saying very little about their opposition to his campaign finance reforms.

The greatest risk in backing Bush so strongly was that, had he lost, the Christian Right might have borne the brunt of criticism for consigning the Republican Party to defeat, just as the heavy push by Christian Right groups for the Clinton impeachment in 1998 hurt the GOP in that year's elections.[33] Bush's electoral-college victory spared the Christian Right from further criticism for harming the party's fortunes.

The General Election Campaign

When campaign polls showed McCain the stronger candidate for the GOP, many observers suggested that the conservative wing of the party had erred badly by delivering the nomination to Bush. In retrospect, leaving aside the electoral college and a divided Supreme Court decision, that suggestion would seem perfectly defensible. Nonetheless, Bush prevailed, however narrowly.

The general-election campaign in 2000 highlighted one of the continuing dilemmas for the Christian Right: how to deliver energy and enthusiasm in both the GOP primary contest and the general-election campaign. In contrast to the substantial energy expended for Bush against McCain, the movement's general-election activity was significantly lower even than its efforts in 1996, when Bob Dole ran a lackluster and futile campaign against Bill Clinton.

Only 14 percent of the 2000 electorate was identified as belonging to the religious right, a decline of more than three percentage points from the 1996 election. Voting by the evangelical core constituency of the Christian Right also declined in 2000. The National Election Studies (NES) show that turnout of white evangelicals dropped by 6 percent from 1996 to 2000, whereas turn-out of white Catholics dropped by 1 percent, and of white mainline Protestants 2 percent. Furthermore, the NES data show a decline in national support for the Christian Coalition, from 15.5 percent in 1996 to 13.7 percent in 2000.[34]

Forms of political activity other than voting also declined among white evangelicals. Compared to 1996, fewer white evangelicals reported that they were contacted by a religious or moral group in 2000. Fewer reported receiving information about candidates in churches. A study by the Annenberg Public Policy Center found that pro-choice groups spent heavily on television advertising in 2000, whereas Christian conservative organizations spent relatively little.[35] However, Clyde Wilcox reported that Christian Right groups actively used their radio programs to communicate with targeted audiences, and that this type of activity has the advantage of reaching its targets much more cost-effectively than television.[36]

The level of activity by the Christian Coalition is in some dispute. Throughout the country there were reports that the organization was practically invisible in key primary states and in the general election. The organization claimed to have distributed 70 million voters' guides on the Sunday before election day, though there is no reliable way to confirm that number. Whether this was good or bad for the Christian Right, Robertson was a constant presence in the news during the 2000 elections, especially during the GOP nomination contest. Some Christian Right political-action committees (PACs), such as Gary Bauer's Campaign for Working Families, were active in 2000. Bauer's group reported receipts of $2.7 million, made significant contributions to GOP candidates, and engaged in independent expenditures.[37] Although Christian Right political activity declined in 2000, and the self-identified religious-right component of the electorate was smaller, the movement was more united for Bush than it had been for Dole in 1996. Exit-poll data showed that 80 percent of that group backed Bush in 2000, whereas 65 percent had backed Dole in 1996. In the historically close 2000 election, the strongly united vote of the Christian Right was crucial to Bush's victory. And the Christian Right was of course more prevalent in the vote in some states than in others. In Al Gore's home state of Tennessee, for example, the religious-right vote was 27 percent of the electorate, and 78 percent of that group backed Bush.

Furthermore, even at just 14 percent of the electorate, the Christian Right in 2000 was on a par with the labor-union household vote and slightly larger than the African-American vote. As both labor and civil-rights groups have shown in the past, strongly united groups of such size in the electorate can be the key to the electoral fortunes of a major political party.

Concluding Observations

In the end, the GOP nomination contest in 2000 showed that, despite many predictions to the contrary, the Christian Right remains an active and powerful force in U.S politics. When the movement is united behind a candidate, as it was for Bush once the race became a two-man contest, the Christian Right can be a true kingmaker in the Republican Party. There is no convincing evidence at this point that the Christian Right is losing influence in that party. As for general-election campaigns, it is too soon to judge whether the declining political activity of the movement in 2000 is the beginning of a steeper decline or was merely an aberration.

What is clear, however, is that the Christian Coalition has lost most of its clout and that there is no one Christian Right organization to take its place today in mainstream political activity. Perhaps the Christian Coalition succeeded so well at training its activist core for mainstream politics that many of those people ultimately left movement politics for Republican party politics. If so, part of the story of the Christian Right today is that whereas interest-group organizations appear to be in decline, the core constituency has become more and more integrated into the mainstream of American politics. But it is also clear that many core activists became disgruntled with interest-group organizations that seem to act like mainstream units of the GOP and ignore the key social issues that mobilized these activists in the first place.

In all likelihood the Christian Right will have to choose between two futures. In one, it supports Republican candidates and bargains for incremental policy changes. In the other, it insists on more fundamental policy changes, perhaps achieving no policy victories but maintaining its ability to serve as prophetic critic of the culture and government. The more probable of these two possibilities is that the Christian Right will continue its course of pragmatism and will therefore continue to lose part of its activist core. Some will leave politics altogether, some will gravitate toward GOP politics, and others will support third parties and more radical organizations. If the movement does lose part of its activist base, it will still constitute a sizable and well-organized interest group in American politics—perhaps as influential as feminists, African-Americans, or environmentalists. This is the normal progression of many social movements.

Ultimately, the fate of the Christian Right is constrained by its policy goals. Its achievements do not match those of other major movements in the United States, such as labor, civil rights, and feminism. Those movements changed America, while the changes the Christian Right has helped to bring about are at the margins of politics and culture. The Christian Right can achieve its core agenda only by convincing citizens that the movement's moral vision is the correct one. Yet in the quarter century since this wave of Christian Right activity started, the public has become more liberal on abortion, and considerably more liberal on gay rights and women's issues.

As long as the Christian Right fails to convince the public of its moral claims, most GOP candidates will either continue to emphasize mainstream issue appeals or be defeated at the polls. And as long as Republican candidates distance themselves from the more controversial social issues associated with the Christian Right, movement purists will find little reason to be enthusiastic in supporting the GOP. The struggle in the movement between pragmatists and purists is certain to continue for a long time to come.

CHAPTER THREE

Conservative Protestants and the Family: Resisting, Engaging, or Accommodating Modernity?

W. Bradford Wilcox

The "family modernization" perspective is one of the most influential theoretical approaches to the study of contemporary family change. This perspective holds that modern structural and cultural developments lead to a decline in the functions, stability, value, and authority of the family. On the structural front, state and market institutions take on many of the functions once handled by the family, such as schooling, leisure activity, and food production. This loss of functions weakens members' dependence on one another, thereby diminishing levels of family commitment. Furthermore, cultural concomitants of modernity such as secularization and individualism undercut the values and virtues associated with family-centered living. Family functions that retain any real purchase on the lives of modern persons have to do with a narrow range of what are called *expressive* tasks: providing affection, psychological support, and companionship, along with some related aspects of child rearing. Family modernization is so potent a force, moreover, that even subcultures organized along family-centered lines cannot resist succumbing to its dynamics.

The most obvious challenge to this theory emanates from conservative Protestantism, which is the largest family-oriented subculture in the nation.[1] Since the 1970s, conservative Protestant institutions have mounted political, cultural, and pastoral attacks on such central features of family modernization as feminism, the sexual revolution, and pro-homosexual movements. Drawing

W. Bradford Wilcox is assistant professor of sociology at the University of Virginia. His research focuses on how cultural institutions influence family behavior, relationship quality, and family stability. He has published articles in several journals, including the *American Sociological Review*.

51

upon its considerable institutional resources and its strong sense of collective identity, conservative Protestantism has established symbolic boundaries and built parallel institutions that enable it to *resist* some aspects of family modernization.[2] At the same time, over the last three decades this subculture has clearly adopted—or at least accustomed itself to—some aspects of family modernization. Some scholars see this as a sign of conservative Protestantism's ability to *engage* the world by adapting to "the conditions of the time" without "bargain[ing] away [its] core beliefs."[3] Others view these developments as faith-denying attempts to *accommodate* to a modernity that is hostile to theological orthodoxy.[4]

My purpose here is not to analyze or judge the theological orthodoxy of conservative Protestantism. Rather, I will draw on these theoretical perspectives to try to determine whether conservative Protestantism is resisting, engaging, or accommodating the logic of family modernization, which—above all else—is characterized by declining personal investment in family life. I will look at three important dimensions: the family-related culture produced and legitimated by conservative Protestant institutions, the family environment children experience in this subculture, and the manner in which gender roles and differences are conveyed.

These matters are of more than academic interest; they have a direct bearing on the public welfare. The extent to which conservative Protestantism is resisting family-modernization trends in divorce and parenting has a signal impact on child well-being, since children benefit from high-quality, stable ties with their biological parents. Also, since almost 30 percent of American adults are evangelical, fundamentalist, or Pentecostal, the extent to which conservative Protestantism is resisting gender egalitarianism has considerable consequences for gender equality in the country as a whole. Finally, these conservative Protestant family practices—especially in areas of fertility, parenting, and marital stability—are also important because of the key role they will play in the future in shaping the subculture's religious strength and public profile.

Responding to the Sixties

Several religious and cultural traditions shaped the conservative Protestant response to the dramatic demographic, cultural, and political events of the 1960s and 1970s. In the 1960s, a commitment to a literal interpretation of the Bible went hand in glove with a commitment to an unchanging and objective biblically based morality. Linked to this biblical morality was a sentimental model of the family that had been institutionalized in the nineteenth century at the high watermark of evangelicalism's cultural influence; this model was thought to embody the divine plan for the family and was seen as the cornerstone of a civilization deeply indebted to the Protestant ethic.[5] Moreover, conservative Protestants were and are inclined toward a "personal influence" strategy of both evangelization and social change that focuses, to a large degree, on the family.[6] A final cultural factor was the social status of conservative Protestants, which put them at some remove from the carriers of cultural modernity: in the 1960s, conservative Protestants were overwhelmingly southern and/or working-class Americans, with little affinity for the ideas and mores of the emerging counterculture.[7]

Not surprisingly, many of the family-related cultural and political developments associated with the 1960s and 1970s came as a profound shock to this subculture. The rise of the sexual revolution, feminism, and the divorce culture struck at the heart of biblical morality and conservative family ideals. Likewise, Supreme Court decisions on school prayer and abortion in the 1960s and 1970s, the Internal Revenue Service's targeting of racially segregated Christian schools in the 1970s, and the 1970s campaign for the Equal Rights Amendment convinced many conservative Protestants that the government was turning on their churches, schools, and families, as well as turning against biblical morality. In response, a host of organizations—from the Moral Majority to Concerned Women for America—were formed in the late 1970s to do political battle with the enemies of the traditional family. Critics of this effort charged that it amounted to an effort to impose Christian morality through the state. But it may be more accurate to see the political mobilization of conservative Protestants as a defensive movement to protect a traditional, family-oriented way of life.

Although the political dimensions of the crusade to save the traditional family have received the most attention from academics and the media, conservative Protestant institutions have also carried this crusade to their own domestic front. James Dobson founded Focus on the Family in 1977 to provide guidance on family matters from a Christian perspective; this membership-supported organization now reaches more than two million people every month through syndicated radio shows, magazines, books, and videos, and has an annual budget of more than $100 million. More than 10 percent of the multi-billion-dollar Christian publishing industry is devoted to family matters.[8] The National Congregations Survey suggests there are more than 26,000 family-oriented ministries—not to mention discussions of family issues in Sunday sermons and informal small groups—in conservative Protestant congregations around the country.[9] These institutional efforts support a family-oriented culture that is substantially independent of cultural trends within the wider society.

These institutions produce two distinct ideologies. The first is *familism*, which depicts the family as the most important institution in society because it is the primary cultivator of virtue, meaning, and sentiment. This ideology holds that norms of familial obligation should govern parental and marital relations, and the family deserves high levels of practical and emotional investment on the part of its members. The second ideology is *gender-role traditionalism*, which advocates a gender-based division of labor in both the family and the workplace on the grounds that men and women have distinctly different talents. Gender-role traditionalism is also associated with an endorsement of male headship in the home. These family-related ideologies have long roots in American life but are now supported most vigorously by conservative Protestants.

FAMILISM: A HIGH VIEW OF FAMILY IMPORTANCE

Conservative Protestant familism has been colored by this subculture's commitment to biblical literalism, its Americanism, its pragmatism, its pietism, and its increasingly therapeutic character, as well as by the cultural upheavals of the 1960s and 1970s. These influences can be seen in conservative Protestant discourse on parenting since the 1970s. For instance, one leader wrote, "If we are to rebuild our nation we must first strengthen our homes and make sure that they are Christ-centered. Husbands and wives must assume the full responsibilities of Christian parents so that children may walk in the ways of the Lord."[10]

This approach to parenting combines a progressive emphasis on an intense, affectionate approach to regular parent-child relations with a stricter, more traditional approach to disciplinary situations. It draws on biblical notions of children as created in the image of God but wounded by original sin to argue that children need to be treated with significant doses of both love and discipline. In the words of Beverly LaHaye, president of Concerned Women for America, parents should give a child "an honest picture of what he can expect from his own Heavenly Father."[11] To comprehend God's love, children should receive "words of encouragement, love, and acceptance from their parents."[12] Parents are also urged to demonstrate God's love to their children by spending a lot of time with them.[13]

At the same time, they are called to embody God's justice. This strict approach to discipline often uses corporal punishment, which is justified by numerous biblical citations such as Proverbs 22:15, "Foolishness is bound in the heart of a child; but the rod of correction shall drive it far from him" (biblical quotations are from the King James Version unless specified otherwise). It is important to note, however, that parents are exhorted to discipline their children in a spirit of self-control, exercising parental sovereignty in a way that parallels God's sovereignty. They are told to avoid harsh physical punishment and yelling, lest they undercut their divinely sanctioned authority: "Chastisement is not a tongue lashing, threats or screaming fits of anger; in other words, adult temper tantrums. These things do nothing but support the child's disrespect for his parents' authority and demonstrate the parents' inability to rule."[14] Thus the conservative Protestant approach to parenting is guided, in large part, by biblical motifs of divine love, sovereignty, and justice.

But therapeutic and pragmatic themes also can be found running through conservative Protestant discourse on family matters. Although leaders often insist that their family advice is drawn from the timeless wisdom of the Bible, the subjective, pietistic tradition of which they are a part has left them open to the therapeutic focus on expressive interpersonal relations and personal fulfillment that was popularized in the 1960s and 1970s.[15] The pragmatic and Puritanical roots of this religious tradition also help to make behaviorist models of parenting attractive. The popularity of modern psychology is apparent in the fact that many leading conservative-Protestant family experts, such as James Dobson and Gary Smalley, are trained psychologists and regularly resort to therapeutic language.

This therapeutic model is evident in the counsel on both expressive and disciplinary behavior that conservative Protestant leaders offer to parents. For instance, they tell parents to praise their children out of respect for a "child's need for self-esteem and acceptance,"[16] and they support these claims by pointing to studies from Harvard, Princeton, Purdue, and UCLA that find children thrive when exposed to a warm, expressive parenting style.[17] The pragmatic-behaviorist line of reasoning is apparent in discussions of discipline. Family specialists like Dobson argue that yelling at one's children is ineffective, especially when compared with the prudent use of corporal punishment: "Parents often use anger to get action instead of using action [spanking] to get action [compliance]. . . . Trying to control children by screaming is as utterly futile as trying to steer a car by honking the horn."[18] Thus, therapeutic and pragmatic modes of thinking have been harnessed to an intensive parenting ethic. At least in this domain, conservative Protestantism has been able to adapt aspects of the broader culture to strengthen its own family orientation.

The Marriage Message

Biblical, pragmatic, and psychological themes also combine in discourse on marriage in this subculture, and this too has been affected by the cultural dynamics of the last thirty years. The marriage message both resists and accommodates the broader society's assumptions about relationships. First, conservative Protestant discourse draws upon a number of biblical texts to depict marriage as:

—a covenantal institution, modeled on the unbreakable relationship between Christ and his church as described in Ephesians 5:21-33, which says in part: "For the husband is the head of the wife, even as Christ is the head of the church. . . . Husbands, love your wives, as Christ also loved the church . . ." (vv. 23, 25);

—a source of mutual spiritual and emotional support for couples; Deuteronomy 24:5, for instance, says the newly married man should not go to war or "be charged with any business" but should be "free at home one year, and shall cheer up his wife . . .";

—the proper setting for the mutual satisfaction of sexual desires; for example, St. Paul's instructions on marriage include the requirement that husband and wife should give each other "conjugal rights" (1 Cor. 7:3, Revised Standard Version); and

—the ideal setting for begetting and rearing children.

This biblically informed discourse is now consciously deployed in opposition to more modern understandings of marriage and relationships. A Southern Baptist report on the family suggests the basic tenor of this opposition: "Marriage, according to Scripture, is a covenant commitment to the exclusive, permanent, monogamous union of one man and one woman, and thus it cannot be defined as a flexible contract between consenting human beings."[19] Here, a theological understanding of marriage as a "covenant" marked by "unconditional love and acceptance" is contrasted with a secular understanding of marriage as a "flexible contract."

Also present in conservative Protestant discourse on marriage are Americanist themes; the traditional view of marriage is good not only for the Christian couple but also for society. James Dobson had this to say about the dramatic rise in divorce since the 1960s:

> Come on, America. Enough is enough! We've had our dance with divorce, and we have a million broken homes to show for it. We've tried the me-philosophy and the new morality and unbridled hedonism. They didn't work. Now it's time to get back to some old-fashioned values, like commitment and sacrifice and responsibility and purity and love and the straight life. Not only will our children benefit from our self-discipline, but we adults will live in a less neurotic world, too![20]

Dobson's comments suggest the linking of familism to an idealized vision of an American past populated by intact homes and governed by "old-fashioned values like commitment and sacrifice." This contrasts sharply with the cultural ethos of the 1960s and 1970s—what Dobson terms "the me-philosophy and the new morality and unbridled hedonism."

But although conservative Protestantism has articulated a distinctly countercultural perspective on marriage, it has also accommodated itself to the recent focus on the expressive character of the marital relationship. Its voluminous advice on marriage focuses overwhelmingly on relational dynamics and emotional character. For instance, Dobson urges husbands to focus on the "provision of emotional support . . . of conversation . . . making her feel like a lady . . . building her ego."[21] Similarly, Gary Smalley argues that "genuine

love" entails meeting a spouse's needs and helping her reach her "full potential in life."[22] And so couples are urged to develop techniques of emotional
support and to help each other toward mutual fulfillment; these recommenda-
tions are completely in keeping with the therapeutic sensibility of the broader
culture.

This therapeutic emphasis has also been allied to a pragmatic approach.
Conservative Protestant discourse on marriage holds out the promise of marital happiness for the partner who attends to the emotional needs of his or her
spouse. Smalley, for instance, tells husbands, "Remember, *you* are the one who
gains when you strive to have a loving relationship with your wife."[23] In fact,
he reminds his readers of Dobson's comment that a husband who "learns to
love his wife in the way she needs to be loved" will be rewarded with a wife
who "respond[s] to him physically in a way he never dreamed possible."[24]
Conservative Protestantism has accommodated itself to the therapeutic and
pragmatic imperatives of modern views of the family.

Accommodating Divorce

This spirit of accommodation has also made inroads in this subculture's approach to divorce. Some conservative Protestant leaders—Dobson is an example—
hew closely to the classical Protestant teaching that divorce is not permissible for
Christians except on the grounds of adultery (Matt. 19:9) or the desertion of an
unbelieving spouse (1 Cor. 7:15). Others, however, perform elaborate herme-
neutical maneuvers to argue that any kind of desertion constitutes a legitimate
basis for divorce; a 1980 poll of Southern Baptist clergy found that 36 percent of
Southern Baptist pastors took this position.[25] Still others invoke biblical motifs of
"forgiveness" and "second chances" to argue that "legalistic" approaches to divorce and remarriage are illegitimate and that churches should decide case by
case whether persons should be allowed to remarry.[26] The 1980 poll found that
36 percent of Southern Baptist clergy agreed with this position. What is striking
about this poll is that it suggests that more than half of Southern Baptist clergy
do not adhere to the divorce ethic suggested by a literal interpretation of the
Bible, or to that endorsed by the Southern Baptist Convention in 1904, that
remarriage was permissible only in cases of adultery. Although the attitude toward divorce is still more conservative than that found in the general culture, it
has moved toward accommodation.

Conservative Protestantism has successfully articulated a message that resists some aspects of family modernization, and this is a testament to its institutional strength and its strong sense of collective identity. At the same time, its
embrace of therapeutic modes of family life has had a mixed effect on its
family orientation. On the one hand, this therapeutic approach seems to have
intensified the focus on parenting; on the other, it has become allied with an
expressive approach to marriage that may lift marital expectations to unrea-

sonable heights. Finally, conservative Protestantism has become more accepting of divorce; undoubtedly, this increased acceptance is linked to the fact that this subculture has been far from untouched by the dramatic increases in divorce since the 1960s.

GENDER-ROLE TRADITIONALISM

Conservative Protestantism has played a key part sustaining a traditional view of gender roles. Its continued commitment to this view has been shaped by biblical tradition, belief in a divinely ordained gender order, and a sentimental view of family relations.

This gender-role traditionalism has two key features: patriarchal authority, and a division of family labor along gendered lines. Male headship is accorded important symbolic weight because of the biblical emphasis on male authority. Numerous biblical passages indicate that men should be heads of their families (e.g., Eph. 5:23, "For the husband is the head of the wife . . ."; 1 Pet. 3:1, ". . . wives, be in subjection to your own husbands . . ."; 1 Cor. 11:3, ". . . and the head of the woman is the man . . ."). Consequently, most conservative Protestant leaders have felt duty-bound to affirm this principle. Conservative Protestantism connects these passages to a divinely ordained gender order that extends to all parts of the social world, including marriage. Drawing on its own biblical tradition, along with a kind of folk wisdom that sees men and women as naturally different in ways that favor male authority, conservative Protestantism has maintained that men were created by God to direct the affairs of the family.

The social disorder associated with the 1960s and 1970s—especially divorce, feminism, abortion, and the sexual revolution—served to heighten this subculture's commitment to order in general and traditional gender order in particular. Institutional and lay support for male headship has remained strong: recent surveys reveal that about 90 percent of conservative Protestant laity and clergy support the principle.[27] A prominent recent example is the 1998 Southern Baptist Convention statement calling upon men to "lead" their families and women to "submit [themselves] graciously to the servant leadership of [their] husband[s]."

In contrast, support for the "separate spheres" doctrine has grown weaker. Proponents of separate spheres rely on expansive readings of a few passages from the Bible such as Genesis 2:18, where God, having created man, said, "It is not good that the man should be alone; I will make him an help meet for him"; and Titus 2:3-5, where older women are to teach younger women to be "keepers at home." From these passages they argue that women should be "keepers of the home." But the biblical warrant for this doctrine is weak; the primary motivation appears to be rooted in a dedication to order and familism. Conservative Protestantism is firmly attached to the notion of a divinely ordained gender order, and the separate-spheres doctrine is the only available gender-based model of family interaction. It also supports an intensive mode of mothering that requires mothers to spend as much time as possible with their young children, preferably by staying home.

The Softening of Patriarchy

But in the last two decades, the patriarchal emphasis has softened. The language used to characterize male leadership has shifted from "male headship" to "servant leadership"—as in the Southern Baptist statement quoted above. Notions of headship are now being linked to male participation—rather than male authority—in the home.[28] And men are now encouraged to attend to the emotional dynamics of their marriages. Smalley, for instance, tells his readers that a husband must "meet a woman's needs from *her viewpoint*" and then proceeds to detail what women want: expressions of affection and praise, an empathetic orientation, and lots of communication.[29] This "soft" patriarchy that is now common in conservative Protestant circles paradoxically accords men symbolic status as leaders for adopting what has traditionally been considered a feminine orientation to family life.

Moreover, while conservative Protestant clergy and laity continue to think mothers of young children should minimize their work outside the home, they are much less likely to embrace the "separate spheres" doctrine that men should focus on work and women should focus on homemaking. For instance, one 1996 survey found that conservative Protestants were twice as likely as unaffiliated Americans to say that pre-school children suffer when their mothers work but no more likely to object to the general principle of women working.[30]

Three developments have contributed to the softening of patriarchy. First, conservative Protestant patriarchy has faced sharp challenges to its legitimacy from both external and internal feminist movements. For instance, Christians for Biblical Equality, an evangelical feminist organization founded in 1987, has challenged conservative Protestants who maintain a patriarchal vision of family life to exorcise any hint of domination in their vision and to stress ways in which women benefit from a properly ordered patriarchy. Second, the marked increases in education that conservative Protestants have enjoyed since the 1970s have dramatically improved the employment prospects and expectations of women; conservative Protestant women are more inclined to seek meaning and status through paid work. Finally, declines in men's real wages since the 1970s have increased economic pressure on families and contributed to a significant increase in the percentage of working wives. And as women struggle to balance paid work and family responsibilities, they seek additional support from their husbands in the domestic arena.

The shift away from the separate-spheres doctrine may be understood as an *accommodation* to family modernization insofar as it is associated with a reduction in the amount of time and attention women devote to the family. By contrast, the softening of patriarchal authority may be judged a strategic *adaptation* to family modernization if it increases male emotional and practical investments in family life and increases women's marital happiness.

Continuing Cultural Resistance

Nonetheless, it is important to note that conservative Protestant family and gender discourse has been marked by a note of resistance to the cultural shifts of the last three decades. This resistance is rooted in its tradition of biblical inerrantism and its absolutist vision of the moral life, its traditional vision of the family, its Americanism, and its privatistic approach to both evangelism and social change.

The posture of resistance is also linked to this subculture's strong sense of collective identity. Social theorists have long noted that conflict with an external foe builds internal collective identity. Conservative Protestant leaders have been able to build support for their institutions by articulating a message that highlights points of conflict with the wider culture. In a guest editorial in the *New York Times*, for instance, R. Albert Mohler, president of Southern Baptist Seminary, argues that the Southern Baptist Convention's (SBC) opposition to homosexuality and abortion, and its support for male headship, are rooted in the desire to hold itself "captive to God's word." But he then goes on to say,

> Southern Baptists are engaged in a battle against modernity, earnestly contending for the truth and authority of an ancient faith. To the cultured critics of religion, we are the cantankerous holdouts against the inevitable. But so far as the Southern Baptist Convention is concerned, the future is in God's hands. If faithfulness requires the slings and arrows of outraged opponents, so be it.[31]

Conservative Protestant discourse regarding family and gender is about more than maintaining fidelity to the Bible. It also represents an important weapon in the war on modernity and its high priests—"the cultured critics of religion." Mohler depicts the SBC as a kind of saving remnant, resolute in its desire to fight for the "truth and authority of an ancient faith," willing to endure the "slings and arrows of outraged opponents," and confident that its "future is in God's hands."

But the fact that this family and gender discourse is so tightly tied to questions of collective identity also raises the possibility that it has little consequence for personal behavior. Toward the end of his editorial attack on modernity and its high priests, Mohler admits that "Southern Baptists experience family trouble like everyone else"; but, he says, "at least they know how God intended to order the family."[32] Mohler's admission—along with his failure to include divorce in his list of modern ills—raises the possibility that conservative Protestant resistance to family modernization may be more symbolic than real.

My content analysis of *Christianity Today*, the leading organ of American evangelicalism, lends support to this hypothesis. From 1970 to 1990, 58 percent of articles dealing with family-related matters focused on hot-button issues like homosexuality and abortion—issues that build collective identity but have little practical bearing on the lives of most conservative Protestant adults.[33] That means that less than half of the family-related articles focused on bread-and-butter issues that *will* affect most of these adults, like marriage, parenting, and divorce. It is possible that conservative Protestant family and gender discourse is oriented more toward building collective identity than toward shaping personal behavior.

Social Capital in Conservative Protestant Homes

The notion of "social capital" has increasingly come to orient the study of parenting. Drawing on the work of James Coleman, scholars of family life have shown how family-based social capital—i.e., the character and structure of family ties—is associated with a range of positive social, psychological, and normative outcomes for children.[34]

Three aspects are particularly salient for child well-being. The first two have to with the character of family ties. First is the extent to which parent-child ties are supportive—represented by both the quality and the quantity of time that parents spend with their children. For instance, children who report close ties to their parents are less likely to report psychological distress. Second is the extent to which parents exert social control over their children. This influences the children's integration into the social and moral order. For example, children whose parents set and enforce clear rules, and closely monitor their activities, are less likely to abuse drugs and alcohol. These first two aspects of family-based social capital also tap the extent to which parents are investing themselves in the family and asserting the family's authority over the child and thereby resisting the logic of family modernization.

The third particularly salient aspect of family social capital concerns the structure of parent-child ties—especially whether parents remain married. This is important for child well-being in a number of ways. Children benefit from relationships with adults who have a long-term horizon of care and concern for them, and who interact with them daily. The higher quality of relationships that children from intact, two-parent homes generally have with their parents, particularly their fathers, helps account for the fact that such children are much less likely to drop out of school, experience serious psychological distress, or end up in prison than children raised in single- or step-parent families. Family stability also is an indication of the success with which families are resisting family modernization by valuing family well-being over self-interest.

Authoritarian Parenting?

Some scholarly critics have argued that the parenting style of conservative Protestants is abusive and authoritarian. For instance, in 1991 Donald Capps delivered a presidential address to the Society for the Scientific Study of Religion provocatively entitled, "Religion and Child Abuse: Perfect Together." Capps argued that the parenting advice offered by figures like James Dobson, with its emphasis on divine justice and authority, leads to a parenting style marked by abusive physical discipline.[35] John Gottman, a leading family psychologist, argues that the rise of the religious right is associated with a trend toward an "authoritarian" parenting style among men characterized by abusive discipline and emotional distance from children.[36] But both of these claims were made without recourse to empirical evidence regarding the actual behavior of conservative Protestant parents.

It is true that such parents are significantly more likely than other parents to value obedience from their children and to resort to corporal punishment in disciplinary situations. Using two measures of biblical orthodoxy, one study found that the most biblically orthodox parents spanked their preschool children on forty-six more occasions per year than the most biblically liberal parents.[37] However, there is no evidence to suggest that this strict approach to discipline is abusive or arbitrary. An abusive parenting style is usually marked by an erratic combination of corporal punishment and yelling. But conservative Protestant parents are less likely to yell at their children than are other parents.[38] They are also more likely to set clear rules on matters like curfew, television watching, and homework.[39] Thus they embrace a strict but controlled approach to discipline that is consistent with their emphasis on human sinfulness, divine justice, and parental authority.

As importantly, the intensive and expressive approach to child rearing embraced by these parents in non-disciplinary situations belies any notion of authoritarianism or emotional distance. Conservative Protestant parents are significantly more likely than other parents to report hugging and praising their children. For instance, one study found that the most biblically orthodox parents were 147 percent more likely than the most theologically liberal parents to report praising and hugging their children "very often."[40] They also report higher levels of involvement in activities like homework and sports with their adolescent children.[41] Thus, conservative Protestants score high on the first two dimensions of social capital. Their neo-traditional approach to parenting, which combines a traditional emphasis on structure and discipline with a progressive emphasis on intensive, warm parent-child relations, means that their children benefit from deep and disciplined *emotional* ties with their parents.

The Prevalence of Divorce

But *structural* ties are something else. Compared with the rest of the population, conservative Protestants are *more* likely to divorce.[42] Statistical analyses
of the National Survey of Families and Households indicate that this effect is
tied, in part, to two factors: age and region. Conservative Protestants generally
marry younger than their peers. Paradoxically, the sentimentalization of family
life, and marriage in particular, may encourage young people to marry before
they have acquired the needed virtues and emotional skills. The divorce rate is
also related to the fact that conservative Protestants disproportionately hail
from the South, where the divorce rate is higher than in the rest of the nation.
Here again, the sentimentalization of marriage may encourage young people
to marry before they are ready for the challenges of married life. Given the
religious dominance of conservative Protestantism in the South, it is also possible that this region has a disproportionate share of *nominal* conservative
Protestants, who may be less likely to have strong moral objections to divorce.

Nevertheless, it is striking that a subculture that stresses the importance of
family, and the value of marriage in particular, has a higher divorce rate than
the rest of the population. Two other factors not easily tapped in surveys of
family life also are, in all likelihood, implicated in this. First, the therapeutic
view of marriage championed by many conservative Protestant leaders may
foster unrealistic expectations of marriage. These expectations may lead couples
to divorce when one or both spouses decides that the marriage is not fulfilling.
Second, as noted earlier, conservative Protestant moral discourse on divorce is
muted and ambiguous—especially when compared with what is said on matters like homosexuality. It may well be that leaders and pastors are more comfortable confronting homosexuality, which probably does not affect many people
in the pews, than confronting divorce, which does. Their unwillingness to
underline theological and moral objections to divorce would appear to be
implicated in this subculture's divorce rate, given the fact that opposition to
divorce is strongly linked to marital stability.

Thus, in stressing parental social control and adopting an intensive, warm
parenting style, conservative Protestant familism has been able to resist and
engage family modernization. However, it has not been tough-minded enough
to resist the increase in divorce associated with this modernization.

Resisting and Engaging the Gender Revolution

The last three decades have witnessed dramatic changes in women's social
and cultural status and in cultural expectations, if not practices, regarding the
role of men in families. Conservative Protestant institutions have probably
been the most important sources of *resistance* to this revolution. They have
articulated a gender ideology that encompasses male headship, differences

between the sexes—especially regarding parenthood—and explicit critiques of feminism. Some family scholars speculate that the religious right is an influential force "pushing men toward authoritarian and stereotypical forms of masculinity and attempting to renew patriarchal family relations."[43]

In two respects, conservative Protestant resistance to the gender revolution is associated with distinctively traditional gender patterns. First, there is some evidence that conservative Protestant mothers of preschool children are less likely to work outside the home than other women.[44] Second, there is more inequality in the division of household labor in this subculture.[45] However, this inequality is tied not to male patterns of housework—conservative Protestant men are no more or less likely to do household labor than their male peers— but to the fact that conservative Protestant women do more household labor than their female peers. Their devotion to household labor is consistent with the high value accorded to family life in this subculture.

But in three other respects, conservative Protestant practice has *accommodated* the gender revolution. First, although fertility was dramatically higher in this subculture than in the nation as a whole for much of the last century, since the 1970s the gap has decreased. Currently, the fertility rate of conservative Protestants is slightly more than two children per woman, just above the national rate of 2.06.[46] The declining fertility rate suggests that for both economic and cultural reasons, women in this subculture are seeking to balance child bearing and rearing with paid work. Indeed, labor-force participation rates among conservative Protestant women have grown dramatically since the 1970s; rates among such women without small children appear to be no different from those in the rest of the population.[47] Thus the second way in which conservative Protestant women have accommodated themselves to the gender revolution is by joining the labor force. Finally, although conservative Protestants express their support for male headship in principle, there is no evidence that these men are more likely to make decisions for their families than other men.[48] That is, although conservative Protestant couples overwhelmingly express symbolic support for male headship, they have accommodated themselves to the egalitarian decision-making patterns of other American couples.

But in recent years, conservative Protestant men have *engaged* the gender revolution by responding to popular and church pressure to dedicate themselves to their families. They have increased their emotional and practical involvement in family life. Currently, these fathers are more likely than other fathers to engage in one-on-one activities like homework help or personal conversations with their adolescent children.[49] They are also more likely to hug and praise their children.[50] And, compared to other husbands, they are more likely to display love and affection to their wives.[51] This active and expressive approach to family life would seem to be a consequence of the familist message stressed by churches and family-oriented organizations since the 1970s.

The paradox is that strong support for a patriarchal ideology coexists with a more feminized style of male behavior in the home. Indeed, some ethnographic work suggests that conservative Protestant women and church leaders have linked male leadership to successful efforts to make men more oriented to domestic life.[52] There is virtually no evidence that conservative Protestant gender ideology is "pushing men toward authoritarian and stereotypical forms of masculinity." Quite the contrary.

From the perspective of family modernization, the key issue is whether the gender practices of conservative Protestants are increasing or decreasing investments in family life. They appear to have increased the practical and emotional investments that men make in family life by linking headship to familial involvement and by stressing the importance of the family to men. With respect to women, however, the trend seems toward diminished investments in family life. Conservative Protestant women continue to devote more time to housework and to the rearing of young children than their peers, but their fertility rate has decreased dramatically. They have also increased their labor-force participation to the point where approximately 60 percent of conservative Protestant married women were in the work force in 1999—very close to the national average of 62 percent.[53] All this suggests that the child-centered, patriarchal family that was characteristic of the twentieth-century conservative Protestant family is becoming a relic.

IS DEMOGRAPHY DESTINY? LOOKING AHEAD

From 1960 to 2000, the ranks of conservative Protestantism rose by more than 50 percent, to the point where this subculture now constitutes almost 30 percent of the U.S. population. In this same period *mainline* Protestantism saw marked declines in its membership and population share.

A recent study indicates that the most important factor driving conservative Protestant growth in the last century was fertility. Hout, Greeley, and Wilde report that approximately 75 percent of this subculture's growth can be attributed to its high fertility rates for much of the twentieth century.[54] Fertility created growth in two ways. First, high rates meant that more and more children came to be raised in the conservative Protestant subculture. Second, given the strong link between parenthood and religiosity, high fertility rates meant that conservative Protestant couples were more likely than other Christians to maintain their commitment to Christianity. By contrast, many other Americans drifted away from religious faith when they postponed or avoided parenthood. As Robert Wuthnow explains,

> During the 1950s, the average time between confirmation class and birth of first child for U.S. young people had been only seven years; by the end of the 1960s, in large measure because of the new contracep-

tive technologies, this period had more than doubled to fifteen years. Since the time between confirmation and parenthood has always been one in which young people could drop out of established religion and turn their attention to other things, the doubling of this period was of enormous religious significance.[55]

The second key factor in conservative Protestant growth in the last century was religious retention. Numerous studies show that this subculture has done a better job of retaining its youth than both mainline Protestants and Catholics. For instance, a 1991 study found that 91 percent of adults who had grown up in the conservative Protestant tradition were still conservative Protestant, while the corresponding figures were 79 percent for mainline Protestants and 85 percent for Catholics.[56]

Although conversions have played a role in the growth of conservative Protestantism, most research indicates that high rates of fertility and religious retention were the most important factors. In effect, this means that success in resisting family modernization for much of the last century contributed enormously to the current institutional vigor, size, and public presence of conservative Protestantism. What, then, do current family trends augur?

The distinctively neo-traditional approach to parenting among conservative Protestants suggests that religious retention will continue to be high. But the increase in the subculture's divorce rate, which paralleled the national rise in the late 1960s and 1970s, will keep down what would otherwise be exceptionally high rates of religious transmission from one generation to the next. Studies suggest that conservative Protestants whose parents divorce are more than 30 percent more likely than their peers to leave the fold.[57] Still, the intensive parenting ethic and strong institutional resources found in conservative Protestantism suggest that retention rates will continue to be high.

Currently, conservative Protestantism is still growing at a higher rate than other religious groups because it enjoyed higher fertility through the early 1970s. A disproportionate number of its current members are women of childbearing age who were born when this subculture had a higher fertility rate than the rest of the population. But if current trends are any indication, once this cohort approaches middle age in 2020, conservative Protestantism's comparative advantage in fertility will disappear. In all probability, it will be lower than the rates among recent immigrants to the United States—especially Catholic and Muslim immigrants.

These demographic trends suggest that the beginning of the twenty-first century could mark the zenith of the conservative Protestant presence in American life. The recent rise in its public profile is largely tied to its increased political power, which in turn is associated with dramatic increases in its population share over the last century—especially since the 1970s. If that population share stabilizes in the next two decades, conservative Protestantism is unlikely to exert much more influence than it currently does on American politics. Of course, demographic projections are speculative. But the recent experience of the Southern Baptist Convention—where high divorce rates and falling fertility rates may be linked to recent declines in its share of the U.S. religious market[58]—suggests that demographic trends can exert a powerful influence on the religious and political profile of conservative Protestantism.

The destiny of conservative Protestantism may well be linked to its success in reining in its divorce rate and increasing its fertility rate. At this juncture, such success seems unlikely. But the religious, cultural, and institutional resources of conservative Protestantism—especially as they relate to the family—should not be underestimated. Conservative Protestants have successfully resisted much that is modern; they may yet resist the high divorce rates and low fertility rates characteristic of late modernity. Given the fact that their ranks include almost 30 percent of the nation's population, any success on their part in bringing down the divorce rate would contribute greatly to the well-being of America's children.

CHAPTER FOUR

The Evangelical Response to Homosexuality: A Survey, Critique, and Advisory

Jeffrey Satinover

Homosexuality is nothing new. It is an ever-recurring feature of human societies worldwide. To a student of history, or to anyone on sufficiently intimate terms with human nature—his own especially—nothing about homosexuality should be horrifying or revolting in the way that, say, betraying the trust of a friend or a spouse should be.

Nonetheless, the hallmark of a society in which all sexual constraints have been set aside is that finally it sanctions homosexuality as well. This point, hotly disputed today, is reflected in the wisdom of the ages. The first-century Greek moralist Plutarch saw libertinism as the next-to-last stage in the life-cycle of a free republic, before its final descent into tyranny. As a historian, Edward Gibbon in eighteenth-century England understood the same principle to apply to ancient Rome. Sigmund Freud emphasized it with respect to many cultures in the West. For Freud, universal sexual repression was the price of civilization; without constraints, civilization would lose its discipline and vitality. And, of course, the Bible repeatedly shows the effects of unconstrained sexuality, in its stories of the rise and fall of Sodom, of Gomorrah, and indeed of Israel itself. Dennis Prager, a Reform Jewish cultural commentator, writes:

Jeffrey Satinover is currently a graduate student and teaching associate in theoretical physics at Yale University with interests in quantum information theory. He has practiced psychiatry and/or psychoanalysis for over twenty-five years, concentrating in the last eight on homosexuality. He previously was a fellow in psychiatry at Yale University and a William James Lecturer in Psychology and Religion at Harvard. Dr. Satinover is the author of *Homosexuality and the Politics of Truth* and of *The Quantum Brain*. He and his family are members of an Orthodox synagogue.

Man's nature, undisciplined by values, will allow sex to dominate his life and the life of society. . . . It is not overstated to say that the Torah's prohibition of non-marital sex made the creation of Western civilization possible. Societies that did not place boundaries around sexuality were stymied in their development. The subsequent dominance of the Western world can, to a significant extent, be attributed to the sexual revolution, initiated by Judaism and later carried forward by Christianity.[1]

There are today some groups in both evangelical and non-evangelical churches that deny the validity or even existence of biblical proscriptions against any form of sexual expression save that in marriage between a man and a woman. The most appealing theological claim is that "Jesus never said anything about homosexuality." Scholars such as John Boswell of Yale advance the claim that sexual proscriptions are a recent invention. "There is no text on homosexual orientation in the Bible," says New Testament scholar Victor Paul Furnish of Southern Methodist University. Robin Scroggs of Union Seminary (New York), also a New Testament scholar, finds that "biblical judgments against homosexuality are not relevant to today's debate. They should no longer be used . . . not because the Bible is not authoritative, but simply because it does not address the issues involved." The influential German theology professor Helmut Thielicke wrote, "Homosexuality . . . can be discussed at all only in the framework of that freedom which is given to us by the insight that even the New Testament does not provide us with an evident, normative dictum with regard to this question."

A considerable proportion of evangelicals in America join their many mainstream Protestant, Catholic, and Jewish brethren (especially among the clergy and lay leadership) in accepting the three propositions that define the modern "pro-gay" point of view, along with a fourth (just discussed) that is pertinent only for the faith communities:

■ First, as a matter of biology, homosexuality is an innate, genetically determined aspect of the human body.

■ Second, as a matter of psychology, homosexuality is irreversible. The attempt to reverse it requires so profound a denial of self—akin to Jewish anti-Semitism or black "passing" (pale blacks passing as whites)—that it causes the higher-than-average incidence among homosexuals of alcohol and drug abuse, depression, and suicide.

■ Third, as a matter of sociology, homosexuality is normal. This point does more than repeat the first, because something may be innate without being normal, as in the case of genetic illnesses.

■ Fourth, as matter of religion, homosexuality was never of any concern during the biblical era.

From these propositions follows the argument in favor of normalizing homosexuality, which runs like this: The historical condemnation of homosexuality by evangelicalism is based on ignorance of recently discovered medical facts and a misreading of the Bible. As research proceeds, scientific discovery has advanced almost uniformly in one direction: toward an ever-greater appreciation of the strength of nature—that is, innate biology—in determining human characteristics. As biological traits are God-given, condemnation of homosexuality has unwittingly made evangelical Christianity complicit in the unjust persecution of an innocent minority. This information is now a matter of widespread public record. Therefore those who persist in thinking of homosexuality as a problem of any kind, let alone as a grave sin, are not merely ignorant: they are guilty of a bigotry that is quintessentially anti-Christian.

The four propositions and the argument that follows from them have demonstrated enormous power, even over evangelicals, and even though they are flatly wrong and mix wholly incompatible domains of discourse (e.g., what *is* has no necessary connection with what *ought to be*). Their power is reflected in the counterarguments with which the evangelical community (really, the traditionalist of any stripe) has responded. These counterarguments, too, are mistaken and confused, and may seem to the unconvinced to contain more than a streak of cruelty:

- First, as a matter of biology, homosexuality is not innate but a *choice.*
- Second, as a matter of psychology, homosexuality is completely *reversible* since it is a choice, even if it has become habitual.
- Third, as a matter of sociology, homosexuality is not normal but an *illness* or a *perversion* of nature.
- Fourth, as a matter of religion, homosexuality is flatly condemned by the Bible as "an *abomination*," in the common translation of the Hebrew term *toevah.*

The Evidentiary Principle of Scientific Inquiry

The fundamental problem, as I see it, is this: The evangelical community has long depended upon an ancient, well-developed set of prescriptions—and proscriptions—with respect to sexuality. These have worked remarkably well. However, apart from citing "the authority of Scripture," evangelicals have long avoided answering the question, "*Why* are we to adopt the biblical prescriptions with regard to homosexuality?" Indeed, they long had no need even to ask it. Once this was no problem, but now it is. The evangelical who engages modernity finds his moral principles in a state of severe tension, tethered at the right by Scripture but stretched ever leftward by the *evidentiary principle of scientific inquiry.* I have chosen this metaphor of "tethering" with care. Let me use it to attack straightaway certain straw men that plague many current debates within religious communities.

1. The leftward-pulling tension is often mischaracterized by traditionalists

as a simple untethering from orthodoxy. But the Christian who cuts loose from his moorings (or the Christian society that does so) is no more "the problem" than is a heart attack. The untethering is the inevitable outcome of a long, often "occult" (in the medical sense, meaning "hidden") underlying process.

2. The pull away from tradition is not simply that of freedom from constraint, though certainly rebelliousness plays its part when opportunity arises and the opposition is weak. The real pull comes from a positive virtue—the evidentiary principle of scientific inquiry. This principle is subtle: Accept nothing without evidence, and to no greater degree than remains after the uncertainty has been *quantified*.

3. Nonetheless, the principle of inquiry should not be confused with science itself, or with any particular theories or working conclusions at which science has arrived (evolution, for example). At issue rather is the principle that we may ever more closely, if always imperfectly, approximate the truth of a matter by devising challenges to try to prove a proposition false, and then deriving from the results a numerically quantified estimate of the likelihood that the proposition is indeed false. This estimate can never be exactly zero. For those who adhere to this principle, claims rooted in scripture, doctrine, tradition, and institution are not exempt from challenge. Indeed, they are perceived as especially proper for it, as the authority they demand is so encompassing.

4. It is not so important to modern debates over religious authority that the seat of authority is being challenged, as that the very rule according to which authority is determined is under attack. For if a matter could in principle be proven false but is asserted to be true, then it surely should be tried and tested and accepted only if it passes the test. Indeed, it should welcome repeated challenges, as a genuine champion will. More accurately, I should say that the rule according to which authority is determined is no longer under attack. It *was* attacked and has been soundly defeated

5. Opponents of religion therefore generally do believe that science per se opposes religion, and they readily draw evangelicals into futile debates predicated on a shared mistake. That this kind of debate is common, and its outcome generally embarrassing for believers, does not mean that it is important. What is important, rather, is that evangelicals form a clear and unequivocal answer to the question, "Are you willing to accept *evidence* as the basis for asserting what is true?" Perhaps evangelicalism will answer no when the subject is directly creedal, " I believe in . . ." But perhaps it will answer yes when the matter is less explicit, e.g., "The Bible says that homosexuality is not a good thing." This, not the absence of a direct quotation from Jesus about anal intercourse, is the heart of the matter.

Let me put this challenge even more pointedly. The evidentiary principle has repeatedly subjected *itself* to its own very stringent criteria and has flourished: there is scarcely an accomplishment of the modern world that is not utterly dependent upon it. As a consequence, and despite sophisticated protestations, the battle to change the rule for determining authority is already over. That the truth may be only imperfectly known, and that there are no claims exempt from being so challenged, is now a part of the philosophical outlook of every modern person (though usually in tacit, not articulated, form), evangelicals included. All that evangelicalism need do to cut the tether entirely and consign itself to oblivion is to refuse, on grounds of traditional authority, to engage in an evidentiary test of its practical claims and the prescriptions for living that flow from them.[2] Religiously serious persons stretched by the tension described above know or intuit that to ask a question such as "Why is homosexuality not good?" and to presume that one is owed a *rationale* for the biblical proscription, is already to have abandoned biblical "authority" as it was once understood. They worry, as decent people, that *if no rationale can be offered, the proscription may well be wrong.* In a post-Enlightenment world with its unprecedented level of mass education, a world in which ideas and arguments both good and bad can propagate with astonishing speed, where the sheer successes of a materialistic philosophy in bettering mankind's material existence are undeniable—in such a world almost no one is satisfied with claims that *could* allow themselves to be tested but refuse to do so by protesting that scriptural authority is sufficient, indeed superior.

Evangelicalism doesn't really have an effective answer to the question "Why shouldn't I be homosexual?" apart from, "Because God said so." But evangelicalism should develop such an answer, one that is perfectly clear to the non-believer and—as evidence requires—is not circularly rooted in the biblical claims that it is expected to parallel.

THE "EX-GAY" MOVEMENT AND THE THERAPY OF HOMOSEXUALITY

Another reason why evangelicalism doesn't yet have an effective answer to the questions raised by homosexuality is that it has no clear idea what homosexuality is. Neither does the rest of society. Nor do homosexuals themselves, by and large.

Long ago a small group of professionals developed a genuine expertise in this area. But those who have once been homosexual and have struggled their way out, following a most complex and moving path, understand it best. From these two groups, the professionals and the "ex-gays," we can learn the accurate counterpoint to the four false propositions of "pro-gay" ideology:

■ First, as a matter of biology, homosexuality is neither innate nor a simple choice. Genetic traits having nothing to do with sexuality proper—e.g., degree of anxiety response—are potential risk factors for homosexuality, as for other configurations of personality, but they are not determinative.

■ Second, as a matter of psychology, homosexuality is more often partially reversed than entirely reversed, though that happens, too. The same can be said for nearly every other human problem. The argument as to the reversibility of homosexuality is a red herring. In theory, all human problems are perfectly reversible with the assistance of a perfect God who follows our orders. Even in psychoanalysis, homosexuality is completely reversible—theoretically. The pro-gay movement thinks it needs to insist that homosexuality is perfectly *irreversible* to sustain its ideology and the political power that it has accrued. If a genuine "gay" really can change, then how can homosexuality be a "God-given gift"? Meanwhile the evangelical movement thinks it needs to insist that homosexuality is perfectly *reversible* to sustain its theology and the authority of its prescriptions. How can you ask someone "born that way" to change himself?

■ Third, as a matter of sociology, homosexuality is a perfectly "natural" instance of human reality. Death in this sense is normal, too, even though it invariably occurs as a consequence of conditions that we consider diseases. It's normal for an aging human being to get sick and to die. It's normal for people to have various problems with their sexuality. The incidence of a particular kind of problem is affected by many factors. For instance, the terrible divorce rate—as bad among evangelicals as among others, or even worse—and consequent breakdown of the family, and of fatherhood, directly increase the incidence of homosexuality (and other problems). Homosexuality is a "disease," or a "perversion of nature," or a "disorder" in precisely the same way that divorce is, or isn't, as you wish.

■ Fourth, as a matter of religion, until the modern era homosexuality had always been seen as a serious problem in both Judaism and Christianity, with their largely shared view of what family life is meant to be shaped into (with considerable effort, not "naturally"). That homosexuality is tempting surprises only the squeamish and those of severely limited imagination. And the moral issues involved in sexuality are not one-dimensional. Homoerotic attachments and fantasies, before puberty, often without explicit sexual content, arise to assuage childhood needs in some children, at a time of life prior to full moral choice and responsibility. The later sexualization of these needs and their conversion into impulses likewise happens without choice or consent; indeed, a combination of shock, fear, and self-loathing is the most common internal reaction when these impulses make their first claims. The capacity both to resist the impulse to action that these needs give rise to, fueled by puberty, and to properly meet the unfulfilled needs that are their source, can hardly be expected to develop in a child in a societal and parental vacuum. To return such prodigal impulses to their proper source requires the intense ministrations of many loving people over a very long time. As I understand it, the New Testament formula has two halves, which bear fruit only when they are made one, not separately. "You are healed" is one half; "Sin no more" is the other. Can you expect to apply the admonition to "sin no more" successfully if you have no idea how to facilitate the healing?

Change: The Crux of the Matter

The idea of homosexual change is not new. Neither is the role of religion in this process. Consider the findings of the following study—of a type all too rare—in the *American Journal of Psychiatry* more than twenty years ago:

> The authors evaluated 11 white men who claimed to have changed sexual orientation from exclusive homosexuality to exclusive heterosexuality through participation in a Pentecostal church fellowship. Religious ideology and a religious community offered the subjects a "folk therapy" experience that was paramount in producing their change. On the average their self-identification as homosexual occurred at age 11, their change to heterosexual identification occurred at age 23, and their period of heterosexual identification at the time of this study was 4 years. The authors report 8 men became emotionally detached from homosexual identity in both behavior and intrapsychic process; 3 men were functionally heterosexual with some evidence of neurotic conflict. On the Kinsey 7-point sexual orientation scale all subjects manifested major before-after changes. Corollary evidence suggests that the phenomenon of substantiated change in sexual orientation without explicit treatment and/or long-term psychotherapy may be more common than previously thought.[3]

Robert Spitzer is the Columbia University psychiatric researcher most responsible for what is called the DSM, the 1973 diagnostic manual that normalized homosexuality. In 2001 Dr. Spitzer presented to the American Psychiatric Association an initial study of 200 persons, the majority of whom experienced very substantial change in sexual orientation.[4] Almost all said their religious convictions and/or participation in a ministry were an important part of their successful change. The Spitzer study had the limited goal of examining whether change is possible, but because of the peculiar political-social dynamic that led to it, it sheds light on the evangelical relationship to homosexuality and the ex-gay movement.

The study was funded by the Department of Psychiatry at Columbia University, where Spitzer is professor of psychiatry and chief of biometrics—i.e., his specific expertise is in the science of designing experiments from which valid conclusions may be drawn. "Like most psychiatrists," Dr. Spitzer told me, "I thought that homosexual behavior could be resisted but that no one could really change their sexual orientation. I now believe that's untrue—some people can and do change." The history behind his change of mind is instructive.

During the American Psychiatric Association's annual conference in 1999, Spitzer was drawn to a group of ex-gays chiefly from evangelical ex-gay ministries staging a demonstration at the entrance to the conference building. The leader of the picketing was Anthony Falzarano, founder of Transformation Ministries in Washington, D.C., and of PFOX—Parents and Friends of Ex-Gays. The picketers were objecting to the APA's just-announced resolution discouraging therapy to change homosexuality to heterosexuality. Some entering psychiatrists tore up the literature handed to them by the protesters, but others stopped to offer encouragement.

Spitzer was skeptical, but on grounds of free speech and intellectual integrity he organized a debate to take place at the next year's convention. (He was, in fact, embodying the evidentiary principle of scientific inquiry, facilitating challenge to his own claims.) The gay task force within the APA managed to partially stifle the debate by having the APA leadership rule that the proponents of gay change could not include in the debate anyone who believed that there was anything wrong with homosexuality. This is an unheard of kind of restriction. But it reflects the fact that the American Psychiatric Association— like many other professional associations, and like most mainline American churches—has abdicated the fiduciary accountability and restraints of a genuine "profession" in favor of the ethics of a covert action cell whose reprehensible means they justify by the purported nobility of their ends. Hoping at least to spark discussion, Spitzer acceded to this restriction, having not yet discovered for himself the political aims, sophistication, and power of the National Gay and Lesbian Task Force (NGLTF) and its offspring—funded collectively to the tune of $9 billion annually[5]—as represented by the Gay and Lesbian Task Force and its offspring within the APA.

In a move that reflects the perfectly honed political judgment at work behind the scenes, the APA abruptly canceled the debate altogether anyway— but only at the last minute. Spitzer was shocked and outraged. That this could happen was to him astounding. (To me it was utterly unexceptional. I had already refused to participate in the debate before its terms were altered so as to exclude anyone with my point of view. It would have been a waste of time to prepare for an event that would never be allowed to occur—a waste benefiting others.)

The Spitzer Study

Once the debate was canceled, Spitzer decided to find out for himself if sexual orientation was changeable. He developed a forty-five-minute structured telephone interview that he personally administered to all the subjects. (This is a standard technique, whose validity has long been established. But the NGLTF and associates later used the phrase "telephone call" to make the Spitzer study sound tendentious and amateur.) Most had been referred to him by two groups: NARTH, the National Association for Research and Therapy of Homosexuality, and Exodus, a ministry for homosexual strugglers that requires an evangelical statement of faith of its component ministries and (with a few exceptions) its speakers. (I was one exception.) To be eligible for the study, the subjects had to have undergone a significant shift from homosexual to heterosexual attraction that had lasted for at least five years.

Most of the subjects said their religious faith was very important in their lives. About three-quarters of the men and half of the women had been married by the time of the study. Most had sought change because a gay lifestyle had been emotionally unsatisfying. Many had been disturbed by their own history of promiscuity, stormy relationships, and conflict with their religious values. Many maintained the desire to be (or to stay) married. Some went so far as to give the well-being of their children priority over their own moment-to-moment emotions.

Typically, subjects said their efforts to change did not produce significant results for the first two years (a fact used by critics to explain the uselessness of "conversion therapy") and that the therapy was "stressful" (a fact used by critics as evidence of the damaging effects of conversion therapy). Subjects said they were eventually helped by examining their family and childhood experiences, and by understanding how those factors might have contributed to their sexual impulses. Same-sex mentoring relationships, behavior-therapy techniques, and group therapy were also mentioned as particularly helpful. None had ever been forced, hours on end, to internalize doctrinal precepts of the conversion movement, as a popular publicly funded PBS series repeats over and over.

"Contrary to conventional wisdom," Spitzer concluded, "some highly motivated individuals, using a variety of change efforts, can make substantial change in multiple indicators of sexual orientation, and achieve good heterosexual functioning." He notes that change from homosexual to heterosexual is not usually a matter of "either/or" but exists on a continuum—that is, a diminishing of homosexuality and an expansion of heterosexual potential that is exhibited in widely varying degrees. The assessment tool he used was developed with the assistance of New York psychiatrist Richard C. Friedman, a gay activist, and myself, referred to by gay activists as an "anti-gay activist."

Spitzer used a structured interview so that others could know exactly what questions were asked, and what response choices were offered to the subjects. The full data file is now available to other researchers. He expressed his gratitude for the help of the National Association for Research and Therapy of Homosexuality (NARTH), and the ex-gay ministry Exodus. Critics of the study argue that the simple fact that its subjects were found through NARTH and Exodus—yet where else could changed persons have come from?—invalidates his findings, as though it is self-evident that evangelical groups and anyone they name cannot be trusted.

Spitzer's request for my input followed an unusual sequence of events pertinent to this discussion. I had referred to him for his study an ultra-Orthodox Jewish patient whom I advised to participate in evangelical ex-gay ministry activities in his area, as none for Jews then existed. At my urging he sought the help of an older rabbi in translating evangelical theological concepts into their Jewish equivalents. Initially, my patient found the frank Christian evangelizing of the group a distraction and a reason to resist its benefits. The participants and the ministry leaders in like spirit insisted that his objective was impossible: to relate and submit to the healing power of God while thoroughly dismissing the Christian conception of Him. But in time he formed an extremely positive impression of the integrity of both the participating individuals and the supporting ministry. This perception led him to an extraordinary degree of openness that was a major step in his healing. That his connection to his fellows happened to be filtered through a different—in many ways flatly opposing and in his judgment rather silly—set of concepts came to be of no importance. It was amazing to his new friends and to the ministry, as well as to the man himself, that he both received and gave so much. In the end, they all agreed not to assume they were privy to how God conceptualizes things or how he operates.

After four years of therapy, this Orthodox Jewish man is free of homosexual impulses and fantasies; he made an excellent marriage and has become a father. As a young man he was identified as a future spiritual leader of his community. After puberty, however, his homosexual desires overwhelmed his capacity for a relationship with God, and his religious life became rote and alienating. Following treatment—and his experiences in the evangelical ministry—his exclusively Jewish religious life returned far more powerfully than ever, and he is indeed becoming a major figure in his religious community.

In any event, the Spitzer study is in many respects the most reliable indicator not only of homosexual change in general, but of homosexual change as influenced by evangelical ex-gay ministries, whether or not the participants accept evangelical theological premises. Spitzer describes himself as an "atheistic Jew with little interest in religion," but he had no trouble adopting a dispassionate, anthropologic point of view with respect to the facts.

The NARTH Study

A much earlier larger study with validity comparable to that of the Spitzer study had been conducted under the auspices of NARTH and published a year earlier.[6] A large proportion of its subjects were motivated and assisted by evangelical principles. However, many were influenced not by evangelicalism but by Mormonism.

The study surveyed 882 dissatisfied homosexuals, of whom 726 had received therapy from a professional therapist or pastoral counselor. Over 67 percent of the participants said they were exclusively or almost exclusively homosexual at one time in their lives, while only about 13 percent of the participants were so at the time of the survey. Of the 67 percent who reported being exclusively homosexual, 45 percent said they had made major changes in their orientation, while 35 percent of all participants said they did not make significant changes. Overall, then, roughly a third of the participants made major changes and a third did not. Those participants who had made changes reported statistically significant reductions in the frequency of their homosexual thoughts and fantasies. They reported significant improvements in other important areas of their lives also—particularly in their psychological, interpersonal, and spiritual well-being.

EVANGELICAL MINISTRIES TO GAYS AND EX-GAYS

The evangelical community is divided into two camps, one saying "You already are healed," the other saying "Sin no more." The ex-gay ministries have arisen in response to the need for struggling homosexuals to be freed from what one ex-gay called the "Christianity/Homosexuality whipsaw."[7] Their mission is to help men and women make the change from homosexual to heterosexual behavior and emotional response "through the power of Jesus Christ." Like most evangelical ministries, they consider their specific mission to be contained within the larger mission of "evangelization."

No one approach is shared by all such ministries. But some consensus on basic principles has formed over the last five years because of (1) the growing influence of Exodus International, an umbrella organization of roughly 125 independent ex-gay ministries nationwide; (2) a natural weeding-out process as experience is gained with different approaches; and (3) a close working relationship between many ex-gay ministries and members of NARTH (the National Association for Research and Therapy of Homosexuality), a non-religious professional organization of psychiatrists, psychologists, and psychotherapists.

The Twelve-Step Approach

Numerous Homosexuals Anonymous (HA) groups have sprung up across the country. Although HA is not the main approach to the spiritual healing of homosexuality as Alcoholics Anonymous (AA) is for alcoholism, it is worth discussing in some detail. It provides a "transitional" model that falls between secular psychotherapy and more fully faith-based approaches.

The development of a twelve- (actually fourteen-) step model is an indication that compulsive/addictive and self-soothing behaviors play a considerable role in homosexuality. As yet there are no solid statistics to indicate overall efficacy rates for HA, but it seems to be approximately where AA was twenty or thirty years ago. Its continued growth is impressive in view of the intensive public campaign to normalize homosexuality, a campaign never waged on behalf of alcoholism.

Homosexuals Anonymous welcomes persons who actively live a homo-sexual life as well as those who have committed themselves to abstinence as a precondition to change. As in AA, persons who are uncertain that they even have a problem suffer a much higher rate of relapse than those who are convinced of their need for change. Nonetheless, it is understood that, as with alcohol and all other addictions, *abstinence is not the cure but merely its precondition.*

The principle that abstinence is a precondition for successful change is also one of the basic principles of psychodynamic psychotherapy. So clearly was this principle adhered to in the early days of psychoanalysis that patients had to agree not to move or change jobs or alter their marital status until their treatment was completed. The treatment was expected to release anxieties that could provoke patients to impulsive, self-destructive acts if they tried to react in any other way than with words.

So long as people allow themselves the habitual, compulsive, self-soothing behavior for which they seek treatment, they will have an escape from the underlying emotional distress that prompts it. When they give up the behavior, the distress remains. Indeed, if anything it is now heightened, because the usual routes of escape have been closed off. "To be healed, our sickness must grow worse," said T. S. Eliot. Only under these somewhat artificial and deliber-ately more difficult conditions can they now acquire *alternative* means of dealing with the distress. They learn to turn to others or to God instead of alleviating the distress with alcohol, with orgasm, or indeed with any form of self-centered soothing.

Within the AA community, alcoholics who have not had a drink for many years still wisely refer to themselves as "recovering," not "recovered." This way of describing one's progress embodies two pieces of folk wisdom. First is the well-known fact that, unlike many purely medical illnesses, an alcoholic's prob-lem with alcohol is permanent: he may always be tempted to replace his spouse or his God with a bottle. This is not because it is impossible to change alcoholism, but because we are human. We can fully erase neither the knowl-edge that a quick fix is available nor the craving for it.

The second and more important fact is that the "problem" in alcoholism is subtler than simply the drinking itself. Properly understood, the act of imbib-ing alcohol is the *outcome* of alcoholism, not its cause. The cause lies in a certain attitude: the individual's heightened temptation and willingness to use alcohol as a solution to the stresses of being human. In Samuel Johnson's words, "he who makes a beast of himself gets rid of the pain of being a man." Put differently, alcoholism is an idolatrous solution to the spiritual suffering that is the essence of the human condition.

This is why not drinking is not the solution to alcoholism but merely the precondition for finding the solution. If the drinking continues, the distress to which it is the response is lessened and even eliminated, at least temporarily. With the distress "solved," there is no motivation to seek other solutions, except abstractly or while briefly in the grip of post-binge depressive guilt, a notoriously fruitless sort of motivation. Only when alcoholics are not drinking, and are keenly aware of the now-free-to-emerge spiritual distress, can they work toward an alternative solution.

HA models itself on AA. Two features are central to its method. One is an acknowledgment of powerlessness over homosexuality—the profound truth of which is supported by what we know of how the brain changes in response to experience. The other is an acknowledged dependence on a "Higher Power." As in AA, the sense of "cure" within HA is appropriately tempered, because no such term is ever used. Rather one is perpetually "in recovery." This description comports with the neurological fact that old habits are never entirely erased, just overwritten with new ones. It also expresses humility in the face of weaknesses, which is a precondition to any spiritual healing.

As with AA, the roots of the HA approach lie deep within the Bible, tapping its view of our common humanity, of our sinful nature, and of our utter dependence on God. Unlike most current AA groups, however, HA still uses explicitly Christian language and theology. To the extent that HA embodies a tacit understanding that compulsion is central to homosexuality, HA can be said to be "good psychology." But to the extent that it manages this compulsion through "fourteen steps," it is a useful—if somewhat condensed and simplified—version of traditional Western salvation, and in particular of Christian surrender.

The strength of HA lies in its emphasis on building up self-discipline and mutual accountability among group members. These are indeed important components in the management and treatment of all forms of compulsive and addictive behavior. But by themselves they are often insufficient. As we know from extensive experience in substance-abuse programs, when rigid discipline and accountability are uncoupled from hope, compassion, and love, they often collapse into abrupt episodes of relapse and rebellion. This is especially true with regard to homosexuality. A compulsion whose roots lie deep within the need to be loved and affirmed may maintain an especially firm and subtle grip on the soul.

Exodus International

The more than 125 separate ministries nationwide that make up the umbrella organization called Exodus International comprise a wide spectrum of openly religious approaches to the healing of homosexuality. At one end of the spectrum are those that, like HA, emphasize self-discipline and accountability, and downplay—or are even hostile to—direct supernatural intervention. These ministries tend to have an authoritarian cast, and for doctrinal reasons they usually reject psychology or psychotherapy as an adjunct to healing. Activists and the press frequently highlight some of these groups as representative of all ministries to the sexually broken, which they are not. As the leaders of Exodus have gained experience (they have always acknowledged the extent to which they have had to "feel their way in the dark," inevitably making mistakes), they have become far more aware of the danger inherent in rigid approaches.

A particular problem arises with those ministries that lack a clear understanding of the healing process. No matter what the setting, there will always be people who seek to change but do not succeed, even after many years of effort. Perhaps understandably, some of these people relapse into a gay-activist posture and become hostile toward the ministries they perceive as having failed, or even deluded, them. Mel White, the former evangelical ghostwriter and author of *Stranger at the Gate*, is a prominent example. Ministries that lack a solid grasp of healing can only assert that sufferers need to remain chaste, to live holy lives, and to submit to God's will. From a traditional Jewish or Christian perspective, this is true as far as it goes. But it is also true that without a realistic hope of regeneration and change, many people will fall into hopelessness and despair or into rebellion.

At the other end of the spectrum are those ministries that do emphasize healing. Most have arisen out of the charismatic renewal movement and depend on direct intervention of the Holy Spirit. Although these ministries certainly accept the importance of responsible choice, self-discipline, and accountability, they also believe in the possibility of profound and lasting change— "regeneration." Most of them have integrated the insights of depth psychology (psychology of the unconscious) into their approach, some with great sophistication and discernment. Alien as such a formulation may appear to secularists and others outside the charismatic tradition, the potential for the transformation of even extremely intractable conditions is repeatedly borne out by experience.

Desert Stream/Living Waters

One of the groups operating under the umbrella of Exodus International is Desert Stream, headquartered in Los Angeles and led by Andrew Comiskey. A former homosexual himself, Comiskey trains leaders to establish ministries in churches around the country through his "Living Waters" program. His book *Pursuing Sexual Wholeness* provides an overview of a biblical approach to the healing of male and female homosexuality. [8] It offers a compelling personal testimony to Comiskey's own difficult journey out of the gay lifestyle into committed marriage and fatherhood. The insights and principles he offers can be directly applied beyond homosexuality. "Does that healing extend only to those who come out of homosexual backgrounds?" he asks.

Gratefully, no! The struggler begins to recognize in his quest for intimacy and identity the struggle familiar to all. . . . Some face heterosexual brokenness, others the sterile temptation to isolation. Whatever the specifics, the struggle to emerge as a whole person upheld by whole relationships applies to every man and woman. . . . "The healing of the homosexual is the healing of all men. . . ." No one is exempt from sexual brokenness—no one is altogether whole in his capacity to love and to be loved. Therefore, no one is exempt from the ever-deepening work of healing that Jesus wants to establish in the sexuality of His people.[9]

A motif repeated continually in ministries such as Comiskey's is that the healing and regeneration process, though perhaps particularly striking in the lives of homosexuals (who become visibly and dramatically different), can take place in anyone's life. Those with an open heart and mind who spend time around these ministries learn an important and moving truth: "homosexuals" are just "us." The particular nature of each person's brokenness, while it must be taken into account in the details of healing, is in the end of little significance. What really counts is the whole person that each may be led to become, out of whatever brokenness.

People who come to Desert Stream/Living Waters for help undergo a screening interview. Those accepted must be strongly committed to change and in most cases may not give evidence of severe psychopathology. Their personal testimony to the depth of their involvement in the gay lifestyle and their struggles to overcome their homosexuality show that they are not merely pre-selected heterosexuals who have mistakenly identified themselves as homosexual. The program is expressly designed for people who have committed their lives to Christ and actively desire the healing of their sexuality through the power of the Holy Spirit, but Comiskey reports that an increasing number of non-Christians now apply for admission. This trend is apparent in similar ministries across the country, largely because there are so few resources outside the evangelical sphere.

On average, seventy-five to eighty persons seek admission to each Desert Stream thirty-week cycle. Of these, twenty or so are refused, primarily because of the nature of their motivation. They may, for instance, be driven by shame in the eyes of others rather than a clear inner determination to change. These are often highly "religious" persons who have stifled their homosexual impulses not so much out of inner conviction as in response to the internalized shame-based strictures of the authoritarian churches in which they were raised. Perhaps three or four other applicants decide on their own not to participate. Thus in each thirty-week cycle around fifty-five people participate in small groups; two-thirds are homosexuals and the rest have other sexual addictions. Of the fifty-five who begin the cycle, it is rare for more than three to drop out, and often none do.

In 1995, Comiskey reported that 50 percent of the homosexuals who start the program complete it with substantial progress out of homosexuality and into heterosexuality; about 33 percent clearly make little or no progress, frequently regressing into active homosexual behavior when they leave the program. For the rest, the outcome is uncertain. While critics have long dismissed such self-reported statistics as self-serving and inaccurate, the outcomes conform closely to what the *American Journal of Psychiatry*, Spitzer, and NARTH studies concluded. Comiskey's long-term experience reveals that approximately 25 percent of the homosexuals in the program marry within eight years and have marriages that last at least as long as or longer than the current national average. Case studies in his *Pursuing Sexual Wholeness* movingly illustrate the many twists and turns that this process takes before it can reach a successful conclusion.

Redeemed Life Ministries

The founder of Redeemed Life, a ministry to people with all forms of sexual brokenness, is Mario Bergner, a former homosexual who had been deeply involved in the East Coast gay and theatrical life. His story, as well as an explication of the combined psychoanalytic and religious principles that guide his ministry, can be found in his moving book, *Setting Love in Order*.[10]

Bergner notes that as a teenager he made two serious attempts at living a Christian life and forgoing his homosexuality. But because in the churches he attended he heard only either condemnation of homosexuality or outright acceptance of it, he remained unaware of the possibility of sexual redemption.

The dominant approach to the treatment of homosexuality today focuses on the critical role of the same-sex parent in generating homosexuality. Bergner's work, while taking this into account, is more sharply focused on the complementary role played by ambivalence toward the opposite-sex parent, a much needed corrective. The therapeutic approach in Redeemed Life combines depth psychology in a primarily group setting with healing prayer. Participants make an eight-month minimum commitment to a small group, which is focused on sexual redemption in Christ. For persons who remain committed to the process for the long haul, Bergner reports success rates of over 80 percent. In principle, however, he believes in 100 percent reversibility, a problematic position.

Pastoral Care Ministries

Leanne Payne founded Pastoral Care Ministries, a healing ministry centered in Wheaton, Illinois. Her work has deeply influenced many in the field, including Comiskey and Bergner. Although Payne's ministry reaches out well beyond "sexual brokenness," much of it deals specifically with homosexuality and other forms of compulsive sexual behavior.

An important influence on Payne's work is the "Healing of Memories" movement. Spiritual healing of the body has been associated with Anglicanism and Pentecostalism since the beginning of the charismatic movement early this century; "healing of memories" extends healing to the domain of the mind. Not since the first few centuries of the church's history has it had this kind of healing as a clear and distinct objective. Its reappearance in the twentieth century parallels—but did not arise from—the discovery of the unconscious. Because of this congruence, and because depth psychology seemed to offer a more scientific-seeming and morally neutral approach than traditional religion, the work of Jung in particular came to be a dominant influence in the healing movement, mostly not to good effect.

Although the healing-of-memories movement did not explicitly join forces with depth psychology, it tacitly shared the understanding that one may *consciously* hold one set of ideas, emotions, values, attitudes, beliefs, and memories while *unconsciously* holding an entirely different set. Our deepest wounds —to which we make our sinful and most guilt-inducing responses—may therefore lie unrecognized and out of sight. Insofar as from a faith perspective confession is the first step in healing, such parts of the psyche—memories of trauma, memories of responses to this trauma, feelings of subsequent guilt— may all remain unconscious impediments to the ongoing work of healing and growth in the life of a believer.

Healing of memories can be thought of as a modern formulation of the ancient process of in-depth confession, the necessary first step toward wholeness before God. Twelve-step programs also recognize the need for the retrieval of such memories in requiring a thoroughgoing, honest inventory of sins (although not called that) and a subsequent confession of those sins both before God and to those who have been wronged. In a Christian framework, one of the primary functions of the Holy Spirit is to bring to the mind of the believer all the sins that need to be confessed, those being committed repeatedly as well as those forgotten.

From the perspective of depth psychology, parts of the self are routinely split off from our conscious awareness, primarily in response to early emotional wounds. This splitting, which we do to protect ourselves from the painful memory of the wounding itself, keeps us from recognizing our sinful responses to that wounding. When the healing of memories takes place, these wounds and our sinful responses to them are remembered, acknowledged, understood for what they are, and then *presented to God for forgiveness and healing*. Thus the retrieval of our wounds and sins through the use of a depth-psychological approach is a way to deepen the process of confession.

But the retrieval and acknowledgment are not themselves curative; they are preparatory. The healing-of-memories movement therefore departs from secular psychological theory in two critical ways: first, healing is made far more likely because of openness to God; and second, healing itself is effected by God. Both of these processes depend on something even more fundamental, which is necessarily lacking in a secular treatment setting: the conviction that conscience is genuine and absolute and not merely the internalization of parental and societal norms.

JUDAISM AND HOMOSEXUALITY

There are two other religious communities whose attitudes toward and experiences with homosexuality are notably compatible with those of evangelicals. The first is Judaism. Because of the well-known high levels of achievement of both Jews and homosexuals, and because the attitudes of most non-Orthodox Jews are considerably more liberal than those of non-Jewish society at large, Jewish gay activists are disproportionately visible. This may leave the false impression that Judaism itself fully accepts homosexuality.

In many respects, Orthodox Judaism and evangelical Christianity have much more in common with each other today than each has with its modern, liberalized variants, just as those liberal variants seem closer to each other than to their own orthodox counterparts. Orthodox Jews and evangelical Christians see the liberal variants less as religious faiths than as sociopolitical ideologies. Equally, many liberals in both religions dismiss their orthodox counterparts as "fundamentalists" who refuse to see that in the last hundred years science has effectively debunked their worldviews. Liberal Christianity (mostly in the mainline churches) and liberal Judaism (in Reconstructionist, Reform, and many Conservative synagogues) view themselves as having grown beyond theological positions supported by Scripture. They treat biblical injunctions as but the culturally relative opinions of the men of the time.

In contrast, evangelicalism remains theologically dependent on both Old and New Testaments "as received," and Orthodox Judaism remains theologically dependent on the Hebrew scriptures "as received"—especially the Pentateuch—and on the Talmud. With their shared dependence on the Hebrew Bible, they therefore both maintain an unbroken chain of belief, going back thirty-five hundred years, that homosexuality is a sin—even if, like other sins, it is an "unnaturally natural" one. Neither would view homosexuality as an illness in the medical sense. The Orthodox Jewish and evangelical positions on homosexuality differ somewhat, but these differences are mostly in emphasis and reflect certain differences in their general approaches to spirituality.

A major portion of the moral theology of the Church derives directly from the Talmud, and some of the early church fathers routinely consulted the rabbis of their time for clarification of scriptural principles. Recall that during the earliest years of the Church, "scripture" meant the Hebrew Bible. The New Testament had yet to be redacted and canonized. The Apostle Paul was a Talmudic scholar, and with few exceptions, his comments about homosexuality directly reflect Talmudic discussions of sexuality. These discussions, in turn, constitute a detailed explication of the rather more terse commandments found in the Pentateuch.

The vast preponderance of Jewish homosexuals are liberal not only in their outlook on life but in their religious attitudes as well. Although homosexuality does occur among Orthodox Jews, it is strikingly uncommon in that faith community. Why is this?

Most telling about Orthodox Judaism is that its marriages are among the most stable in the United States—even though divorce is not forbidden, only strongly discouraged. They are stable even though many marriages (especially in ultra-Orthodox or Hasidic communities) are arranged—a method that cuts directly across the "natural," desire-based method of selecting partners. Beyond that, lengthy sections of the Talmud are devoted to the precise obligations, including sexual ones, that each partner in a marriage owes to the other. Failure to meet these obligations is laid out in the Talmud as legitimate grounds for divorce.

The homosexual impulses that naturally occur in any population of human beings are constrained to a degree among Orthodox Jews by their way of life. Given the biblical mandates to marry, to fulfill one's spouse, and to raise many children, it is inconceivable that large numbers of homosexuals could remain "closeted," and it would be extraordinarily difficult to carry off mere marriages of convenience. What occurs instead is a self-reinforcing process: stable family life reduces the incidence of the kinds of problems that increase homosexuality; reduced levels of homosexuality help stabilize family life. In America as a whole, the widely decried breakdown of families increases the likelihood of all forms of sexual pathology. Father problems especially cause an increase in male homosexuality, and the increase in homosexuality in turn contributes to the breakdown of families in the next generation.

On the matter of homosexuality, the Jewish population is more sharply divided than the evangelical, falling into two distinct camps: the liberal and secularist majority, among whom homosexuality is present and widely accepted, and a large Orthodox minority, among whom homosexuality is uncommon. Because the majority accepts it and the minority has a low incidence of it, no Jewish groups have arisen to "treat" homosexuality, as do evangelical ministries like Exodus. The Orthodox person struggling with homosexuality will be referred instead to one of the psychiatrists or psychotherapists who continue to treat homosexuality as a resolvable mental-health problem, while the non-Orthodox Jewish homosexual commonly accepts the gay-activist position that the problem is not homosexuality itself but the desire not to be homosexual.

Judaism recognizes sexuality as an enormously powerful force. Because it is so powerful, it needs to be hedged about with many constraints. But Judaism does not deal with the potential for evil inherent in man by rejecting the natural altogether. It lacks entirely any ascetic tradition, so much so that a great sage who does not marry is criticized as in some measure having failed. Its approach, rather, has always been to sanctify the merely natural, to make it holy. It is the guidelines of the Torah, written and oral, that teach man how to do this. Such sanctification invariably involves constraint.

Because of the natural power of sexuality, those who fall prey to it are seen as less morally culpable than those who fall prey to less compelling temptations, such as speaking ill of another person. Indeed, he who condemns the homosexual *person* for his behavior, rather than the behavior itself, commits the far more grievous sin—a notion that strikes at the root of all judgmentalism. Orthodox Judaism thus holds that, although homosexuality cannot be condoned, mitigating circumstances may exist that temper our condemnation of it. And a great many other sins are far worse than homosexuality. It is worth noting that the Hebrew word *toevah* has passed into English translations as "abomination." Thus many modern translations of Leviticus, and almost all Christian ones, condemn homosexuality as "an abomination." But this is misleading. Driving on the Sabbath is *toevah* as well. Indeed, anything is that detracts from the pursuit of holiness.

Thus, despite the apparent legalism of the Orthodox Jewish approach, it contains a specific and precise *scale* of compassion. Although Orthodox Judaism unflinchingly calls homosexuality a sin, it does not condemn it in the tone that some Christian groups have used. But this rigorous compassion bears little resemblance to what now passes for "tolerance"—its standardless, liberal counterpart.

In spite of the compassionate attitude of Jewish teachings on homosexuality, Judaism today has for all intents and purposes no practical resources for dealing with it. Homosexuality is so thoroughly accepted in Reform Judaism that diversity of opinion is forbidden, and dissent is harshly condemned. In Orthodox Judaism, homosexuality has become enough of a problem to arouse concern only very lately, and Orthodox institutions are completely at sea when it comes to offering practical assistance. A few believing Jews have therefore turned to evangelical resources, naturally with trepidation. Jews rarely turn to Courage, the Catholic ministry to homosexuals, because of its emphasis on celibacy; only now is Courage beginning to incorporate healing as a possibility and goal.

In summary, then: (1) The attitudes toward homosexuality contained within Orthodox Judaism are extremely nuanced. The evangelical world could gain much by studying these ideas carefully—not from "Old Testament" scholars but from modern-day, well-respected teachers of Orthodox Judaism. And (2) Orthodox Judaism is in desperate need of assistance in establishing native counterparts to the very well-developed evangelical ministries to homosexuals.

LATTER-DAY SAINTS AND HOMOSEXUALITY

The other faith community with which evangelicals can find common ground on homosexuality is the Church of Jesus Christ of Latter-day Saints. Both because of the deliberately self-contained nature of the LDS community and because of the poorly disguised distaste with which LDS theology is often viewed by other Christians, LDS activity is little known in the wider world. But the church is very actively engaged with questions of homosexuality. Its methods reflect the nature of its culture and its theology as played out in its distinct institutional structure. The most pertinent features are:

First, to a degree unparalleled in the modern West, the church and the social institutions of the LDS community are intimately bound together. As a result, decisions by the church have a much more direct impact on social mores and policies, much as was once the case with the Catholic Church.

Second, Brigham Young University maintains a high standard of excellence, considerably higher than most outsiders think. While other religiously affiliated schools are on a par—Georgetown University, Notre Dame University, Yeshiva University—and therefore compete well in the wider market, none maintains nearly so strong an adherence to the precepts of the faith upon which it depends.

Third, to a degree that is matched only by serious Orthodox Jews, the LDS community is intact. Divorce rates in the United States are now around 50 percent, up from 43 percent in 1988. The divorce rate among all LDS members is now at about 30 percent and at 6 percent for those married within a temple (i.e., with religious vows). A 1993 study published in *Demography* found that 8.2 percent of LDS members are likely to cohabit, compared with 24 percent of (all) Protestants, 23.1 percent of Catholics, 32.5 percent of (all) Jews, and 44.8 percent of non-religious Americans.

Fourth, somewhat along the lines of the Catholic Church, the LDS church is a structured hierarchy. Perhaps because it is smaller, its processes and decisions are even more cohesive and uniform than those of the Catholic Church. It deliberates at the irritatingly glacial pace of most institutions founded on contemplative virtues (by contrast to, say, a band of guerrillas), but once it decides to do something, it can mobilize a large body of people and institutions with little fear of being undermined from within.

The LDS leadership spent approximately seven years carefully considering homosexuality: what it is, what causes it, whether it can be changed, and whether, among all the various problems to which the church *could* direct resources, it *should* direct them at this particular one. In the end, the LDS committed itself fully to addressing homosexuality. It immediately allocated an extraordinary amount of time and money, in conjunction with its far-flung network of social-service agencies, to seek advice from all sources on how best and most compassionately to help those seeking to rid themselves of homosexual attraction.

In Brigham Young University, the LDS church has an extremely valuable scientific and academic resource. The church and BYU provided much of the financial and all of the statistical, analytical, and computational resources for the NARTH study. The church is also constructing a universal database of materials on homosexuality.

Having decided that homosexuality was indeed a problem that needed treatment, the LDS church promptly set about designing, with outside advice, a training program for professionals in its social-service clinics and at BYU. To my knowledge, there is no training program remotely comparable anywhere in the world. And in my own experience of teaching and presenting to both lay and professional groups in Salt Lake City, I never detected even the slightest inclination to assert theology.

Nonetheless, the LDS community is small, and it cannot exert the kind of influence at wide that evangelicals can. While relations between LDS ex-gays/ strugglers and evangelical ex-gays/strugglers are predictably very good, the evangelical community at large often views the LDS church quite negatively. In sum: The LDS church provides the best current model for an evangelical approach to homosexuality, but it is too marginalized by Christendom at large to have a significant impact outside its own circle.

Concluding Observations

If evangelicalism is to play an effective and positive role in addressing the challenge of homosexuality in modern America, it will need to take a number of steps that will be difficult, both practically and in principle. In my opinion as an outside observer, these are:

1. It must sacrifice the primacy it grants to "evangelizing" in favor of providing concrete assistance. And it must not think that faithfulness in evangelizing can substitute for concrete assistance it is unable to provide.

2. Where it does not know how to provide assistance, it must humbly seek advice from others.

3. Where it has developed reliable strengths, it must offer assistance without strings attached and allow the act, attitude, and outcomes to speak for themselves.

4. Evangelical leaders should work more closely together to devise effective strategies for dealing with homosexuality on both the political and the personal level. But they should realize that the personal level—the healing of homosexuality—is vastly more important.

5. The evangelical community should raise its level of intellectual discourse. It should establish an academic center modeled on BYU or Yeshiva University that demands the highest level of achievement, and should seek advice from

these institutions. Alternatively, Wheaton College should be dramatically increased in size and scope to become a full-fledged university..

6. The evangelical community should seek criticism from both its outside friends and its enemies.

7. It should allocate significant resources to Exodus International—but with strings attached: Experts able to increase the skill and accountability of Exodus ministries should be funded to provide guidance, regardless of their faith.

8. It should devise an educational campaign to teach pastors and other church leaders a humane approach to homosexuality and homosexual change. Cruel condemnation should be swiftly and publicly quashed.

9. The evangelical community should accept responsibility for having contributed to the spread of homosexuality through its failure to measurably help stabilize family life.

10. Finally, and most importantly, the evangelical community should set itself the goal of in fact stabilizing family life for the next generation. It should establish measurable benchmarks along the way. Whenever it fails to reach those benchmarks, it should be prepared to question *any* of its premises and correct its course.

CHAPTER FIVE

Evangelicals and the Same-Sex "Marriage" Debate

David Orgon Coolidge

The same-sex "marriage" debate is a topic I come to not only as an interpreter but also as a participant.[1] This means that in discussing evangelical involvement in this debate, I have a fairly specific idea of what I will *not* be dealing with. I will not attempt to address a whole host of issues related to marriage and family more generally or to homosexuality more generally. Nor will I focus on the annual "wars of religion," as they have been called, going on within the mainline Protestant denominations over these questions. While evangelicals are indeed central players in these dramas, the stage is different.

Furthermore, I am not going to focus on the *internal* debates within evangelical circles about these general issues, for a simple reason: *there is no significant division within evangelicals on the specific question of same-sex marriage.* As I see it, there are three sets of evangelical opinion on "gay rights," although for practical purposes there are only two views within evangelicalism today. The first comprises those who have *morally* "converted" to a gay-affirming stance—which makes support for "gay rights" a religious duty. Remember, in an earlier generation the Metropolitan Community Church (MCC) was founded by the Reverend Troy Perry, an evangelical pastor. In this generation, the Reverend Mel White, who taught at Fuller Seminary, has become a major evangelist for the same-sex cause through his group Soulforce.[2] But these persons prove the rule: those who move in this direc-

David Orgon Coolidge founded and directed the Marriage Law Project at the Columbus School of Law (Catholic University of America) and the Ethics and Public Policy Center, Washington, D.C. He held an M.A. from Howard University School of Divinity and a J.D. from Georgetown University Law Center. He died from a brain tumor in March 2002, and this book is dedicated to his memory. Margaret Nell and Jeremy Dys rendered valuable help with this project.

tion either marginalize themselves within evangelical settings, melt into main-line churches, or strike off on their own. Evangelicaldom has rejected the "morally converted" views.

This leaves two other groups of opinion, which for want of better terms I will call "liberal" and "conservative." The "liberals" are basically those from what was once called "the evangelical left." They affirm the historic view of sexuality and marriage, but they may have a variety of views about specific "gay rights" legislation. Their views are, however, based in evangelical reflection. I'm thinking here of such prominent persons as Mary Stewart Van Leeuwen, Richard Mouw, Stanley Grenz, and Ron Sider. They set the tone in some evangelical circles, but not in the legal-political debate.[3]

The "conservative" body of opinion sees a fundamental contradiction between the "gay agenda" and the traditional view of sexuality and marriage. This view assumes that there is truly a "culture war" going on, that evangelicals should be on one side of it, and that "compromises" with the gay agenda are bad for evangelicals and for American society in general. This "conservative" view is not considered politically correct within some evangelical circles, but as social and legal conflicts intensify, it is coming to be the outlook of many evangelical leaders. It is certainly the view of leaders of many conservative evangelical civic and political organizations, which may help to explain why the media almost always confuse "evangelical" with "Christian Right."

But these are broader matters. What I am after is much narrower: a manageable slice of evangelical involvement in the same-sex marriage debate that can give us a feel for real events. One option would be to look at evangelical involvement in the successful 1996 campaign to pass the Defense of Marriage Act. But that was mostly an effort by national groups. The same-sex marriage debate has been mostly state by state, not nationwide. In the states there have been roughly three kinds of debate about same-sex marriage: (1) lawsuits causing drawn-out constitutional debates lasting several years (Hawaii and Vermont); (2) nationally noticed debates lasting a year or less (Alaska, California, and Nebraska); and (3) debates in the other states where defense-of-marriage legislation has been introduced (thirty-five states have now passed such acts).[4] All three of these settings merit a great deal more scrutiny. As far as I know, they have hardly been studied at all, except for a few pieces written by scholars and journalists seeking to "explain" the "Christian Right."[5]

The tales of the multi-year campaigns in Hawaii (the first) and Vermont (the most recent) are fascinating, but they take too long to tell, and to a certain extent they have been told elsewhere.[6] In those states we would especially need to explore the important role of evangelicals in *legal work*, both directly as litigators and indirectly as groups filing *amicus curiae* briefs. This is a major area of increased evangelical presence that is rarely mentioned in the frequent obituaries of "Christian politics." The key thing to note here is not only the proliferation of evangelical public-interest law firms but also the pivotal role of the Alliance Defense Fund, which serves as a referee and grantor among these groups.

What I will focus on, however, is the more manageable one-year campaigns in Alaska, California, and Nebraska. They have several structural similarities. Each involved a popular vote, either on a constitutional amendment (Alaska and Nebraska) or on an initiative statute (California). Each therefore involved a genuine public debate in the sense that every member of the public was a potential voter. Although each state had first conducted debates at the legislative level, the campaigns themselves had to appeal to a much wider audience. In all three I was directly involved as a participant and observer. But I was not "in charge" of anyone's work, and I feel free to characterize the campaigns as I see them.

Alaska: The Marriage Amendment

Senator Loren Leman is one of Alaska's most prominent legislators, and he is an evangelical. When a trial judge thought he had found a right to same-sex marriage in the Alaska constitution, Senator Leman's top staffer, Mike Pauley, went to work drafting a constitutional amendment.[7] Pauley is a conservative Catholic who used to work for Representative Chris Smith of New Jersey, and his friend Kevin Clarkson is an evangelical lawyer who has litigated pro-life and religious-liberty cases in the Alaska courts.

In the past, most of Alaska's gay-rights battles had been fought city by city, mostly in Anchorage. In that setting, large evangelical congregations such as the Anchorage Baptist Temple could have a big impact on local politicians. But this time the entire state was involved. Religious participation in Alaska is relatively low, and the portion of religious practitioners who identify themselves as evangelical is low as well. So the campaign to pass the constitutional amendment could not be aimed just at evangelicals or religious people.

The key players were inclined to work with a broad coalition. Senator Leman and Kevin Clarkson gathered together a prominent Latter-day Saint attorney, the Catholic archdiocesan priest in charge of ecumenical affairs and the diocesan attorney, and several local civic leaders. They hired a devout Lutheran to open an office, organize the campaign, and do press work. Volunteers from all religious communities poured in to help.

The Alaska Family Coalition, as it was named, was not officially connected to any religious community and did not use "religious" rhetoric. Its leaders were uncomfortable with publicly using scriptural or theological language to make their case. There had been that kind of testimony in the legislative session, and it had backfired. Insisting that every citizen had a right to participate with his or her own voice, the coalition leaders sought themes that would connect more broadly with the electorate. The two they stressed were the importance of marriage and the importance of self-government versus rule by judges.

The Catholic archbishop and his fellow bishops issued a pastoral letter on marriage and conducted voter education, while Latter-day Saints and evangelicals supplied volunteers and votes. There were three forms of national involvement that I could identify. First, the campaign took place at a time when Gary Bauer was cranking up his presidential campaign, and his campaign gave money to pay for a temporary staff person. Second, James Dobson's Focus on the Family did mailings to its Alaska list of around 8,000. (Alaska's population is approximately 630,000.) Third, the American Center for Law and Justice filed an *amicus* brief with the Alaskan supreme court on behalf of the amendment.

The coalition kept its campaign mainstream, even convincing the *Anchorage Daily News*, a generally liberal newspaper, to endorse the Marriage Amendment. The *News* editorial urging a yes vote, which came as a surprise to both sides, enhanced the coalition's showing of broad public support. On election day 2000 the amendment passed by an a large margin, 68 to 32 percent.

Five things stand out about evangelicals' involvement in Alaska. First, they played leading roles as public officials and litigators. Second, evangelical citizens were willing to submerge themselves in a larger coalition, working with Catholics and Latter-day Saints in support of marriage. Third, the campaign rhetoric was non-theological. Coalition members realized and articulated the importance of marriage to every Alaskan, not just those of religious faith. Fourth, the campaign focused on marriage and judicial activism, not on homosexuality. This created a positive focus, allowing those in favor of the amendment to be "for marriage" rather than against homosexuality or same-sex marriage. Fifth, national evangelical organizations such as the Christian Coalition were not major players. The pro-marriage efforts remained primarily local. National organizations played only a supplemental role, informing their constituencies through their mailings or radio programs, and were not viewed as invasive or self-promoting.

California: Protection of Marriage Initiative

Proposition 22, the Protection of Marriage Initiative, involved a long struggle but a relatively short campaign. Efforts to pass a defense-of-marriage statute in the California legislature had failed in the mid-1990s. Then a top staffer for Representative (now Senator) Pete Knight from southern California decided it was time for an initiative. Andy Pugno is a conservative Catholic who was going to law school at the time and now practices law in Sacramento. Through his work he had strong connections to politically active evangelicals in California, especially the Capitol Resource Institute, a state-level family-policy council affiliated with Focus on the Family. He also was familiar with, but more distant from, evangelical advocates such as the Reverend Lou Sheldon of the Traditional Values Coalition.

The campaign in California went through two stages, with two types of evangelical involvement. The first stage was gathering signatures to get the initiative on the ballot. Prominent evangelical funders chipped in, and Focus on the Family sent petitions to the 270,000 Californians on its mailing list. During this stage there was no significant involvement from other groups.

Once the signatures were gathered and the initiative was certified, the broader public campaign began. Catholics and Latter-day Saints came to the table. Rob Stutzman was chosen as head of the Proposition 22 campaign and Robert Glazier as its press spokesperson. Stutzman is a Nazarene who had served as spokesperson for former California attorney general Dan Lundgren, a conservative Catholic. Glazier is a Latter-day Saint who had worked in Washington, D.C., and was politically knowledgeable.

This new campaign team made a strategic decision: Proposition 22 was only about marriage. It would have no effect on existing state gay-rights laws on such matters as anti-discrimination and domestic partnerships, and the campaign would not address other issues.

Each religious community contributed to the campaign in its own way. The California Catholic Conference put together a resource packet for parishes, and Cardinal Roger M. Mahony of Los Angeles released a public statement. Many Latter-day Saints canvassed neighborhoods to inform and advocate. Evangelicals got a big boost with one of Dr. Dobson's nationwide monthly letters. But while local groups chipped in, overall the evangelical participation in the final campaign was weak. Evangelicals did not raise the amount of money or recruit the number of volunteers expected. People with whom I spoke attributed this to the reluctance of pastors to speak publicly about the issue. There are as many as 15,000 evangelical churches in California, but they were not recruited and mobilized into a force their sheer numbers might suggest was possible. Confronted with Proposition 22, some of the many established evangelical players jumped on board, while others did not. Those who did were the ones with more extensive political credentials, more used to working on the political inside as well as more used to working with other religious communities.

Nevertheless, in March 2000, Proposition 22 passed 61 to 38 percent. Even this substantial margin understates the political victory it represented. The initiative passed in 52 of the state's 58 counties, including Los Angeles County, Sacramento County, and even San Mateo County. The only counties that defeated it were four in the San Francisco Bay area (San Francisco, Alameda, Sonoma, and Marin), Santa Cruz, which is between San Jose and Santa Barbara, and Yolo, near Sacramento.

Nebraska: Initiative Measure 416

The most recent state to wage a successful campaign for a marriage amendment is Nebraska. Here the dynamics were different from those of Alaska and California, because there were different kinds of evangelical players. For a number of years there has been a Nebraska Family Council (not affiliated with Focus on the Family), whose arguments on family issues are based on explicit scriptural grounds. The council has also emphasized homosexual issues, often combining public-policy advocacy with a summons to homosexuals to seek healing from a sinful lifestyle.

Over a number of years, efforts had been made to pass a defense-of-marriage act in the unicameral Nebraska legislature. Senator Jim Jenson, an evangelical, had led these efforts. His top staffer is Jeff Santema, who has both a seminary degree and a law degree. As part of his legal training Santema studied under Professor Richard Duncan of the University of Nebraska Law School, one of the most prominent evangelical scholars writing on homosexuality and the law. Santema also worked closely with the Nebraska Catholic Conference. The problem was that another senator, Ernie Chambers, continually blocked the legislation, and because of his seniority he could not be stopped. Since the state's legislature has only one house, there was no other place to introduce legislation.

When Guyla Mills of the Nebraska Family Council saw what was happening in Hawaii and later in Vermont, she decided that Nebraska needed to stop working with the unicameral legislature and pass a constitutional amendment. (Nebraska amendments do not have to go through the legislature first.) So she enlisted a local attorney, who began to circulate possible drafts, and she registered the text with the Nebraska secretary of state. Her grass-roots church contacts were such that in only six weeks she was able to gather enough signatures to put the initiative on the November 2000 ballot. (By comparison, in California it took several months to gather the signatures necessary to place Proposition 22 on the ballot.)

After the proposition was certified, Family First (the Nebraska branch of Focus on the Family), the Nebraska Catholic Conference, and local Latter-day Saints formed a coalition to support Initiative Measure 416, as it was now called. The Nebraska Catholic bishops declared themselves in favor of the measure, and Focus on the Family did mailings to its list in Nebraska.

The issue became how supporters of marriage should make their case to the wider public. Guyla Mills continued to emphasize homosexuality as a sinful lifestyle, while the coalition chose to base its case on the protection of marriage from the courts. While there was wide support for the coalition, the Nebraska press typically called only Guyla Mills for public statements.

Initiative Measure 416 did something that no other marriage amendment had done—it proposed to prohibit state recognition of "civil unions, domestic partnerships, and similar same-sex relationships." The coalition offered an interpretation of the amendment that would not prohibit agencies from offering benefits to a broad range of unmarried persons, but would only prohibit singling out same-sex couples. This undercut claims by the opposition and the major newspapers that homosexuals would now be under siege in Nebraska. In the end, everyone pitched in and won the battle: in November 2000 the amendment passed 70 to 30 percent.

Concluding Observations

I have sometimes heard it said that the Catholics give prestige, the Latter-day Saints give money, and the evangelicals give time, energy, and enthusiasm. While this has some truth to it, it is an inadequate and perhaps overgenerous characterization of these communities. Let us consider just one issue in this regard: the question of authority, in the sense that church leaders can both speak credibly to the wider community and encourage lay involvement in social policy.

I would say that the LDS leaders have *real* authority, because when the church announced its support for the initiatives, members responded by giving unequivocal support and assistance.

The Catholics generally have what we might call *timid* authority. Partially because of their numbers, they are more legitimate within the wider society. This makes them more reluctant to use their authority in controversial situations. Pro-life issues are the big exception, but even then bishops can be reluctant to offer guidance. Everyone knows that dissent is rampant in Catholicism, and no bishop enjoys being pitted in public against his own priests, sisters, or laypeople.

I would say that evangelical leaders have *dispersed* authority at best. Specific ministries, such as Focus on the Family and its affiliated family-policy committees, can have a great influence on the people who listen to them. Beyond that, the only authority evangelicals seem to respond to is their local leadership. Since no one group speaks for evangelicals as a whole, you have to know specifically whom you are dealing with to determine their beliefs and commitment. Moreover, because calls to action can come from ministries, either church or para-church, they may be loaded with the fiery rhetoric that their enemies love to use in cartoons. And many evangelicals do not seem motivated to participate in public life for its own sake, on its own grounds, with its own language, and with modest goals.

Yet there *are* evangelical persons in public life now who can counteract these negatives. For the most part they are not trained by elites from the evangelical subculture. They are a different breed from the preachers and political ministries. Generally trained in such professions as law and public policy, they have learned to participate in public life through work on issues, political campaigns, and/or government service. They know how to work under conditions of intense pluralism, through coalitions, with or without the use of religious words. They no longer supply just "time, energy, and enthusiasm." As individuals, they supply vital leadership.

At the same time, they cannot necessarily bring the larger evangelical community with them. They have to relate to evangelical ministries and parachurch activists in a way that both takes the participation of the ministers and activists seriously, on their own terms, and also channels the groups in broader and more constructive ways. When this works, it can be formidable. When it doesn't, the insiders and the outsiders go their own way, and their people stay at home. I have seen this in Alaska, California, and Nebraska. I have also seen it in abundance in Hawaii and Vermont, although, as I said, that tale would take too long to tell.

I wish some bright, young Ph.D. students would explore this sector more deeply, delving into such questions as: Where do the newer evangelical leaders get their training, not only professionally and practically, but also in their approach to public policy? How have they been affected by working in coalition with Catholics and Latter-day Saints? How do they sort out which issues should be accommodated and which must be fought? How do some maintain a vital link with their grass-roots constituents while others fail? Where do they go in challenging moments when they need resources of various kinds? To what extent do national evangelical organizations succeed or fail in assisting them?

Finding answers to questions like these could do a lot to strengthen the contribution of evangelicals to public-policy issues, not least the debate over same-sex marriage.

CHAPTER SIX

Evangelicals and Abortion

Clyde Wilcox

The abortion issue has aroused passions, inspired activism, and influenced votes for more than twenty-five years. The passions it has aroused have led to angry confrontations on the steps of the U.S. Supreme Court, and even to the murder of abortion providers. Abortion has also inspired ordinary citizens to extraordinary activism, including such endeavors as blockading abortion clinics or ushering women through such blockades. Abortion creates activists out of citizens who would otherwise be apolitical.[1] It influences votes in presidential, congressional, and state elections, and has even led to a realignment of partisanship among some voters.[2]

Scholars and journalists often depict the abortion debate as part of a "culture war" between highly religious Americans and secular Americans. Organized opposition to abortion is indeed concentrated among highly observant white evangelicals and Catholics, although some black evangelicals are also strongly anti-abortion. The Christian Right has made abortion a central element in its policy agenda, and moderate public statements by Christian Coalition founder Pat Robertson on abortion in the United States and China led to widespread resignations of Coalition state and local chairs.

Not all evangelicals are aligned with the Christian Right, and some take relatively liberal positions not only on economic and foreign policy issues but also on social issues. Previous research has suggested that there is a

---

Clyde Wilcox is professor of government at Georgetown University, Washington, D.C. His research interests include religion and politics, public opinion and electoral behavior, and the politics of social issues such as abortion and gay rights. He is the author of *Onward Christian Soldiers? The Religious Right in American Politics* and *God's Warriors: The Christian Right in Twentieth-Century America*, and the co-author or co-editor of numerous other volumes.

substantial pro-choice contingent among American evangelicals.[3] Yet there has been little recent research on the politics of abortion in the evangelical community.

In what follows I will examine the attitudes of evangelicals toward abortion, and the political consequences of those attitudes. My primary focus will be on the attitudes and behaviors of white evangelicals in the United States from 1972 through 2000. I will identify evangelicals by their denomination, although I will also examine the impact of evangelical doctrine on the abortion attitudes of those who attend evangelical, mainline, and Catholic churches. I will compare the attitudes of evangelicals to those of other white Christians, to help understand the distinctiveness of evangelicals.

I will first describe the data used in the study, and then briefly discuss abortion attitudes in the general public. Next, I will compare the attitudes of white evangelicals with those of other white Christians—mainline Protestants and Catholics—to see if evangelicals hold distinctive attitudes. I will then explore the sources of abortion attitudes among these three groups and, finally, the partisan and electoral consequences of those attitudes.

The Data and the Six-Point Scale

The data for this study come primarily from the General Social Survey (GSS), a large omnibus survey conducted annually or biannually by the National Opinion Research Center. Since 1972, the GSS has routinely asked whether abortion should be allowed under six circumstances: (1) if a woman's health is in danger, (2) if the fetus is severely defective, (3) if the pregnancy is the result of rape, (4) if the family is too poor to support additional children, (5) if a woman is single and does not wish to marry, or (6) if a married couple wants no more children. Respondents can approve or disapprove of each of these circumstances independently. From these responses I have created a scale ranging from 0 (disapproves in all six circumstances) to 6 (approves in all six circumstances).

The GSS also includes measures of church attendance, commitment to a denomination, and (in the latter years) views of the Bible. It contains a rich variety of social indicators and attitudes, including attitudes toward sexual morality, euthanasia, ideal family size, and women's roles. The three-decade-long existence of the GSS makes it possible to aggregate a number of respondents and to examine differences of attitude among different theological communities within the evangelical tradition. In addition, I will use data from a *Los Angeles Times* poll on abortion and gay rights, conducted in June 2000. The survey does not identify those who attend evangelical denominations, but it does include one item measuring a basic evangelical religious doctrine (belief in the Bible) as well as a question about whether the respondent self-identified as Pentecostal or charismatic Christian.

Abortion and Public Opinion

Abortion has polarized American political elites, who generally support either an absolute right to fetal life or a woman's absolute right to make decisions concerning her body. This "clash of absolutes," especially evident in the courts, is also a feature of interest-group mobilization, campaign rhetoric, and partisan clashes.[4] Yet public opinion does not mirror this sharp division. The GSS data from 1972 through 2000 show that between 5 and 10 percent of Americans oppose abortion under all circumstances, and between 33 and 44 percent support abortion under all six circumstances. Thus the totally anti-abortion contingent is quite small. These data suggest a much larger totally pro-choice cohort. Yet when additional questions are included in other surveys, they reveal that the portion of the public that supports an unlimited abortion right is also small. For instance, in the June 2000 *Los Angeles Times* poll, fully 40 percent of those who consistently supported abortion under a variety of circumstances also opposed all second-trimester abortions. These otherwise pro-choice respondents also favored a variety of restrictions on abortion, including the requirement that a woman get the consent of the biological father before undergoing an abortion.[5]

A majority of Americans are "situationalists" whose position on abortion is, "it depends."[6] It depends on two main factors. First are the reasons for seeking an abortion. There is overwhelming support for allowing abortion for physically traumatic circumstances such as danger to the woman's life or health, severe fetal defect, and rape, and there is overwhelming opposition to abortion for sex selection. The public is more divided on economic and social reasons such as poverty, single motherhood, and desire to limit family size or to plan professional development; approximately half of the public opposes abortion for any of these reasons. The second main factor is the gestational stage of the fetus. A clear majority of all *LA Times* respondents opposed abortions in the second trimester, and it is safe to assume that an even larger segment would oppose abortions in the third trimester.

The public draws these distinctions because it values both fetal life and a woman's right to control her fertility. In the *LA Times* poll, 49 percent of men and 63 percent of women indicated that life begins at conception, while another 36 percent of men and 26 percent of women said life begins sometime between conception and birth. Moreover, fully 60 percent of all respondents said that abortion is murder; yet of those, nearly half also said that the abortion decision should be left to the woman in consultation with her doctor. This indicates considerable ambivalence toward abortion, brought about by conflicting values.[7] Many Americans seek to balance these competing values by supporting abortion in some but not all circumstances.

But these are not the only two values in conflict in the abortion debate. The

LA Times survey also asked whether legalizing abortion has encouraged people to become sexually promiscuous, and a narrow majority said yes. Thus abortion involves not only the value of fetal life and of women's autonomy but also more general values of sexual morality. Although the public in general may seek to balance competing values, some religious communities will emphasize one or more of these values over others. It is therefore likely that evangelicals, mainline Protestants, and Catholics will come to different decisions about abortion. The *LA Times* data, for example, show that more 57 percent of white Pentecostals *strongly* believe that legal abortion encourages promiscuity, compared with 36 percent of other white Christians.

Evangelical Positions

Attitudes of many white Christians toward abortion are likely to be influenced by the official position of their denomination, or by that of their local pastor or priest. Evangelical denominations, mainline Protestant denominations, and the Catholic Church differ somewhat in their official positions on abortion and in the sources of those positions.

The National Association of Evangelicals (NAE) adopted a pro-life resolution in 1972 that allowed for moral ambiguity in circumstances of rape, incest, and danger to the life of the mother. Yet there was little evangelical activism during the 1970s, even after the 1973 *Roe v. Wade* decision legalizing abortion on demand. In May 1980, *Moody Monthly* magazine devoted an entire issue to abortion, with an editorial that sharply contrasted the quick Catholic mobilization on abortion with the evangelical response. Lamenting "no real outcry . . . no protest," the editorial asked, "Isn't seven years long enough? . . . The deeper horror is the silence of the evangelical." Liberal evangelical leader Jim Wallis proclaimed a pro-life position in 1980 as well.[8]

Today most evangelical denominations have adopted resolutions condemning abortion, usually with an exception for cases where the life or physical health of the mother is in danger. Some also make an exception for rape or incest or (less commonly) fetal defect. Not surprisingly, these resolutions generally link the official church position to Scripture. The Bible does not explicitly mention abortion, so denominational statements ground their opposition in a penumbra of verses that speak of God's forming persons in the womb (for example, Psalms 139:13-16), and of the mother of John the Baptist feeling the child "leap" in her womb when she was greeted by Mary (Luke 1:40-44).

Central to the scriptural case is Exodus 21:22-25: "If men strive, and hurt a woman with child, so that her fruit depart from her, and yet no mischief follow: he shall be surely punished, according as the woman's husband will lay upon him; and he shall pay as the judges determine. And if any mischief follow, then thou shalt give life for life, eye for eye, tooth for tooth, hand for hand, foot for foot, burning for burning, wound for wound, stripe for stripe."

The interpretation of these verses varies across denominations, centering on the meaning of "mischief." Many evangelicals believe the verses mean that if the fetus is born prematurely but lives, then no "mischief" has occurred, but others (and most mainline Protestants) believe that "mischief" is the death of the mother. Some evangelical Bible guides argue that this passage is directly about abortion, but many interpret it to be about a miscarriage induced by fighting men.[9]

Most evangelical denominational statements on abortion address only that issue. But sermons, magazine articles, and other publications frequently discuss abortion in the larger context of a general decline in sexual morality, and a breakdown in traditional gender roles.

Mainline Protestant and Catholic Positions

Mainline Protestant denominations generally take moderately pro-choice positions. Most condemn abortion used as birth control or for trivial reasons such as sex selection, but ultimately maintain that abortion is a personal decision that must be made by a woman after much prayer and thought. Scriptural arguments are less common in mainline position statements than in evangelical statements; abortion policy seems instead to flow from more general social, economic, and political positions. The United Methodist Church, for example, gives its position on abortion within a more general discussion of sexuality and gender equality. The statement concludes, "Therefore, a decision concerning abortion should be made only after thoughtful and prayerful consideration by the parties involved, with medical, pastoral, and other appropriate counsel."[10] Several mainline Protestant denominations support the Religious Coalition for Reproductive Choice.

The Catholic Church has long opposed both contraception and abortion. Contemporary Catholic teaching on these matters is based upon the 1968 encyclical by Pope Paul VI, *Humanae Vitae*. Like most Catholic teachings, the encyclical does not base its positions on scripture but instead relies on natural law—the process of uncorrupted reasoning about God's plans and purposes. The encyclical argues against contraception because the purpose of human sexuality is procreation, by which human beings participate in the divine act of creation. To interfere with the possibility of procreation is to pervert the purpose of human sexuality. The encyclical restates the opinion of Pope Pius XII that the fetus acquires a soul at the moment of conception. The Catholic condemnation of abortion is clear and has been consistently enunciated, although no pope has addressed the subject *ex cathedra*. A sizable pro-choice contingent in the Church is well organized and visible, however.

Within the American Catholic Church there has been considerable emphasis on a "seamless garment" of pro-life policies that includes opposition to abortion, to the death penalty, and to nuclear weapons, along with support for social welfare programs. The Church has supported gender equality in many aspects of public life, but it has maintained that women have special skills as mothers and has therefore supported different gender roles in families.

Abortion Attitudes and Faith Communities

From the official positions of churches in these traditions, we would expect evangelicals and Catholics to be less supportive of abortion than mainline Protestants. Those who attend church regularly are most likely to be exposed to these messages, and therefore more likely to hold distinctive positions. Among evangelicals and mainline Protestants, abortion attitudes are likely to be linked to attitudes about sexual morality and feminism, whereas among Catholics, attitudes on other issues are likely to be important predictors of abortion attitudes.

Figure 1 shows the average score for evangelicals, mainline Protestants,

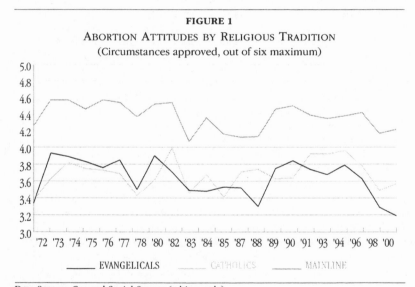

FIGURE 1

ABORTION ATTITUDES BY RELIGIOUS TRADITION

(Circumstances approved, out of six maximum)

DATA SOURCE: General Social Survey (whites only).

and Catholics on the six-point GSS scale on abortion attitudes, 1972 through 2000.[11] The data here confirm our expectation that mainline Protestants are more supportive of abortion than either evangelicals or Catholics. By the early 1990s, evangelicals are less supportive of abortion than Catholics, and their attitudes show a steady decline throughout the latter portion of the decade.

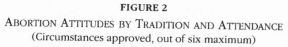

FIGURE 2

ABORTION ATTITUDES BY TRADITION AND ATTENDANCE
(Circumstances approved, out of six maximum)

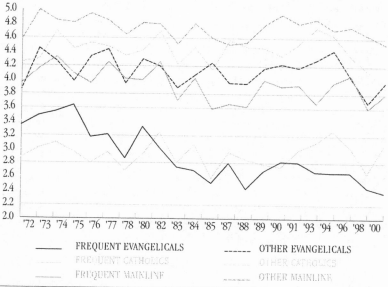

——— FREQUENT EVANGELICALS	- - - - - OTHER EVANGELICALS
········· FREQUENT CATHOLICS	········· OTHER CATHOLICS
············ FREQUENT MAINLINE	- - - - - OTHER MAINLINE

DATA SOURCE: General Social Survey.

Some trends occur across religious traditions. Support for abortion increased among all three groups after 1972, most likely in response to the 1973 *Roe v. Wade* decision.[12] Support declined among all three groups in 1978 but increased again in 1980 and 1982. Then from 1983 through 1988 support was lower among all groups, but in 1989, the year of the *Webster* decision that seemed to threaten abortion rights, support increased. It remained high until the mid 1990s, when it began to drop again. These trends do differ a bit by tradition: Catholics appear to respond more slowly to the trends that produce increases in support for abortion, and evangelical support declined more rapidly in the late 1990s.

Figure 2 compares adherents to the three religious traditions who attend church at least two to three times a month with those who attend less often. Among all three, those who regularly attend church are less supportive of abortion than those who attend less often. This is true even among mainline Protestants, who are less likely to hear anti-abortion messages from the pulpit. But religious opposition to abortion is clearly strongest among evangelicals and Catholics who worship regularly. Frequently attending evangelicals were the least supportive of abortion during the 1990s, and their support declined steadily over the decade.

Although evangelicals and Catholics who attend regularly are less supportive of abortion than those who do not, these differences are not large. The scale measures the number of circumstances under which abortion should be permitted, and the difference between frequently attending evangelicals and infrequently attending mainline Protestants in 2000—the greatest difference observed—is two circumstances out of six. Frequently attending evangelicals do not oppose abortion under all circumstances. Even in 2000, when their support was at its lowest, they on average approve of abortion under three of six circumstances—generally for the physically traumatic ones: to protect the health of the mother, in the case of severe fetal defect, or when the pregnancy is the result of rape. On average, infrequently attending mainline Protestants approve of one additional circumstance, most often poverty.

Figures 1 and 2 show averages; all three of the faith communities contain members who oppose abortion always, or who support an unlimited right to choose. Figure 3 shows the distribution of opinions on abortion by religious tradition and frequency of attendance. Among evangelicals who attend church regularly, an absolute majority supports abortion for some

---

FIGURE 3

DISTRIBUTION OF ABORTION ATTITUDES BY TRADITION AND ATTENDANCE
(Circumstances approved, out of six maximum)

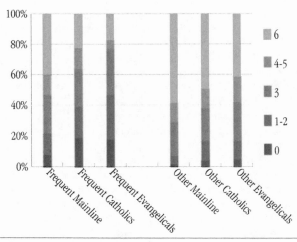

DATA SOURCE: General Social Survey, 1989–2000.

or all of the physically traumatic circumstances; the rest are roughly equally divided between opposing abortion under all circumstances and allowing abortion under all circumstances. What is striking is that three in four observant evangelicals support abortion for *no* additional circumstances beyond the three physically traumatic ones. In contrast, a plurality of less observant evangelicals, observant mainline Protestants, and Catholics support abortion for all six circumstances, as does an absolute majority of less observant mainliners.

Explaining Evangelical Distinctiveness

Of the many possible explanations for why evangelicals are less supportive of abortion than mainline Protestants, religious differences are the most likely. Evangelicals generally believe that the Bible is inerrant and attend churches that interpret Scripture as opposing abortion. They are also more likely to attend church regularly—often more than once a week—and to show other evidence of religious commitment.

But evangelicals differ from mainline Protestants in other ways as well. They have lower levels of education and income, are more likely to have been raised in the South and in rural regions,[13] and are more likely to be conservative on a range of issues that includes sexual morality, gender roles, and general ideology. Each of these characteristics is associated with pro-life positions in the general public.

One way to examine the sources of evangelical distinctiveness is to successively control for various factors on which evangelicals and mainline Protestants differ, comparing, for example, evangelicals who believe the Bible is inerrant and who attend church weekly with mainline Protestants who share that doctrine and level of attendance. I did this, using data from the General Social Survey, 1989–2000. First I looked at the overall difference for both evangelicals and Catholics from mainline Protestants. In a second model, I added controls for religious characteristics, essentially comparing evangelicals, mainline Protestants, and Catholics with similar ideas about the Bible, similar levels of church attendance, and similar commitment to their denominations. Third, I also controlled for such demographic characteristics as education, sex, geography, and age. Finally I added controls for political and social attitudes.[14]

In the first model, using the six GSS questions on circumstances under which abortion should be allowable, I found that evangelicals support abortion for almost one fewer circumstance than mainline Protestants, while Catholics on average support abortion for two-thirds of a circumstance less than mainline Protestants.[15] In the second, with doctrine, religiosity, and denominational commitment held constant, evangelicals and Catholics are still less supportive of abortion than mainline Protestants, but the difference is smaller.

When evangelicals are compared with mainline Protestants with the same level of religious involvement and the same doctrine, they support legal abortion for two-thirds of a circumstance less on average. Thus about a third of the distinctiveness of evangelicals is explained by their religious doctrine and practice.[16]

Belief in the inerrancy of the Bible—a key evangelical doctrinal tenet—is a very powerful predictor of opposition to abortion. Not all who attend evangelical churches hold this doctrine, and many mainline Protestants and a significant minority of Catholics do believe it. But the belief is far more common in evangelical congregations. Presumably its power as a source of opposition to abortion is that it gives an ultimately credible source in which to ground pro-life messages.[17] Church attendance and commitment to the denomination are also significant predictors of abortion opinion. (Born-again status, also very important in evangelical doctrine, is another important predictor, but early GSS surveys did not include an item to measure this.)

The third research model added controls for demographic characteristics—education, gender, geography, and age. Finally, the fourth model also controlled for attitudes related to abortion opinion—opposition to euthanasia as a measure of pro-life sentiment;[18] attitudes toward sexual morality, gender equality in families, and the ideal number of children; and general ideology and partisanship. By this point the distinctiveness of evangelicals is much reduced but remains statistically significant.

This final model is telling, for it has controlled for many of the things that make evangelicals unique—their high levels of church attendance, belief in the inerrancy of Scripture, traditional sexual morality, support for traditional gender roles, and conservative ideology. Yet even with these controls, those who attend evangelical churches are slightly less supportive of abortion than mainline Protestants with these same characteristics. This suggests that evangelical churches communicate a uniquely pro-life sentiment, perhaps through the official position of the denomination or through messages from the pastor. This remaining distinctiveness might also result from the more homogeneously pro-life ethos in evangelical churches: mainline Protestants who hold orthodox doctrine and conservative values attend churches where others in the pews may not reinforce those values, but evangelicals are likely to find their pro-life sentiments supported by their fellow churchgoers.

Sources of Attitudes within Religious Traditions

Evangelicals are distinctively less supportive of abortion than mainline Protestants and only slightly less supportive than Catholics. But it is likely that the *sources* of abortion attitudes will differ among the three traditions. For example, attitudes toward the Bible's authority might be strong predictors of attitudes toward abortion among evangelicals but might be less useful in predicting attitudes of Catholics, because the Bible is less central to Catholic teachings on abortion. For Catholics, commitment to the denomination might well serve as a strong predictor, as a proxy for belief in the authority of the Pope to speak on matter of faith and morals.

In this second part of the study I used the same predictors of attitudes that were used in the first part plus, for evangelicals, an additional one: attending a Pentecostal denomination. The data show remarkable similarities in the sources of attitudes across the three faith traditions, but also some interesting differences.

For all three groups, belief in the inerrancy of the Bible is a powerful predictor of abortion attitudes, as is frequency of church attendance. Yet denominational commitment is a predictor of abortion attitudes only for Catholics, presumably signaling their support for Catholic theology.[19] Among evangelicals, those who attend Pentecostal denominations are significantly more conservative on abortion than other evangelicals. Additional analysis reveals that those who attend Assemblies of God churches are the most pro-life of all denominations in the General Social Survey.

Among evangelicals and mainline Protestants, higher levels of education lead to more pro-choice attitudes, but this is not true among Catholics. Catholic schools may be responsible for this distinction, although the GSS data do not permit us to test this hypothesis. It is also striking that, all other factors being equal, younger evangelicals and Catholics are more opposed to abortion than older members of their faiths. This effect is larger for evangelicals—indeed it is twice as large for them as for Catholics. It is important to remember that on this point *all else is held constant*, for the younger evangelicals are somewhat *less* conservative than their elders on sexual morality and gender roles. Yet these data suggest at the very least that generational replacement will not lead to more liberal evangelical attitudes on abortion and might result in even more conservative attitudes over time.

For each faith tradition, several key social and political attitudes are associated with abortion opinion. Opposition to euthanasia and support for traditional sexual morality are significant predictors of opposition to abortion; in both cases this is most true for Catholics and least true for mainline Protestants, but the relationship is always quite strong. Only among evangelicals, however, is opposition to abortion linked to support for non-egalitarian gender roles within the family. In all three groups, those who believe that large families are ideal are less supportive of abortion. Predictably this is most important for Catholics, who are exposed to unique teachings against contraception. For Protestants but not for Catholics, opposition to abortion is significantly linked to general conservative ideology. A significant number of pro-life Catholics are liberal on other issues, and indeed the "seamless garment" of pro-life policies includes many liberal positions.

Overall, however, these data suggest that the broad outline of the abortion debate is similar across faith traditions. Those who are regular churchgoers and take a high view of Scripture are more likely to oppose abortion, whereas better educated and less observant congregants are more likely to hold pro-choice attitudes.

Abortion and Realignment among Evangelicals

Greg Adams reported that the abortion issue has evolved in American politics and served as the basis of some partisan realignment.[20] He argued that House members from the two parties began to stake divergent positions on abortion in the late 1970s, and that Senate votes followed suit in the early 1980s—presumably as the result of focused group activity in recruiting candidates and helping them win nominations. Once the party positions were sufficiently distinct, then some strong partisans began to change their positions on abortion, while some with strong positions on abortion began to change their partisanship.

Evangelicals were attracted to the Republican Party by GOP positions on school prayer, the death penalty, gun control, race, and defense spending.

FIGURE 4

CORRELATION BETWEEN PARTISANSHIP AND ABORTION OPINION
Negative: Pro-life respondents more likely Democrats.
Positive: Pro-life respondents more likely Republicans.

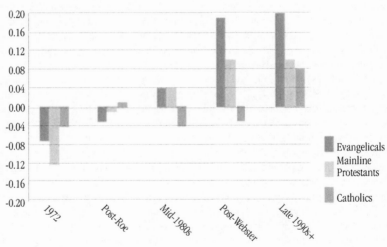

DATA SOURCE: General Social Survey.

Did the party's stand on the abortion issue also contribute to the realignment of white evangelicals to the Republican Party during the past two decades?

If abortion has been a source of realignment, then we should expect to see the correlation between partisanship and abortion opinion increasing over time. Figure 4 shows that correlation for five time periods. In 1972, the correlation is negative for all three groups, which means that pro-life respondents from all faith traditions were more likely to be Democrats than Republicans. In the post-*Roe* period (1973–82) and the mid-1980s (1983–88) the correlation was close to zero. But in the post-*Webster* period (1989–95), evangelicals and mainline Protestants who favored sharp limits on abortion were much more likely to be Republicans, and this effect was by far the greatest for evangelicals. By the late 1990s and beyond, Catholics too had begun to exhibit consistency between their partisanship and their abortion views, but the effect was still far greater among evangelicals.

Of course, there are other reasons why abortion and partisanship should line up more clearly for white evangelicals in the late 1990s. The Christian Right organized itself during the 1990s as a Republican recruitment vehicle, and the party took a variety of other positions that would appeal to this constituency. The question is whether abortion had any special appeal to white evangelicals pondering a switch to the GOP.

The GSS data do not permit a definitive test, but my research suggests that abortion is indeed part of the Republican realignment among white evangelicals. In regression analyses of factors predicting partisanship for members of each faith tradition, I controlled for demographic factors such as education and income, father's education, geography, and gender, as well as for other issues that might underpin partisanship, such as attitudes toward gun laws, the death penalty, race, defense spending, and homosexual relations, along with general ideology. The results show that abortion attitudes are a significant source of partisanship for evangelicals but not for mainline Protestants or for Catholics. This suggests that abortion is the major element in a more general moral and religious realignment among evangelicals.

Concluding Observations

By the latter part of the twentieth century, evangelicals were less supportive of abortion than members of the other major religious traditions, and their attitudes were trending toward even more conservatism. The most observant evangelicals were even less likely to support unlimited access to abortion. Evangelical attitudes were slightly more conservative than those of Catholics with similar levels of religious devotion, and were much more conservative than those of mainline Protestants.

Evangelicals are distinctively opposed to abortion for several reasons. They interpret the Bible as banning abortion, they are likely to attend church regularly, and religion is likely to have great salience in their lives. They are slightly less educated, more Southern, and more rural than mainline Protestants and Catholics. They also hold more traditional views of sexual morality and gender roles, and are more likely to call themselves conservatives. Each of these factors contributes to evangelical uniqueness, but even when these factors are all held constant, evangelicals remain less supportive of abortion than mainline Protestants. This is probably because of the sermons and other messages about abortion in evangelical churches, which are starkly different from those in mainline Protestant churches.

This does not mean that all or even most evangelicals totally oppose abortion. Between 1989 and 2000, only 11 percent of evangelicals opposed abortion under all circumstances; the figure for observant (regularly attending) evangelicals was 18 percent. Approximately 30 percent of observant evangelicals either opposed abortion always or supported it only to save the health of the mother, a position consistent with the teachings of most evangelical denominations. Among all evangelicals, slightly more support abortion under all circumstances than oppose it under all circumstances. Overall, when compared with mainline Protestants, evangelicals disapprove of only one additional circumstance, and that distinctiveness drops to a fraction of an item once other factors are held constant.

Yet evangelical support for abortion is declining, and so that gap may widen over time. One of the most interesting and subtle differences between evangelicals and other Americans over time is in support of abortion for rape and for fetal defect. Evangelical groups and denominations have articulated clear positions opposing abortion under these two circumstances, but the General Social Survey has found very steady support for these circumstances among the general public over the past twenty-eight years.

Indeed, it is only frequently attending evangelicals who have decreased their support for abortion under these two circumstances. Their support for abortion when the pregnancy results from rape has decreased from 70 percent in the post-*Webster* period to 58 percent in the late 1990s, and support for abortion when the fetus is severely defective has declined from 77 percent to 56 percent, a truly huge change. This decline did not occur among less observant evangelicals, nor did it occur among Catholics and mainline Protestants, regardless of their level of attendance.

Yet the dividing line for public battles over abortion is over the social conditions. More than three-fourths of Americans support abortion for the mother's health, fetal defect, *and* rape, and a narrow majority of even frequently attending evangelicals do as well. But only half of the public supports abortions for other reasons, as do fewer than one-fourth of observant evangelicals. The physically traumatic circumstances are thus a likely minimum for any viable state law limiting abortion, but they account for only a tiny minority of all abortions. These data suggest that evangelicals are likely to be enthusiastic supporters of state laws to limit abortion to these circumstances. Should evangelical activists push to limit abortions even more severely, however, they are likely to encounter resistance not only from outside the evangelical community but from within that community as well.

The data presented here also show that abortion has been a source of partisan realignment among white evangelicals. Although most accounts of party change among Southerners have focused on race politics, these data suggest that moral issues have been more important in recent years. There is ample room for this trend to continue, but if abortion becomes highly salient (if *Roe* is overturned, for example), then some pro-choice evangelicals might move back to the Democratic Party. Indeed, there are today more pro-choice Republican evangelicals than there are pro-life Democratic evangelicals.

Overall, evangelical churches, pastors, and activists have engaged the culture in a debate over abortion. The issue has mobilized evangelicals to join groups, sign petitions, and march, and to change their partisanship and their voting habits. In the process, many evangelicals have joined forces with Catholics, which no doubt has led some to rethink their evaluations of that faith.

As for the future, abortion is likely to continue to be an important source of evangelical political engagement, especially in battles over nominations to the Supreme Court.

CHAPTER SEVEN

Evangelicals and Bioethics:
An Extraordinary Failure

Nigel M. de S. Cameron

A volume of essays boldly titled *God and Culture* and published a decade ago aimed to articulate an evangelical vision in the major areas of the academy. The volume was offered as a *Festschrift* to Carl F. H. Henry, dean of evangelicals for half a century and long a steadfast advocate of cultural embrace on their part; regrettably, his imaginative plan for an evangelical research university ultimately foundered a generation ago.[1] In my contribution to *God and Culture,* I attempted to focus attention on the need to develop a distinctive agenda for bioethics, one that would embody the Christian worldview and build on the moral vision of the Western medical tradition. The essay, "Bioethics: The Twilight of Christian Hippocratism," also offered a candid acknowledgment of the general failure of evangelicals to engage an area that is of central importance to their own world-and-life view, one in which opportunities for leadership and influence continued to be great.[2] Now, a decade later, it is sobering to note the conservative Christian community's continuing lack of interest in that cultural question in which it arguably has the largest stake.

This disinterest is paradoxical for several reasons. The great awakening of evangelical social-political interest in the past generation has owed most to the emergence of elective abortion as a focus of both moral and political concern. It was abortion that first catalyzed twentieth-century evangelical engagement with public policy (while at the same time fertilizing the growing evangelical-

Nigel M. de S. Cameron is dean of the Wilberforce Forum in Reston, Virginia, and directs its affiliated Council for Biotechnology Policy (BiotechPolicy.com). He previously was at Trinity International University/Trinity Evangelical Divinity School, where he initiated the Center for Bioethics and Human Dignity. He has published widely in the bioethics field, including his keynote book *The New Medicine: Life and Death after Hippocrates* (new edition 2002).

Catholic rapprochement, which makes it increasingly difficult to isolate "evangelical" approaches). But just what did the abortion issue catalyze?

For one thing, it initiated what we might call the multiple–single-issue approach of Christian conservatives that was most evident in the rise (and fall) of "moral majority" attitudes toward public policy. This approach has failed to mature into anything resembling organic cultural engagement. *Roe v. Wade* appears to have become a fixed point in the firmament of American jurisprudence, while developments in biotechnology have radically transformed the nature and scope of bioethics and its stakes. Yet the early years of the third millennium find evangelicals hardly any more engaged even in the policy questions of bioethics than a generation ago. Abortion, which seemed to offer a historic starting-point for evangelical participation in bioethics and in wider cultural-political questions, now seems close to marking an end-point in the same process.

The term "bioethics" was coined a mere generation ago. Under its rubric has emerged an interdisciplinary field that draws on ethics, philosophy, law, medicine, public policy, and, increasingly, the biosciences for its subject matter. Bioethics forms a bridge from the old "medical ethics," with its clinical focus on narrow patient-care issues (now largely supplanted by the term "clinical ethics"), to a broader discussion of implications of the biosciences and, indeed, of such cognate fields as robotics and nanotechnology (the development of extremely small devices that will give us the capacity to enhance and control human beings; we already have nano-implanted rats that can be controlled for emergency rescue activity). Coinage of the term wrenched the American conversation out of the professional and traditional context of medicine. The term both symbolized and helped to effect a raw new context for these questions in which the congruent Judeo-Christian and Hippocratic traditions were set aside. (In Europe "medical ethics" remains the term of choice, and the discussion is still more clearly rooted in the profession and its role.[3])

So what is new? The impression is widely held that new questions have called forth a fresh approach, both within clinical medicine (where the development of such life-preserving techniques as intravenous nutrition and hydration and the use of ventilators has revolutionized end-of-life care) and within the wider biosciences (where the conquest of the human genome and the advent of such techniques as mammalian cloning have granted us unheard-of powers to use for good or ill). But to view today's bioethics simply as a response to these new capacities is to be mistaken.

A Promising Start Aborted

Twenty years before the term "bioethics" was coined, Joseph Fletcher, who later came to great and undeserved fame as a harbinger of "situation ethics," delivered a series of prescient lectures that were published in 1954 as *Medi-*

cine and Morals.[4] In the introduction to the book Fletcher offers two fascinating comments: first, that he is claiming a new and wider meaning for the old term "medical ethics" that will embrace such major substantive issues as euthanasia and abortion, and not simply the professional medical issues to which it has generally referred; and second, that he has no option but to discuss his approaches to these questions within the context of the Christian tradition—curious testimony to the power and near unanimity of that tradition as the second half of the twentieth century opened.

In this respect Fletcher anticipated the Princeton ethicist Paul Ramsey's dogged and brilliant attempts—in such influential volumes as *The Patient as Person* (1970)—to tie "medical ethics" to the common moral tradition of the West.[5] Ramsey was swiftly, though respectfully, pushed to one side, and in bioethics discussions of the late 1970s and 1980s he seemed already to have assumed a strangely anachronistic character. One plain and sad reason was the almost total failure of Christians of any hue to take up the challenge of a bioethics for this new generation that would start where Ramsey did. The emerging bioethics "community" moved rapidly on to forge "principlism" and the other generally autonomy-focused models that have dominated the landscape since.

Since those same decades marked the rise of the pro-life movement and its capture of the evangelical heart, it is perplexing to find so little connection between that movement and the larger bioethics agenda. From the vantage point of today this is particularly striking in light of the confluence of several factors. First, the United States is home to the world's most vigorous and influential pro-life movement, and evangelical participation is a substantial component. Second, the United States is the bastion of worldwide evangelicalism and the source of most of its resources. Third, institutional life in the United States, especially in higher education, is uniquely flexible and accessible to the distinctive religious communities. The many reasons for this include historical patterns of immigration, uniquely generous non-profit funding, and the vigorous life of supporting churches. Through hundreds of colleges, seminaries, Bible schools, publishing houses, and broadcasting networks, American evangelicalism maintains an extraordinary—though little used—capacity to generate not only intellectual leadership for the churches but also intellectual challenge to the culture. Fourth, the United States was the first mover in the bioethics enterprise and continues to dominate its conversations worldwide with almost monopolistic force.

The moral and political issues facing the pro-life movement today go far beyond abortion. The bioethics agenda may be generally divided into two parts: the "life issues" that most controversially focus on abortion and euthanasia, and the new manipulative issues of biotechnology that focus less on *taking* human life and more on making and designing and controlling human life. In general, euthanasia has attracted only a small fraction of the interest that evangelicals have shown in abortion, even though it has close parallels with abortion and was hailed by pro-lifers a generation ago as the next threatening challenge. As for issues of biotechnology, these have proved to be of very modest interest to evangelicals. The prospect of human cloning, one of the great issues of our generation, is a matter of some concern, though chiefly because its mechanisms—either for purely "experimental use of the embryo, or for perfecting the process of "live birth" cloning of babies—inevitably involve the destruction of early human life. It is unclear what the response would be if the live-birth option were perfected, let alone if it were proved to be "safer" than natural conception. The paradigm has been set by abortion and the elective or reckless destruction of the embryo-fetus, rather than by any overarching understanding of the dignity of human life, of life created in the image of God.

The Evangelical Absence

The bracing intellectual questions that are rapidly reshaping the context of medicine and the biosciences have yet to be properly engaged from a Christian perspective, and indeed, except for the work of Jacques Ellul,[6] evangelicals have little to draw on. At an academic and professional level, there have been very few evangelical participants in American bioethics. Allen Verhey of Hope College, Michigan, has been perhaps the most distinguished and productive. One of the chief means by which bioethics has been discussed and disseminated has been through compendiums of articles and essays; as a movement, bioethics has generated only limited monograph publication, finding its life force in conferences, consultations, journals, symposiums, and other ephemera (a characteristic that marks it as a quintessentially post-modern discipline in its social character). Verhey is established as a leading compendiast.[7] In my own book *The New Medicine: Life and Death after Hippocrates,* I sought to elaborate a paradigm for a renewed professional vision that found its roots in the Hippocratic tradition.[8] John F. Kilner in *Life on the Line* developed a fresh and distinctively Christian context for clinical decision-making.[9] More recently, two vigorous critiques of current thinking have appeared over the name of attorney Wesley J. Smith, a close associate of Ralph Nader and longtime general counsel to the Anti-Euthanasia Task Force. In *Forced Exit* Smith addresses "The Slippery Slope from Assisted Suicide to Legalized Murder."[10] In *Culture of Death: The Assault on Medical Ethics in America* he assails the move from Hippocratism to utilitarianism that he thinks characterizes mainline bioethics.[11]

But these writers have participated as individuals; there has been little institutional development, and there was none at all until the early 1990s.[12] Evangelical colleges (of which there are now more than one hundred affiliated with the Coalition for Christian Colleges and Universities) and seminaries have done little.[13] Similarly, foundations have shown only modest interest in the development of bioethics projects.

At an invitational meeting convened at Trinity Evangelical Divinity School in 1993, a dozen key persons gathered to discuss the evangelical neglect of bioethics.[14] Some were scholars in the field while others worked with related agencies. From that meeting emerged a plan for the first evangelical bioethics center in the United States, the Center for Bioethics and Human Dignity. The center is hosted by Trinity International University, the school of the Evangelical Free Church of America, though it operates with a broad-based advisory board. Several parallel projects have begun to develop subsequently, including the Concordia Bioethics Center at Concordia University in Milwaukee, directed by Richard Eyre, D.Min.; the Center for Bioethics in the Church, based in Oakland, California, directed by Jennifer Lahl, R.N. (thecbc.org); and the St Louis Bioethics Center, directed by Barbara Quigley, R.N., and Cindy Province, R.N. (bioethicscenter.org). All four of these leaders are graduates of Trinity's bioethics programs.

Parallel with the development of the Center for Bioethics and Human Dignity, Trinity established a series of academic programs, the first such developments in an evangelical school in the United States. Current programs include: required bioethics courses in the college pre-med curriculum; an undergraduate bioethics minor (the only such program in any American university, according to *Peterson's* guides); a Doctor of Ministry specialization in bioethics and a bioethics concentration in the M.A. in Christian thought at Trinity Evangelical Divinity School; and, most significantly, an M.A. in bioethics at Trinity Graduate School, offered in modular format and with significant take-up by senior physicians, including several medical-school faculty and other leaders in Christian medicine.[15] One telling commentary on the evangelical predicament is this: when these programs were initiated, it was anticipated that other evangelical schools would soon follow suit. That has not happened.

Moreover, evangelicals continue to have remarkably little influence on, even presence within, the conferences and journals that define the bioethics enterprise. The Center for Bioethics and Human Dignity, as the single major evangelical catalyst during most of the past decade, has focused almost exclusively on cultivating networks within the evangelical community. Its annual conference and associated volume of papers have been addressed to that community; and while others have sometimes listened—some of the books have been reviewed in major medical journals—the audience has been almost entirely internal. The reasoning has been tactical: first galvanize the thinking of our own community. But it has also proved the easiest path, especially as it has been forged in close collaboration with other organizations that generally share such values and have shown limited interest in engagement or collaboration with secular and liberal Christian opinion.

The evangelical predicament is especially dire in relation to the advent of the biotechnology agenda, where huge new issues are arising—such as cloning, genetic alteration (both therapeutic and for enhancement), germline intervention (i.e., altering the genetic makeup of reproductive cells so that changes are inheritable), nanotechnology—that will soon overshadow the issues of the "old" bioethics in scope and significance. The failure of evangelicals to develop a community in which these matters are considered is the single most evident strategic failure of the Church in our generation.[16] The failure is highlighted in a recent volume by an evangelical who, with considerable sophistication, offers essentially a justification for a range of these new options.[17] By contrast, scholars broadly identified with "progressive" political positions, with the participation of mainline and liberal Christians but not evangelicals, have devoted considerable energy to the articulating of positions highly critical of some current trends in biotechnology.

A Few Encouraging Signs

One interesting recent development is a growing alliance between key conservative Christian thinkers and "progressives" on these questions. Sparked initially by the cloning debate, it now extends across a wide swath of issues, with special attention to genetics (genetic discrimination, gene patenting, germline intervention). Participants fear that, in the absence of policy based on a clear understanding of the dignity of human life, the biotechnology industry will bring to market the fruits of its research in a manner that will be fundamentally subversive of the human good.[18]

Several other fruitful projects exist. The journal *Ethics and Medicine* has been published three times a year since 1983, and remains the major evangelical-led publication of its kind. Publishing peer-reviewed papers, it is circulated primarily in continental Europe, the United Kingdom, and the United States chiefly by arrangement with three Christian bioethics centers.[19] Its editorial boards include physicians, nurses, and academics. *Ethics and Medicine* is currently edited by C. Ben Mitchell, a professor of bioethics and contemporary culture who is bioethics consultant to the Ethics and Religious Liberty Commission of the Southern Baptist Convention.

Annual conferences of the Center for Bioethics and Human Dignity have spawned an extensive book series published by Eerdmans as well as other publications.[20] Contributors to these publications have included public figures such as Francis Collins, director of the Human Genome Project, and Sir Brian Mawhinney, former U.K. secretary for health; prominent scholars noted elsewhere in this essay such as Allan Verhey and Gilbert Meilaender; those associated with the work of the Center for Bioethics and Human Dignity such as executive director John F. Kilner, senior fellow C. Ben Mitchell, and me; and several dozen others, the majority of whom are physicians, although there are also theologians, nurses, and persons who work in public policy.

The issues of embryonic stem-cell experimentation and human cloning have focused major public and political controversy on the implications of biotechnology for human dignity. It is characteristic that evangelicals were not prepared for this debate, though leadership has been forthcoming from an avowedly evangelical President whose commitment on the bioethics agenda puts the best efforts of most of his co-religionists in the shade. The stem-cell and cloning discussions have had the effect of generating fresh reflection and activity on their part. As one result, the Council for Biotechnology Policy has been formed as an affiliate of the Wilberforce Forum.[21] Fellows of the Center for Bioethics and Human Dignity took a leading role in the drafting of a declaration on stem-cell research, now posted with other materials at stemcellresearch.org. A parallel project is under development at cloninginformation.org. Evangelicals have played a major part in the political process surrounding these questions.[22] Senator Sam Brownback (R-Kans.), who has taken a leading role on Capitol Hill on human cloning legislation, addressed the 2001 conference of the Center for Bioethics and Human Dignity.

As with abortion, it has taken major public-policy challenges to begin to mobilize the evangelical constituency. The dominance of stem-cell and cloning issues in the public mind has stimulated evangelicals to take a growing interest in both their policy implications and the ethical and theological questions that they raise.

Concluding Observations

At the heart of every culture lies a set of assumptions that define its vision for human dignity and identity, its wisdom as to what it means to be human. That may be set out in stories, legends, and histories; it may be articulated in constitutional documents; it may be defined theologically. At the heart of Western culture lies the vision of humankind made in the *imago Dei*, the inordinate dignity of God himself imparted to the creature. As in other cultures, the practices and artifacts of every day are essentially unwound from those determinative assumptions.

The turmoil into which Western culture has been thrown by its steady repudiation of the Judeo-Christian past is nowhere so clear as in the development of bioethics, as from Fletcher on the steady process of rewriting the ground rules of human nature has been brought to an increasingly sharp focus. This gives unity to the diverse issues addressed in the ambit of bioethics—all treat the question of what it means to be human.

The evangelical engagement in the debate over abortion was focused essentially on one symptom of this broad and confused shift in understanding, on whether "unborn human life" is "human life." This question of "when life begins" remains the major preoccupation of evangelical engagement with medicine and bioscience and related policy. While it may have been the key to the debate of a generation past (its presenting problem, at least, was the continuity or discontinuity of born and unborn human life, and the respective rights therefore of fetus and mother), it is not very relevant to the debate in progress today. That debate treats the character of the unborn only incidentally; its subject is the nature of human life as such, and its focus is typically procedural, addressing particular issues without candid acknowledgment of their anthropological assumptions.

Clearly, evangelicals have a huge stake in the outcomes of these ethics-policy discussions. What is also clear is that they face an unprecedented opportunity, for they are uniquely qualified to address the nature of human life, and they live in a culture in which confusion and fear are present on every hand. They are challenged to articulate a Christian vision for human dignity, and to apply it to the biotechnology questions confronting the culture. The Judeo-Christian worldview has never before been under such a threat; and it has never before had such an opportunity for a hearing.

CHAPTER EIGHT

Evangelicals, Welfare Reform, and Care for the Poor

Kurt Schaefer

M y task is to review the recent approaches that influential American evangelicals have taken when considering poverty and the role of the state in alleviating it. But first, three words in the previous sentence require some clarification: *evangelical, recent,* and *influential.*

Setting a boundary to distinguish *evangelical* work from other work is somewhat difficult for at least two reasons. First, important contributions to the conversation about faith and culture have come from orthodox Christian sources not generally considered "evangelical." These would include, in recent years, the work of Roman Catholic authors like Michael Novak and Father Robert Sirico, many publications of the Evangelical Lutheran Church in America, and several dozen doctoral dissertations from non-evangelical seminaries. And second, there are other contributors whose personal practice is evangelical but whose work is not self-evidently influenced by this personal practice. In the interest of clarity and brevity, I will adopt a narrow definition: authors widely regarded as evangelical ("If it looks like an evangelical . . ."), who write self-consciously as evangelicals ("and sounds like an evangelical . . ."), whose writings can be identified by others as indebted to the evangelical heritage ("then it *is* an evangelical").

As for *recent*: a full review of evangelical work on poverty and welfare would be a hefty volume indeed. But if we limit our attention to work recent enough to be informed by the full scope of U.S. attempts to combat poverty, then our time span condenses to the last decade and its experiments with

Kurt Schaefer is professor of economics at Calvin College. His current research involves the use of mathematics and statistics to evaluate public policy. Dr. Schaefer is co-author, with W. James Bradley, of *The Uses and Misuses of Data and Models: The Mathematization of the Human Sciences.*

welfare reform. (This of course presumes that we consider only the United States; groups such as evangelical economists' associations in Australia and the United Kingdom, and an emerging group in German-speaking Europe, could enrich our discussion, but they are beyond our scope here.)

Finally, *influential.* Influence too often is inversely proportional to integrity, or even to quality. For our purposes here, however, it seems appropriate to focus on work recognizedly influential in shaping both evangelical approaches to culture and non-evangelicals' perceptions of evangelicals. And, in the interest of order and clarity, we will limit our range to books and exclude journal articles.

Given these guidelines, we can cover the waterfront by looking at four representative books. Three of them offer broadly visionary discussions of how evangelicals should think about poverty and welfare: Marvin Olasky's *The Tragedy of American Compassion,*[1] Ronald J. Sider's *Just Generosity: A New Vision for Overcoming Poverty in America,*[2] and John Schneider's *Godly Materialism: Rethinking Money and Possessions.*[3] The fourth book is tactical, weighing the practical things congregations can do to combat poverty: *Restorers of Hope: Reaching the Poor in Your Community with Church-Based Ministries That Work,* by Amy L. Sherman.[4] Each of the four authors brings a particular angle of vision to the discussion. They come from different academic disciplines (and none are economists), and they have affinities to different schools of thought regarding economics and political organization. I will attempt to summarize their arguments, giving page numbers occasionally with both paraphrased and quoted material.

THE TRAGEDY OF AMERICAN COMPASSION BY MARVIN OLASKY

Olasky's 1992 work is the most widely cited and apparently influential. His position has, in broad strokes if not in all details, become the political mainstream. The United States has ended welfare as we knew it by imposing work requirements, essentially ending general relief for able-bodied males, and imposing lifetime limits on federal support. As a result, welfare rolls have fallen dramatically. If Olasky's analysis of the harm done by the welfare system is correct, we should expect a dramatic renovation in the American work ethic, the state of marriage, and the extent of philanthropy. This book is representative of the thinking that has shaped both conservative Christian opinion and general federal policy in the 1990s.

Olasky gives an account of how poverty and the underclass are to be defined, of what has worked and has not worked in addressing the problems of the underclass, and of the interrelation of poverty and the human spirit. The core of his argument runs as follows: In an era when human needs were met voluntarily and holistically by other human beings, poverty was more severe, yet social breakdown more rare. The *way* in which people are helped affects their spirit and behavior, and spirit, not poverty, is the core cause of modern social disintegration. Bureaucratic spending exacerbates such problems, as it is fundamentally out of touch with the needs of the human spirit that drive social dysfunction. Authors who argue that the free market itself can solve the problems of poverty also fail to appreciate the crucial place of genuinely compassionate persons and groups in fighting poverty (p. 4). Both sides neglect pre-twentieth-century moral understandings of what is required for a well-functioning social order. As a result, American cities are now in cultural, economic, and moral crisis, and our political discussion of welfare is at an impasse, primarily because of the public hijacking of compassion. In sum, poverty-related problems are improving, however slowly, but reliance upon public assistance has by its nature created more poverty and undermined the human spirit.

Historical American Models

Olasky builds his case by discussing the exercise of American compassion chronologically, beginning with his interpretation of the early American model. The earliest colonial approaches to generosity stressed personal aid to the sick, home-opening hospitality to those suffering from disaster, and denial of benefits to those judged openly indecent or unwilling to work when work was available. In fact, the English approach of granting benefits to all, without regard to cause of poverty, was sometimes viewed as resulting in "stingy" benefits, whereas the worthy poor (such as widows and orphans) should be relieved "amply" (18). The disorderly or idle could find support in strict workhouses, in which punishment for refusal to work was viewed as a way of treating all human beings as members of a community with responsibilities, rather than as animals (11). "Charity schools" were founded to teach the young good work habits and fear of God, and in the Northwest Territory justices of the peace were appointed "overseers of the poor," setting up poorhouses maintained by the work of their inhabitants and withholding benefits from all who did not lodge and work in the poorhouse. Families were viewed as the central means of support; immediate relatives who did not offer support to needy family members were fined heavily.

Olasky believes that this model of compassion, like other models, was directly related to the general cultural theology:

> Cultures build systems of charity in the image of the god they worship, whether distant deist, bumbling bon vivant, or "whatever goes" gopher. In colonial America, emphasis on a theistic God of both justice and mercy led to an understanding of compassion that was hard-headed but warm-hearted. Since justice meant punishment for wrongdoing, it was right for the slothful to suffer. And since mercy meant rapid response when people turned away from past practice, malign neglect of those willing to shape up also was wrong [8].

These theological understandings led to other subthemes in early American compassion. God's personal involvement in the creation implied that God's people should go beyond "clockwork charity" to give their hearts and love to the needy; the better off should know the poor as individuals with distinct characters, backing the mistreated but chastising the indolent. In fact, charity should be withheld when it would support a descent into idleness and dependence. Some charitable societies agreed that families of drunkards, who "may be without food . . . and wholly innocent in respect to the causes of their destitution," should not receive money, and should be given other aid such as food only to cover "the demands of unquestionable necessity" (20). Political hardness was based on the belief that some needed to suffer in order to become willing to change, though no one was left to starve without any means of support. Shame and stigma toward the voluntarily poor seemed appropriate. The belief that God's good law informed all of life meant that the most important need of the poor was to know of God's expectations for his creatures; material help would fall flat without spiritual formation and God's gracious alteration of the courses of human lives.

This model, reinforced by sermons and other spiritual admonitions, was appropriate in part because "in practice, since work was readily available, there was no talk of structural unemployment. . . . The major type of poverty . . . was caused by a calamity . . . or crippling accident or early death (often by disease)" (11). An expanding border provided growing opportunities for able-bodied workers, at least those of European extraction. As cities grew, more organization was also necessary to help those who were marginalized through no fault of their own. Yet cities were generally still compact, and rich and poor lived near each other and worshipped together; thoroughgoing economic segregation was rare (17). Orphanages were established (sometimes with state support), groups provided small monthly allowances for working widows (often after checking on the applicant's means and character, and on the availability of relatives who could help), and aid was generally given in kind rather than in cash. Through the nineteenth century, most support was offered voluntarily, given in kind and with personal involvement, and aimed at those who were in difficult situations against their own will and were cooperating in trying to change things.

But by the end of the nineteenth century the country stood in need of a new model: "American social conditions of the past seemed almost paradisaical to charity leaders slouching through crowded urban slums" (21). The early American model of charity whose praises Olasky sings seems to have been a flop at solving the problems of the emerging urban nation, the kind of nation we now live in. No doubt the difference in population density partly explains, not only changes in the American approach since the last century, but also the difference between the early American model and its contemporary European counterpart.

New Urban Pressures

Olasky says that the future-minded who saw the emerging cities' problems looked to the experience of the British Isles, where they observed the detrimental effects of "outdoor relief," aid given to persons who continued to live in their homes rather than in poorhouses. They worried that this practice would lead—in fact had led—to dependence, to support of those not truly in need and a concomitant reduction in aid to the truly deserving, and to donor fatigue at seeing resources used unwisely. As a counterexample Olasky offers the relief work of Thomas Chalmers in Glasgow in the early 1820s. Receiving permission to experiment in a 10,000-person district, Chalmers limited aid to those judged deserving (not poor through their own unaltered behavior, and willing to work and save and live an upright life). He stressed small-scale personal involvement of the better-off by dividing the area into twenty-five districts under deacons' leadership. Voluntary collections increased and costs fell, to the extent that a parish school could be staffed with the surplus.

This theme—restricted access, judged by small-scale volunteers—carries through Olasky's entire analysis of the needs of America's emerging cities. Impersonal, indiscriminate, "promiscuous" charity is the villain that reduces benefits to the deserving, reduces the incentive for personal saving and insurance, and cuts everyone off from the potential benefits of personal contact and moral development. Aid was to be restricted to those whom it might physically and morally elevate, and given by persons who suffered alongside recipients in whom they had a personal interest; those who were idle or intemperate should be left to suffer the consequences (28).

By the 1840s and 1850s societies organized roughly along Chalmers's principles were being founded in every major American city, often providing aid in kind rather than cash. The goal was "to make city relations as much as possible like those of the countryside" (29). Olasky argues that the possibility of religious conversion was the motive that called forth sacrifice on the part of the volunteers, and that the need for religious renovation was the underlying cause of recipients' poverty. Professionals could be facilitators of aid, bringing giver and receiver together, but not major suppliers.

Acknowledging that this approach often failed—in cases of recessions that caused urban jobs to dry up, or for the hundreds of orphaned and abandoned children roaming urban centers—Olasky suggests that the nineteenth-century response was to "send the city into the country" (32). Private organizations subsidized mobility for adults and arranged for children to be sent westward. The children worked on farms in return for room, board, and education—in the best case, arranged by a local board that supervised the child's treatment. The private organizations also established residential schools for abandoned children. Olasky emphasizes overcrowding, fueled by high tax rates, as the core material cause of New York's urban problems.

The Breakdown of Consensus

Olasky then chronicles objections and threats to the nineteenth-century consensus about charity. The first threat, apparently imported in part from England, was the notion of "outdoor relief," relief not tied to doing work or living in a poorhouse. Calls for this surfaced in the journalism of the 1840s. Earlier commentators warned of problems with outdoor relief: the disincentive to working and saving that calls forth more paupers even as the charity-givers try to reduce their number; the inability of rationalized government to adjust support standards to the nuances that should make an individual eligible or not; and the inability of such aid to touch the personal causes of poverty (most often, in this era, intemperance) in the way that personal, voluntary aid could. Turning a matter of love into one of litigation might also result in donor fatigue and might harm the character of the well-off by stimulating jealousy and cynicism. Thus public aid might reduce, not increase, the amount of help going to the worthy poor.

But some mid-century journalists, beginning with Horace Greeley, challenged this consensus. Olasky ties Greeley's support of relief for able-bodied persons who did not work to his universalism and his belief in the natural goodness of all people. Both salvation and prosperity were seen as the right of every person. The corrupting influences of capitalist society were to be overturned by communal associations, including redistribution through collective agencies—an "unimpeded, unpurchased enjoyment" of each person's natural right to an "equal share" of the world's wealth (52). In contrast to the earlier anti-poverty emphasis on the personal moral transformation of individuals, Greeley promoted an early Social Gospel: the centerpiece of Christianity is communal living and material redistribution, to be accomplished by changing the economic environment along socialist lines to abolish the causes of poverty. Human desires, being good in themselves, must be given full scope. The result will be "universal happiness . . . a perfect Society . . . 'the Kingdom of Heaven'" (54). Thus Greeley put forth, to a large audience in the northeastern United States, the moral case for universal redistribution. Partly owing to his influence, justifications for public welfare multiplied in the 1850s. Olasky cites published reports that by the late 1850s, both "outdoor" relief and poorhouse relief were rising, primarily because of changes in donor attitudes and opportunistic legislators.

Immigration, urbanization, and rapidly growing urban populations after the Civil War also resulted in economic segregation—sharply defined areas of rich and poor, with the rich riding from home to work rather than walking through diverse neighborhoods. The wealthy, and their churches, were less likely to meet the needy personally; instead, they learned of them through the press. Voluntary aid became less tuned to the actual needs of the poor. Without personal contact, social "help" became less realistic or even destructively indiscriminate. Compassion fatigue set in.

Evangelicals Fight Back

This was a context ripe for Social Darwinism and its argument that social policy should allow the economically unfit to fail and die rather than being artificially preserved. And spread it did, throughout the 1870s into the 1880s. Orthodox believers were engaged in beating back both Social Darwinism and indiscriminate "outdoor" aid. Granting the emergence of involuntary unemployment and other causes of poverty that were not the fault of the poor, they nonetheless maintained that open-handed charity without a work requirement was likely to worsen the problem by creating willing paupers. Compassion should instead consist of suffering with the marginalized; donors should become personal workers who met more than physical needs. This was especially important in anonymous urban settings. Aid sometimes took the form of an interest-free loan, and the recipient was linked to a church or individual whose work it was to move that person toward self-sufficiency.

The new evangelical approach required an outpouring of volunteers to become effective. Olasky lists dozens of urban organizations, quotes from their charters, and relates numbers of recipients to whom some form of aid was dispensed, in order to demonstrate that the outpouring of volunteerism was significant enough to constitute a sufficient response to urban poverty. Some cities saw tens of thousands of engagements between the needy and volunteers in the course of a year.

Olasky identifies attributes that fueled these works of compassion: (1) *affiliation* (fighting the tendency of men and other family members to abandon their families; rebonding the marginalized to the community); (2) *bonding* (with volunteers, when no other communal tie could be reinforced); (3) *categorization* (ensuring that charity went to the willing-to-work or otherwise worthy, including children whose one parent was unable to support them); (4) *discernment* (which allowed categorization, through personal knowledge of the poor and "the benign suspicion that came naturally to charity workers who had grown up reading the Bible" [107]); (5) *employment* (eventually if not immediately for all able-bodied heads of households, though this emphasis "would have been savage had jobs not been available" and if "alternatives to begging did not exist during short-lived periods of unemployment" [109–10]); (6) *freedom* (defined by Olasky as "the opportunity to work and worship without governmental restriction," bribery, or restrictive licensing requirements [111]); (7) and *God* (accounting for spiritual needs and sources of problems and for the possibility of conversion and change, and emphasizing "suffering with" on the part of donors). These seven attributes form Olasky's framework for asking what has gone wrong with American compassion.

The Great Descent

Late-nineteenth-century charity, Olasky says, was marked by upward movement among the deserving poor, which he contrasts with intergenerational dependency today. Yet despite the good done by personal volunteerism at the turn of the century, much of urban life remained stubbornly dysfunctional. The beginning of the great descent (near the turn of the century) was the desire "to do more." Olasky argues that the call for public initiatives was precipitated by a universalist, Social Gospel theology, with its denial of the fallenness of human beings and their need for personal conversion and moral regeneration:

> Underlying this demand for mass transformation was the belief that man was naturally good and productive unless an oppressive system got in the way. . . . Ignoring the experience of the 1860s and 1870s, and harkening back to the commune spirit of the 1840s and the Greeleyite message of that era, their faith was clear: the only reason some people did not work was that they were kept from working [120].

Hence a call for unconditional aid, and an embarrassment with evangelical calls for personal regeneration. These emphases "became the inspiration of governmental social work programs of the 1930s and community action programs of the 1960s" (125).

Beginning with the Theodore Roosevelt administration, Olasky documents the slow development of a federal presence in welfare policy, and the growing emphasis on professionalism (and displacement of volunteerism) in social work. He associates this professionalization of social work with liberal theological commitments (143-46). Donors distanced themselves from recipients, both geographically and empathically; boards of charities became fund-raising bodies; "bonding" was reduced to the viewing of photos of grateful clients; "discernment" was lost in self-satisfying reports to donors. The more secularized relief efforts (such as the settlement-house movement) tended to lose their initial stress on personal contact. Large-scale social change was stressed over personal involvement and conversion. Many religious programs had become functionally secularized; there seemed no reason but "conservative stinginess" to oppose massive new governmental systems (149), especially when private agencies had difficulties responding to the mass needs and reduced donations of the 1930s. Thus through theological liberalization and the long-term depersonalization of charity, the stage was set for large-scale change under the New Deal.

Slowly, over the decades since 1930, cold public entitlement has displaced effective voluntary compassion, in Olasky's view. He acknowledges that the unemployment of the thirties was not due to personal problems in need of individual care. Yet a stigma against public relief persisted (which Olasky applauds), aid was generally given only when no relative could support the needy, and federal programs were proposed as short-term solutions primarily aimed at widows, orphans, and the disabled, not as enduring entitlements. The alternative of choice, the Works Progress Administration, tried to provide income while maintaining a work ethic. The social-work profession organized itself, emphasizing the professionalization of compassion and the permanence of the need for its programs; it gained influence in the Roosevelt administration.

Olasky also identifies three subtle changes that directed America toward a universalistic welfare system with no work requirements: a decreased sense of personal responsibility and increased emphasis on collective action; a trend toward impersonal urban service rather than personal contact and true "suffering-with" compassion; and an ideological leftism among social workers that trivialized individuals, viewed income as entitlement, and neither valued work nor feared pauperization. Olasky dismisses studies during the following twenty years that claimed stipends do not harm independence and self-respect, or found that federal involvement reduced administrative abuses, inefficiency, and political control (163-65). He finds little popular support for universal entitlement throughout the 1940s and 1950s, and concludes that the New Deal's primary effect was to establish an organizational basis for social revolution, not the revolution itself.

The Sixties: A "War Against Shame"

That revolution came in the mid- to late 1960s. Olasky affirms that even through the early 1960s, "many of the old values were retained by both welfare workers and recipients" (167). Workers in New York were still told that withholding assistance was often as important as giving relief; applicants had to verify eligibility; often unwed mothers had to promise not to have male callers under improper conditions. Shame was still a healthy motivator. "As late as the mid-1960s, only about half of those eligible for welfare payments were receiving them" (168).

This means that Olasky's analysis of the 1960s is crucial to the case he is building that American compassion has taken a tragic turn for the worse. He blames the 1960s for a sea change in *attitudes*. The "key contribution of the War on Poverty," he says, was "the deliberate attempt to uncouple welfare from shame by changing attitudes of both welfare recipients and the better-off" (174). "Great Society legislation, not so much by extending benefits as by funding advocates to change that consciousness, helped sever welfare from shame in the minds of many dole-holders" (175). Public doles became not a humiliation but a way to preserve dignity. A war on shame was waged, underlain by "the theologically liberal tendencies within social work (and related fields)" (169). Categorizing individuals as "deserving" or "undeserving" lost support (169). Activism for state intervention was fueled by a combination of philosophical materialism, economic relativism, and progressive sentiment, which combined to produce the conviction that eliminating poverty was merely a matter of passing out dollars to bring all households' income above the poverty line (170–72, 174). Mainline churches approved of the open-handed attitude toward impersonal support, holding to a social cause and therefore a social solution for poverty. In the process, many of the traditional private social agencies were compromised in their commitment to principles of mutual obligation (176). For self-serving reasons, the legal profession encouraged the movement away from categorization and discernment (181–82); it became difficult or impossible to declare recipients employable and therefore ineligible, or to require that female recipients not have a "man in the house."

Thus President Johnson's expansion of public welfare through the Great Society programs—a sudden replay of the New Deal from a position of economic strength (173)—showed a rosy disregard for real-life effects and attempted to replace shame with a conviction that the system was the enemy (178). The result was a dramatic increase in the number of welfare recipients from the mid-1960s to the mid-1970s, driven by a dramatic increase in the proportion of eligible families who decided to apply for benefits. "The Great Society's War Against Shame was a success" (183).

Olasky finds several big losses from the entitlement revolution. By 1980 social mobility had declined, not because of lack of opportunity but presumably because of the change in attitudes that Olasky attributes to the 1960s. The "remnant of private, challenging organizations" was marginalized (185). And marriage declined as a viable bond of mutual obligation. Olasky argues that "government entitlements . . . did influence heavily the choice of whether to choose parenting or adoption, whether to marry or not, and whether to live at home or in an apartment" (187). Marital obligations decreased as governmental obligations increased, making it feasible to raise children alone.

Olasky ends with a discussion of how personal compassion can make a difference in the difficult poverty-related problems of homelessness and abandoned women and children. Here I think he will find few critics of the notion that personal, costly compassion is preferable to mass-produced, impersonal relief. Yet we may be left wondering whether such personal compassion is truly feasible on a large enough scale, and how churches might begin to point the way toward such compassion now that the political system has essentially accepted Olasky's analysis. (Later we will look at a practical guide to how churches can achieve compassionate, personal involvement with the needy.)

The many potentially serious weaknesses in Olasky's book have been thoroughly explored elsewhere. Some have emphasized the paucity of documentation or data to support many of the central theses, aside from quotations from contemporary journalistic sources. I would like to add a word about some more principial inclinations of the book.

I wonder about Olasky's emphasis that relief must involve personal conversion and moral renewal. These things are of great importance; no doubt they are the ultimate answer to many of the problems of the poor. But do we require the same emphasis in our other social institutions? Does anyone criticize the grocery store for not emphasizing that we do not live by bread alone? Do we fret that gas stations do not lobby their patrons to quit speeding? Would we back a corporation that withheld salaries until the employees agreed to tithe? No. Isn't this because our common sense teaches the difference between the "common grace" institutions that make civilization possible among a variety of worldviews, and the "special grace" institutions that press the Gospel into culture? If so, I would need a careful argument that the institutions by which we assure care for the marginalized should be considered special-grace institutions. Personal renewal absolutely must happen, but does this mean that these institutions must be involved in the renewal?

I suppose yes, if public charity always displaces private compassion and erodes the moral sensibilities of the recipients. That is Olasky's claim. But it is not enough to say that this happened in the particular historical circumstances of the United States in the twentieth century. Olasky claims that this is a universal truth—we must choose one approach or the other. Why can't the two be complementary? I think of driving around my medium-sized city. Safe and efficient travel absolutely depends on hundreds of small voluntary acts of charity, self-discipline, and empathy on the part of the drivers surrounding me. Do we displace this innate private philanthropic goodness when we ordain posted speed limits, enforcement police, weather advisories, and road-repair crews? It would be impossible, I believe, to exercise civility while motoring if driving conduct were left *entirely* to a spontaneous social contract. Public enforcement of policies in the interest of the public welfare, in this case, makes more private charitable acts possible.

JUST GENEROSITY BY RON SIDER

We turn from the leading spokesperson for evangelicals who are politically conservative to the leading spokesperson for much of the rest of the evangelical political spectrum. Ron Sider's work will be familiar territory for those who follow America's evangelical public intellectuals. During the last generation, Sider's widely discussed *Rich Christians in an Age of Hunger* has gone through four editions with various publishers. From his academic post at greater Philadelphia's Eastern Baptist Theological Seminary (he is professor of theology and culture) he presides over Evangelicals for Social Action, which might be thought of as a think tank supported (mostly) by evangelicals who would not identify themselves as politically conservative.

Though Sider is best known for his opinions about poverty outside North America, *Just Generosity: A New Vision for Overcoming Poverty in America* brings the focus home. Its organization and approach mirror those of *Rich Christians*. First the author sets forth his direct, personal connections to poverty and paints vivid pictures of the daily lives of the poor; then comes his understanding of Scripture's vision for the poor and God's strategy for their restoration; next he develops a detailed policy agenda; and finally he issues a rousing call to action. In the foreword Sider shows he is aware of two great weaknesses of this approach: that an author might presume to read policy directly from Scripture without bothering to study the world of natural revelation, and that an author might claim *ex cathedra* authority for a favorite faddish policy. Sider acknowledges the possibility of errors in his biblical exegesis, and claims even less authority for his social analysis and policy prescriptions.

The book presents itself as a new, comprehensive strategy that is neither conservative nor liberal, to correct a situation that is unnecessary and immoral. The first two chapters present, through data and anecdotes, a sobering vision of life at the poverty line—low wages, broken families, lack of health insurance, poor education, general insecurity, and a lack of options. Along the way, Sider challenges a number of stereotypes about American poverty. Only 12 percent of the poor live in urban ghettos; only 27 percent are African-Americans; 20 percent of poor families include an adult working full-time year-round, and over one-third are headed by a married couple. Sider also argues that America's rich have become richer while the poorest have become poorer, and that there is no more social mobility in America than in France, Italy, or Scandinavia. But he does not dodge points that de-romanticize poverty, such as the possibility of substantial unreported incomes, and the part played by shortsighted and immoral personal choices. In the end, Sider argues that poverty has four broad causes: structural causes (such as falling low-skill wages, falling union membership, racism), poor personal decisions (drug use, poor school performance, violence, pre-marital sex), sudden catastrophes, and permanent disabilities. This web of causes requires a holistic approach.

Sider's chapters on biblical theology strike themes that will be familiar to readers of his other work. Human beings are to revel in the goodness of the material world as its stewards, and "any economic structure that prevents persons from producing and enjoying material well-being violates our God-given dignity" (51). Also, "any economic structure that subordinates labor to capital thereby subordinates spiritual reality to material reality" (52). Because "our communal nature demands attention to the common good," says Sider, "individual rights, whether of freedom of speech or private property, cannot be absolute." Personal "choices have consequences," and "completely equal economic outcomes are not compatible with human freedom" (52).

Sin has entered the creation and affected both individual persons and the economic structures they create. Therefore justice will involve more than fair procedures (procedural and commutative justice); there must also be some notion of a fair distribution of power and resources (distributive justice) and, sometimes, communal action to redress distributive injustices— legitimate claims of ownership need to be restored, and restored with the force of law rather than through voluntary charity. The search for a practical summary of the requirements of distributive justice takes Sider through the Old Testament texts addressing Joshua's conquest, the year of Jubilee (which Sider still takes to be a radically redistributive teaching), the sabbatical year, and various other legal provisions of ancient Israel. In the end, Sider takes Scripture's standard for justice to be this: "Every person or family has access to productive resources (land, money, knowledge) so they have the opportunity to earn a generous sufficiency of material necessities and be dignified participating members of their community" (67). People should "normally have the opportunity to earn their own way," and this was assured in Israel by methods that "encouraged work and responsibility, strengthened the family, and helped the poor return to self-sufficiency" (67, 70). This standard of justice involves more than lifting the poorest to a minimal level of sufficiency, since "great inequalities of wealth and therefore power lead to oppression" (75). Thus a relative, not absolute, definition of poverty and need is called for. While the state should "enable other institutions . . . to carry out their responsibilities," sometimes "the depth of social need exceeds the capacity of nongovernmental institutions"; then the state "rightly acts to demand patterns of justice and provide vital services" (73).

Responsibilities of Civil Society

Sider endorses civil-society approaches as a "third way" between statist tinkering with the structures of society and anti-statist emphases on personal moral choices. Both (political) liberals and conservatives have "thought that all we had to do to get the right behavior was switch the economic incentives and change the external environment" (21), but Sider portrays a moment in American history in which a holistic, multi-institutional approach is possible, "in which . . . faith communities, businesses, the media, and government all contribute what each does best." Thus his solution includes a role for civil society, particularly for faith-based organizations: they teach "the attitudes of heart and mind that both prevent poverty in the first place and also help the poor escape poverty once they have fallen into it," and they also could administer poverty-related programs that would be evaluated and (largely) funded by government. Sider addresses most of the rest of civil society as well:

■ *Businesses* are castigated for paying low wages, not offering health insurance to all employees, promoting consumerism and sex via advertising, not assuring that jobs are offered to everyone, undermining family life by inflexible work rules, and generally treating workers "as merely an economic input" (88). Several employee-friendly businesses (ServiceMaster, for example) are held up as better models.

■ Strong *unions* are promoted as a way to balance the corruption of power. The "enormous power" of "top business executives . . . offers vast opportunity to use it for selfish advantage unless other power counterbalances corporate power"; by comparison, "individual employees are mere ants" (89). Although unions have at times misused power, they "have often been effective tools, helping the poor to demand a living wage" (89).

■ The *media* are faulted for promoting consumerism, sex, and violence while becoming "often the primary moral teachers for our children" (98).

■ *Universities*, while conducting helpful poverty-related research, generally harbor a culture of agnosticism that leads to "a biased neglect of the role of religion" in their work (90). Yet Sider relies upon their research capability to evaluate faith-based poverty programs: "Are faith-based programs usually more successful than secular ones? Are Buddhist and New Age programs as effective at drug rehabilitation as Jewish and Christian ones? Are thoroughly faith-based programs more successful than nominally faith-related programs? . . . We need honest, objective answers to these and other questions" (91).

Responsibilities of Government
What of the proper role of government?

When a social problem emerges, the first question should *not* be, What can government do? The first question should be, What institutions in society have primary responsibility for and are best able to correct this problem? . . . Government must play a significant role in alleviating poverty, but not the only role, and in many cases, not even the primary role. Our society cannot long survive unless the family is renewed, and government can play only a modest, supportive role here. . . . When government does act, the first question should be, What institutions in society are best able to solve this problem? And second, How can government strengthen rather than weaken these institutions? . . . There are some things, however, that only the government can do. Even when [it] uses nongovernmental providers for social services, [it] must write the guidelines, demand, fund, and publicize careful evaluations, and provide much of the finances. . . . Government should rewrite divorce laws . . . act as a last resort when other institutions do not or cannot care for the poor . . . tax us all so it can provide funding for effective programs . . . [become the catastrophic] insurer of last resort . . . [91-93].

The rest of the book, with chapters on family incomes, family structure, health insurance, education, and direct welfare payments, takes up the task of showing how a properly constructed welfare state might succeed at these duties. Since "neither economic changes by themselves nor behavioral changes in family life by themselves can solve contemporary poverty" (102), Sider proposes changes on both fronts:

■ On the economic front, any family in which a total of forty hours per week is spent in paid employment should be assured of an income of 130 percent of the poverty level, with subsidized health insurance for those under 150 percent. This is accomplished by some combination of (1) an expanded (refundable) earned-income tax credit (which creates better work incentives than direct welfare payments), (2) increases in the minimum wage, and (3) expansion of the food-stamp program; the mix among these three should be determined by economists (107). This combination should be supplemented by expansion of a refundable low-income dependent-care tax credit, a refundable child tax credit, and (for those unable to find work elsewhere) a guaranteed government job (preferably in partnership with civil-society organizations, with a wage a bit below the minimum wage to discourage dependency, in consort with job training programs). Together these initiatives raise the forty-hours-per-week after-tax income to the desired target.

■ For changing family life—particularly the absence of one or both parents, which is "the best predictor of who will become poor"—all segments of society are called upon to "promote the norm for a family assumed by virtually all civilizations for millennia: a mother and father united in lifelong marital covenant, with their children, surrounded by a larger extended family" (123). Since "business and government have undermined marriage and parenting in the last several decades" (126), Sider advocates an end to the marriage tax penalty (while discouraging an assured child-support payment to single parents, as this penalizes two-parent families where at least one parent is working—better to use a tax-credit system), and a redirection of the home-mortgage tax deduction toward lower-income families (including a refundable home-ownership tax credit).

■ Socialized health and unemployment insurance complete the just compensation package. Though government should guarantee health-insurance coverage, it might not operate the delivery system; the choice among a single-payer plan, mandated job-related insurance, or mandated worker purchases of private insurance is left to specialists, "who must carefully assess the relative merits of each and clarify the options for us" (146). Sider is quite sure that medical savings accounts are not a just option (148-49), as they would siphon off the healthiest from conventional insurance and might create tax breaks for the wealthy.

Other Proposals

Turning from compensation to general social policy, Sider offers three chapters of policy proposals. The first deals with **education**. Urban schools should be made better, through some combination of increasing funding, ending racism, reducing drug use, improving dysfunctional families, improving nutrition, shrinking administrative bureaucracies, improving teachers' unions, and altering peer pressure; parents should be allowed to choose the kind of education that is best for their children; every religious tradition should be treated equally in the process; and there should be a common curriculum in the basics with standardized testing. Sider proposes that we "invest several billion dollars in a massive five-year test" that pits voucher-based reform against comprehensive, incremental reform of the public school system, to gain the information we must have to decide which approach is best (163).

Sider next offers his proposals on **welfare**. Recent changes in the entitlement programs should be adjusted: non-working healthy adults without children should be offered an entitled job rather than a payment, and welfare payment policy should be altered so that mothers could keep more of an absent father's support payments, as an incentive for those payments to continue. Faith-based organizations should be more active in shepherding those making the transition from welfare programs. Given the existence of guaranteed government jobs, the current time limits for TANF (Temporary Assistance for Needy Families) recipients would be justified, and receipt of such assistance should also require job and financial-planning training. For healthy adults with serious, long-term problems, in a "very small number" of cases the time limits might be extended, but "we certainly should not design the welfare system around their needs" (191). For the vast majority Sider advocates essentially the same standards for all: "Many people who think they cannot work will discover there are jobs they can do. . . . Mothers and fathers so addicted to drugs or alcohol that they cannot keep a job are likely unfit to care for their children. However painful at the beginning, adoption or foster care would probably be better for the children in the long run" (191).

A third chapter of policy proposals deals with **miscellaneous issues**. All neighborhoods should be safe; Sider suggests a long list of initiatives, from gun control to community policing. Taxes, portrayed as relatively low in the United States, should be paid gladly for funding anti-poverty measures. Value-added-tax (VAT) and flat-tax proposals are criticized for their regressive structure. Social Security must be strengthened but not privatized, because diverting some or all of payroll taxes into personal retirement accounts would mean that currently guaranteed benefits would have to be cut, the size of pensions would not be guaranteed, and political support for low-income benefits would be eroded. Government-subsidized "individual development accounts"—stock/bond investment and savings instruments—are advocated as a way to build capital among the poor. Changes in zoning laws and in metropolitan incorporation and annexation habits are encouraged to create more metropolitan-wide governance and tax bases. And faith-based organizations are urged to engage in direct community organizing to help neighborhoods shape their future.

A final, relatively hopeful chapter summarizes Sider's vision of the current opportunity and the roadblocks in its way. The secular policy elite is open to faith-based options, the cold war has ended, and various Christian groups seem to be softening their evangelism-only or social-action-only instincts to come together around common concern for the poor. The economy has been booming, and there are many models of successful ministry to be learned from. Sider raises three remaining obstacles in the last three pages of the book:

- Can we afford everything this book has proposed? Sider suggests that these proposals amount to a redirection, not increase, in welfare spending, to be financed by cuts in the $125 billion in "corporate welfare," $33 billion in mortgage tax credits given to those with annual incomes over $100,000, and $60 billion in tax benefits to middle-class and upper-class people via untaxed health-insurance benefits, along with savings on social programs as the poor are empowered.

- Can a long-divided Christian community come together to work on a common agenda? Sider offers anecdotal evidence that a consensus is forming.

- Do enough Christians really care about the poor? "Suffocating materialism and narcissistic individualism have wormed their way into so many Christian hearts and congregations. Fearfully, I wonder if most Christians may not sleep through one of the most amazing opportunities in our history" (220). Sider closes with encouragement to pray daily, minister to the poor at least an hour weekly, study further at least monthly, and do a personal-reflection retreat yearly on the topics raised in the book.

Some Observations

My comments on the book will be organized around the final three concerns.

First, on *financial sustainability:* The book's proposals will remind economists of similar discussions in the Netherlands around the turn of the last century, in Scandinavia between the world wars, and in America during the negative-income-tax (NIT) experiments around 1970. Each of the European experiments was, in its way, creating a welfare state that relied upon a partnership between church and state to maintain moral character while alleviating poverty in the context of a policy impasse. The Dutch experiment explicitly endorsed a version of the kind of religious pluralism Sider envisions. All three experiments, but especially the American NIT experiments, raise serious questions about the effects upon work incentives of an earned-income tax credit of the size Sider is proposing. It would be helpful for the book to revisit those experiments, particularly the European strain that in the end produced highly secularized societies with social programs that, by many accounts, were not sustainable. What went right there, and what went wrong? How are the current proposals similar, and how are they different? Prudential considerations like these deserve more than the half page Sider gives them (219).

Here's one quick example of a lesson from the NIT experiments. Let's say we adopt Sider's proposed target of 130 percent of the poverty level for minimum-wage earners, and also accept the idea (which he advocates, if I read him correctly) that the tax code should be no less progressive and no harder on work incentives than it currently is. I take that to mean that those receiving support should not face a higher effective income-tax rate than 15 percent, the current middle-income rate. Taken together, these things imply (here I rely on Table 3, page 115) that the minimum-wage earners in a four-person family would receive a subsidy of $10,643 per year; and at the national median household income ($42,467) families would still receive a subsidy of $5,981 per year. In fact, four-person families up to an income of $82,340 would pay no taxes and receive a subsidy. The total national subsidy (roughly figured from Table 2, page 42) would be about $377 billion, paid for entirely by the top fifth of the income distribution (those with family incomes above $82,340). If we were willing to raise tax rates to 40 percent from 15 percent, subsidies would extend up to incomes of around $31,000, at a total cost of around $165 billion. In other words, after a point there is no way around the trade-off between supporting incomes and maintaining incentives to work. To raise support while making the system affordable, you have to raise effective tax rates, and that discourages work effort, which makes the system less affordable. That paradox is worth some consideration.

Next, on the possibility of *bringing together Christians of various political predilections:* The book presents itself as a third way between conservatism and liberalism. This is done, as much as is metaphysically possible, by including everything from both agendas. For example, "It is time to get beyond the silly argument between liberals and conservatives about whether it takes a village or a family to raise a child. Hillary Clinton and Kay James are both right. It takes both" (218). Of course, there are some cases in which the two instincts cannot be commingled. In these instances Sider is consistently a social conservative (except perhaps on gun control; he is anti-pornography, anti-abortion, pro–traditional marriage, critical of Hollywood morality, generous toward faith-based initiatives, respectful of the power of personal virtuous moral action); he is also consistently a political/economic liberal (advocating a welfare state that might make Ted Kennedy blush). Of course, his proposals amend the welfare state's most egregious incentive-corrupters—with tax credits rather than direct payments, for example—in a strategy that mirrors that of New Labour in Great Britain and the former New Democrats in the United States. Whether this conglomerate is sturdy enough to form a consensus I do not know. But I expect that there are many more political/economic liberals who have discovered the virtues of social conservatism than there are social/ political conservatives who will be persuaded by the call for an expanded welfare state. Judging by the contents of the ideologically diverse comments on the cover and a front page, the book seems to arouse more polite respect than committed assent.

On *the need for Christians to care more:* This seems to be the central claim of the book. Actually constructing policy to solve poverty is presented as a technical matter to be worked out by the economists, once we all care enough to do something. The result is a book that is short on serious historical policy evaluation but long on condemnation of self-absorbed middle-class Christians who do not live in the right neighborhoods or volunteer for the right causes or see the world in the right way. No doubt there is a sleeping mainline-denomination giant that may never be roused; but the book's evangelical audience is, by the objective academic studies with which I am familiar, the most generous subpopulation of volunteers and financial contributors that one could reasonably hope for. Show them that you have addressed prudential concerns about how the poor are best helped, then give them latitude to use their own gifts rather than yours, and they will respond.

And finally, since we are considering evangelical resources in this review, a word about the resources that went into the writing of this book. The acknowledgments cite a funding foundation, two editors, two research assistants, an administrative assistant, eight Evangelicals for Social Action staff, twenty academics (who wrote the scholarly volume from which much of the social analysis is nominally drawn), and forty intensive reviewers at academic centers and think tanks. The Olasky book was produced at a Washington think tank, using, I would suppose, a similar entourage. Perhaps my admiration for Lincolnesque simplicity is out of place in the post-modern world. But I do still wonder if the right person holding a few well-considered words scratched on an envelope might, with malice toward none and charity toward all, go further in redirecting a culture.

GODLY MATERIALISM BY JOHN SCHNEIDER

The author of our last broadly visionary book does not aim at prescribing a strategy or taking a political posture. Instead, John Schneider presents a theological analysis of many of the ideas that emerge when poverty is discussed, and in the process has something informative to say to all the other voices in the debate. While most of Schneider's writing has consisted of scholarly efforts in theology, *Godly Materialism* is directed to a broader audience. It rounds out our discussion of economics, aiming to be more a biblical study than a consideration of policy or history or best practices.

Schneider writes "to reach Christian people who have more than enough money but not enough sense of direction in their economic lives" (8), out of

the conviction that many "rich" Christians feel guilty about having money
and privilege in an age of suffering. In Scripture, he says, God seems to side
with the poor, which many extrapolate into a condemnation of capitalism as
a system structured for evil, requiring that we practice downward rather
than upward mobility. Yet there is something right and good about a system
that encourages and liberates people to work hard and be productive, to
dream and pursue dreams, to live in safe neighborhoods with solid schools,
to take delight in material goods (14-15). Therefore many Christians struggle
with their economic identities.

In the contemporary literature of the Church, the pleasures of middle-
and upper-class life are often pitted directly against the life of compassion.
But Schneider asks, "Is there a kind of delight that also embraces justice?" "Is
true godliness possible for people . . . who enjoy the good things of life in a
world of hunger?" (17). He believes there is indeed a "godly materialism,"
and in search of it he undertakes what is essentially a chronological study of
Christian experience (possessions as understood by the Church throughout
its history) and biblical revelation (from Genesis through the book of Acts).

The Three Models

Schneider identifies three plausible models of Christian economic identity:
Historic Catholicism, Historic Protestantism, and New World Theology. The
third came into being after the democratic, scientific, and industrial revolutions that the other two did not foresee. Those revolutions generated wealth
and freedom for many more persons, and a measure of power and control
over life that reached lower levels of the social ladder, than ever before.

The economic teaching of **Historic Catholicism**, rooted in the work of St.
Augustine, may be thought of as three pillars. In the first pillar, basic affirmations,
Augustine affirms the goodness of the creation and the God-given dignity of
work, commercial activity, productivity, and possession of property. This pillar
has rarely been challenged, though it has come under some scrutiny from
twentieth-century theologians attracted to communism (32).

The second pillar established "utilitarian" moral reasoning about the use
of wealth. Augustine distinguishes between *enjoyment* and *use*. He argues
that material goods are to be used, not enjoyed; we may use them in order to
comprehend the eternal and spiritual, but they are not to be enjoyed in
themselves, lest they distract us from concentrating on our heavenly home.
Therefore luxuries, goods purely for enjoyment, are not appropriate. To take
pleasure in simple goods like food or drink indicates a fixation on the world,
not joy in God's good gifts. Living and working in the world and possessing
property are acceptable if we distinguish between needs and wants, and
avoid the unnecessary. "When you possess the superfluous you possess what
is not yours" (31). And so Augustine teaches utilitarianism, stresses social

utility in meeting the greatest needs, and condemns the enjoyment of luxuries while others are poor.

The third pillar uses the notion of supererogation to elevate poverty to a higher station than wealth. Rather than pit monastic life against ordinary life, Augustine affirms both as necessary, but orders them as higher and lower goods. Ordinary life is good, but the monastic life is the ideal. While all Christians must meet certain obligations, acts of supererogation—not required by biblical law but morally good—improve our standing before God. Those who freely choose to follow Christ's example of poverty and communal ownership by living in the monastery perform an act toward spiritual perfection and sainthood.

Historic Protestantism essentially accepted the first two pillars of Historic Catholicism, but vigorously challenged the third.

New World Theology forced a radical re-examination of the second pillar, the utilitarian principle. New institutions of government, learning, and business had done the unimaginable: liberated whole populations from tyranny and poverty by making it possible to gain without doing so at the expense of others—even while actually serving them. This new order brought a powerful shift away from viewing material goods as mere instruments for seeking spiritual realities; now they become goods to be enjoyed as blessings from God, to be delighted in as expressions of human dignity and Christian prosperity (36). The acquisitiveness, credit dependence, and speculative investment of the middle class lost their moral stain. Private property gained theological status through its connection with personal liberty; it was seen as something to be shaped in the image of the owner, as an expression of that owner's imaging of God himself.

The basis in Scripture for this revolution was a rediscovery of the teaching of the Old Testament (38), including the vision of human domination on earth and this-worldly blessing. A theology of guarded, morally rigorous triumph displaced the classical theology of the cross. This world was the Christian's true home and domain, not a passing stage. Charity toward the poor was to have the goal of actually ending poverty; the donor was not to be content with giving alms but seeing poverty self-perpetuate.

Schneider finds two extremes evident at present. Within popular American religion, some have evolved from New World Theology to the triumphal position that true faith brings worldly success, and that the American system is the one God favors. They rarely discuss the suffering of the righteous, or the world's real inequities, or the evils that perpetuate them, or the obligations of the wealthy toward them. At the other extreme are those—especially in intellectual circles—who react fiercely against New World Theology, reviving the traditions of austerity and utilitarianism (and sometimes large-scale communal ownership). Often they do this through a "liberation theology" that emphasizes redemption of the poor. More often than not this is accompanied by hostility toward the middle class and its vision of the good life.

The Biblical Basis

Schneider devotes the rest of the book to a study of Scripture. The creation accounts sharply distinguish Creator from creation, and set human beings apart with supremacy in dignity and value. The material realm and bodily life are affirmed as very good, and this approbation includes human work, cultivation, productivity, and the enjoyment of life. Taken together, the Genesis emphases suggest just what kinds of enjoyment might be "selfish materialism." Human beings, made in God's very likeness, are given dominion and commanded to be fruitful, and to fill and subdue the earth. Unlike the ancient pagan understandings of king or queen as the divine presence incarnate, Christianity elevates each person. Each bears a royal identity with royal obligations, representing God's rule over the earth (51).

And how does this God govern? "The God of Genesis first creates out of sheer delight in the goodness of his creation. . . . When he creates he both enriches himself and glorifies everyone and everything else" (52). His delight is other-centered; he rules with great compassion. We are to be his co-workers, taking delight in the goodness of his world and gifts by engaging in productive work, enjoying abundance, and flourishing. "The whole person, who works, conserves, cultivates, nourishes, protects, but also does so as the one who rules, orders, dominates, and simply enjoys at his or her good pleasure, is the original, majestic human being" (55). The "luxuries" that might be condemned by utilitarian ethics may in a sense be considered necessities (58-59), essential for healthy self-esteem and an expression of God's glory, human dignity, and the goodness of life in this world.

With God's good gifts came limits and responsibility, however, to which human beings proved unequal. Wishing to become autonomous, they pulled themselves away from God and goodness. Yet they have not entirely lost their goodness, and God is still redeeming the creation. In the Noah narratives God re-establishes the essential order of the creation, albeit with several accommodations to life as it is after mankind's fall into sin rather than life as it ideally should be. The ground is again established as good, human beings are blessed with the duty to multiply and fill, and they are reaffirmed as bearers of God's image. Our basic instinct should be not toward separation and counterculture but toward engagement.

The Just Society

The Exodus carries on the theme that the physical world matters to God, that physical circumstances are real and essential to the moral order, not just unpleasantries to be endured or ignored. It teaches that evil is sometimes expressed through social institutions and systems. God liberates through the shaping of just societies, and God's people must represent him in this work. But just what is a just society? What are we to be liberated to? Schneider considers Israel's law as the pattern for an answer. Its constant refrain is God's compassion for powerless people; concern for the poor and powerless is in the very soul of the law, essential to the biblical vision of delight and shalom (68-69).

Schneider gives a thoughtful response to theologians who presume that this drive toward justice and compassion validates socialism or a welfare state that loosens private-property rights. The focus of these claims has been the sabbatical and related laws, often interpreted to teach that God ultimately owns everything and persons are "only" stewards. Schneider thinks this emphasis radically weakens the individual's right to use and enjoy wealth, while strengthening the rights of the community to distribute wealth as it wishes. He answers by pointing out that there was not an initially equal division of property in the promised land; that redistribution was not carried out according to need but actually excluded many of the poorest; that Jubilee—the designation of every fiftieth year as one in which slaves were freed, property was restored to former owners, and the land was left untilled—made rights to land not relative but permanent and absolute, only temporarily suspended by leases between jubilees; and that there was no jubilee expectation of the rich to sacrifice their "luxuries" to serve the needs of the poor but rather a restoration of land to the old landed families, whether they needed it or not.

The establishment of the Jubilee also comes in the context of laws that affirm banking, lending, and general productivity, which make little sense apart from affirmation of commercial enterprise and property rights. "The purpose of the release was to protect the Israelite families from poverty and to empower them for both lives of redemptive action and delight in the abundance of the land" (75). The theme of delight is actually reinforced by the tithing laws, which do not promote simpler living to share with the poor, but actually mandate a party of lush thanksgiving, involving "whatever you desire" with a tenth of one's income each year, in which the poor of the land are to be included.

The Exile brings about a reversal of the Exodus: the slaves have become merciless oppressors, and are sent again into captivity. The main reason for this exile was economic immorality (84). The prophets' teachings expose the nature of this immorality, and apply the lessons both to Israel and to the surrounding nations. Schneider focuses on the prophet Amos; although his message comes at a prosperous time of religious observance in Israel, Amos accuses the Israelites and judges them more harshly than their pagan neighbors. Compassion had left, he said, and the sacred life of liberation, dominion, and delight had been twisted into narcissistic exploitation of the weak. Schneider finds in the prophecies not a moral judgment against enjoyment of fine things, even in times of hunger, but a judgment of demonic self-absorption.

Schneider's consideration of the Wisdom literature turns on the question of whether and why the righteous suffer. He argues both against a simple reading that righteousness produces wealth and poverty is a punishment for evil, and against the simple alternative that the world system is so corrupt that righteousness generally results in poverty, and so the poor are the true people of God. Proverbs does portray being rich as good, and God does want his people to prosper; to say otherwise is to "weaken the whole Christian vision of dignity, worth, and rights for people" (93). Yet wickedness often pays in this world, too, and, as the book of Job teaches, poverty is not necessarily the result of wickedness.

The Example of Jesus

Turning to the life of Jesus and his followers, Schneider argues that a misconception about Jesus' basic place in the social culture of Palestine is a serious problem for our understanding of economic life. In stunning contrast to the typical view that Jesus identified with the poor and was himself a man of the righteous poor who opposed the unrighteous rich, Schneider argues that Jesus, his circle of disciples, and most of the early church were drawn from a diverse lot who primarily represented the "small businesses and trades that belonged to something like the Palestinian 'middle class'" (103). "Businesspeople were the backbone of the church, not objects of its contempt" (117). No one in his own culture would have classified Jesus as poor, either economically or socially (109-10). He in fact had many advantages—a first-born male inheriting a firm that supported an apparently large family, a guaranteed education as a result, a stable home life rather than orphaned life on the streets, good health, an inheritance, to mention a few—that most of his contemporaries lacked.

The poor to whom Jesus came to proclaim release are those poor in spirit, a condition all of these social groups share with those poorest economically (120). Jesus identified with the ordinary, uncomplicated, hard-working, productive, humble, and happy people around him, leading the relatively privileged into new lives of economic redemption and redemptiveness, and placing them in contact with the suffering world in a new community of grace. The result was not egalitarian leveling but a life of economic dynamism and renewed compassion (121).

Jesus was not ashamed of being part of the middle class, relatively sheltered and privileged to enjoy good things, even as others suffered. Schneider's view here is a welcome counterpoint to the views of the popular Christian authors who routinely condemn American middle-class life as a polar extreme from Jesus' incarnation. Jesus could have "identified himself with the really poor. But he did not. The loving heavenly Father took care that his Son had an environment where he 'became strong' and was 'filled with wisdom'" (112).

Furthermore, it is very likely that Jesus' wealth was in large part due to the public-works projects in his area commissioned by Herod Antipas (110, 113). To those who would raise "structural evil" to a level morally indistinguishable from "personal evil," this sounds a strong note of caution. Even God's own Son benefited to some degree from sinful systems without directly trying to change them. Jesus did not speak out against these structural evils even when given the opportunity to do so, and he associated with tax collectors and others deemed most typical of cultural godlessness, while condemning others for their lack of grace toward these persons (115). While some systems (such as selling drugs, prostitution, and pornography) are so essentially evil that involvement in them is ruled out, we should not accept the notion of guilt by implication through cooperative work within systems that include evil (116).

Schneider then struggles with the "two Jesuses" sometimes drawn from the scriptures: the Jesus of radical condemnation and negation regarding wealth and comfort, and the Jesus of compassion and delight who was criticized as a celebrative drunkard, accused of being an indulgent who enjoyed life rather than observing the Torah, and arrested as the wanton, disobedient son who should be put to death (Deut. 21:20). Schneider argues that we have here a single, integrated personality. In his negation statements, Jesus prepares his followers to initiate the kingdom of Christ on earth (141), to experience dark times after his crucifixion, and to learn dependence on the power of God alone. Jesus' need to teach the disciples both profound meekness and extraordinary bravery explains the theme of physical deprivation and separation from the cares of the world. Their adopted life with Jesus was aimed eventually at dominion and rule with the Lord.

Schneider then examines four of the central parables in Jesus' teaching about wealth and poverty. The foolishness of the rich fool is in his philosophy of life, the disposition behind his otherwise prudent actions, not in the actions themselves; he is motivated by greed and lonely isolation, not creative and redemptive love. The rich man who gave only cool indifference to Lazarus is condemned for not hearing Moses and the prophets, for not representing the vision of the Exodus; through compassion, the rich must enter into the world of the poor and touch it with liberating power, though Jesus does not provide a template explaining exactly how (152 ff.). The story of the dishonest manager teaches that, at moments of anxiety that might launch us into isolation, hoarding and hiding from the world, faith must drive us to engage others instead, to open up and give. And the parable of the ten pounds teaches us of God's desire for creative, redemptive uses of economic power, even in situations that seem insignificant. We are to enlarge and dignify whatever realm God has given us.

Economics in the Early Church

Schneider concludes by considering the economic life of the early church, primarily as revealed in the early chapters of the book of Acts, along with Paul's engagement in collections for the Palestinian believers and James's exhortations about wealth. Schneider takes the remarkable transformation of economic life among Jerusalem's believers, which broke the "strongholds that deprived people of decent food, clothing, shelter and simple human delight" (167), to be a story not so much about the poor and their liberation as about the rich and their role as liberators. This was not an experiment in disinvestment and communalism. Having "all things in common" did not mean abolishing private property, or setting up communal mechanisms of ownership. Profits from sales of property remained in the sellers' hands to distribute. It was the voluntary nature of the system that made the actions of Ananias and Sapphira (who "sold a possession and kept back part of the price") so disgusting; their sin was not ownership but deceit and hypocrisy. The text tells us nothing about what proportion of wealth people gave away, and the church itself did not behave in a utilitarian manner in its distribution of donations. Giving was limited by "nearness," within which freedom and delight might abound for everyone; giving went to other believers, with "not a trace of moral panic about the world outside, the global poor." Thus the rich became "powerful liberators without destroying their power to liberate" (177). The church remained a place of celebration and delight.

Schneider then turns to a general indictment of what he sees as the utilitarian instinct of many commentaries on these passages. By utilitarianism Schneider means "the view that enjoyment of superfluous wealth is morally wrong in a context where others have unsatisfied basic needs. Utilitarianism is, and must be, always suspicious of what we have called delight" (171). Human need is a bottomless obligation, so that utilitarianism leads to an obsession with moral justification of all actions and enjoyment. It provides no coherent strategy for liberation. Moreover, "to whatever extent we become poorer we create degrees of poverty and (in one fashion or another) we foster the powerlessness that comes with being poor. Oddly, by so identifying with weakness, we reduce our power to liberate" (174). Obligations toward the poor arise not from a system of "need" but from a vision of royal abundance in life and a discerning awareness of the needs that are near us.

Schneider has made a provocative contribution to the conversation about wealth and possessions. He avoids the mistakes of promoting a health-and-wealth gospel and building a case that excludes compassion and sacrifice. But one might argue that he has done more to clear away old rubble than to construct a compelling alternative. Surely we don't believe that the New World experiments with economic orders are so utterly unprecedented as to require an entirely new theology, with little to learn from Calvin, Luther, or the rich resources of others who have considered these questions. There have always been markets, and there has always been the possibility of gain, in some forms, without patronage or tyranny. Moreover, none of the New World experiments is so pure that it can justify all forms of modern wealth acquisition as equally under God's blessing of dignity and delight. Thus there's a great deal of nuance yet to be explored.

RESTORERS OF HOPE BY AMY SHERMAN

Broadly visionary books, like the three we have considered, do well to remain closely tethered to the realities they attempt to analyze. Churches today find themselves in a new world of welfare reform and charitable choice, and there is a great need for well-informed, practical advice on navigating this sea change in American social policy. We now turn to the best of these guides.

In her Ph.D. thesis, published by Oxford University Press, Amy Sherman chronicled her field work in Central America, investigating the effects of evangelical conversion on economic culture. Her interest subsequently migrated toward domestic poverty, and after finishing her degree she took a position as director of neighborhood ministries for an evangelical church in a moderate-sized American city. *Restorers of Hope: Reaching the Poor in Your Community with Church-Based Ministries That Work* is the first publication that reflects on this work, and others' similar work, in engaging the problems of poverty at the level of grass-roots Christian ministry. She documents the work of many ministries that are doing exactly what Olasky advocates: reaching out to broken people and places with the transforming love and mercy of Christ. These congregations, which she calls "restorers,"

unlike most government agencies, many secular programs, and even some well-intentioned but misguided churches, treat needy people personally, flexibly, and creatively. Restorers build friendships . . . , challenge "can't-do-it" attitudes, . . . counteract cultural messages of hedonism, promiscuity, and moral relativism, . . . build self-esteem, wield moral authority, and care for people in ways that encourage self-sufficiency rather than prolonged dependency.

Why Poverty Persists

Sherman argues that the public debate about welfare policy has swung around to a position that leaves many Christian churches wondering how they can undertake ministries to the poor. An earlier generation emphasized the materialist viewpoint that economic or structural factors (such as discrimination, poor schools, and lack of medical care) are ultimately behind behavioral problems. But grave disappointment with material-aid-only welfare programs has led even secular commentators to affirm the place of spiritual factors in the causes and perpetuation of poverty. At the other extreme, some overemphasize moral-cultural factors (an entitlement mentality, illegitimacy, bad work habits, substance abuse, materialism, negative attitudes toward learning). Both extremes "miss the mark" (18).

Recent welfare reforms have tried to acknowledge the possibility of moral-cultural factors in persistent poverty, imposing penalties for irresponsible parenting or poor work habits, while addressing some of the real structural difficulties, like the high cost of daycare for working poor families. Such reforms, "though necessary, are insufficient. . . . Personal transformation . . . requires 'holistic ministry'—that is, attention to a person's 'whole' being (his/ her emotional, physical, mental, and spiritual state)" (20). To show churches how they can implement a life-transforming ministry among the poor, Sherman examines the work of several effective church-based ministries. All emphasize God's love in both word and deed, and all believe that poverty is ultimately rooted in sin—both personal (moral failings) and social (institutional greed, racism, and materialism) (29). Successful ministries counter ghetto culture with biblical values, deliberately incorporate evangelism and discipleship into their outreach efforts, and "enlarge" the world of inner-city residents.

Sherman's analysis of the "street" culture that challenges holistic ministry identifies several destructive themes. First, street culture is lived by "the code," rooted largely in inner-city residents' profound distrust of the police and the criminal-justice system. Residents feel justified in taking extraordinary measures to protect themselves and seek respect, viewed as a zero-sum commodity: for me to get more, someone else must have less. Second, "the code" grows out of an overwhelming sense of alienation from mainstream society, fed by racism, lack of work opportunities, and poverty. Mainstream values like educational achievement, respect for authority, and hard work are viewed as irrelevant to *their* world. A third source undergirding the code of the streets is "the media's constant proclamation of American society's 'consumerist gospel': health, happiness, and status through material possessions. The pervasive low sense of self-worth felt by many ghetto residents makes them even more vulnerable to this message" (41), and the inner city's isolation and alienation drown out other voices that tend to breed healthy skepticism of consumerism in more balanced neighborhoods.

Street culture is characterized not only by its own code and oppositional values but often by a culture of dependency, entitlement, and stasis, partly engendered by years under the federal welfare system. This mind-set inhibits normal motivations for exiting the system. And all these tendencies are amplified by "concentration effects": through a combination of forces, often urban neighborhoods that formerly included families from a variety of economic classes are now often home to only the most marginalized. In neighborhoods where concepts like marriage, work, and fatherhood are losing their plausibility and the non-poor rarely enter in, even the many families who attempt to live by a higher standard than "the code" find their ability to challenge street culture limited.

What "Restorers" Do

Restorers seek to transform this culture from the inside out, by avoiding the extreme views of poverty as exclusively a personal-behavioral issue or exclusively a social-structural issue. Their prescriptions are inclusive: Challenge the behavior and worldview of street culture by strengthening families, shoring up neighborhood schools, exposing the myths of the consumerist gospel, breaking down the demographic isolation of the ghetto, and countering dependency by refusing to help in a way that discourages personal responsibility (48-56). Do this in a personally supportive way that leads people to real repentance and belief in Jesus Christ, not to a vague, self-constructed "spiritual component."

Simultaneously, restorers address the structural problems that contribute to the persistence of poverty, namely crime, unemployment, substandard housing, and poor schools. They aim to enlarge ghetto residents' worlds. They provide sanctuaries that are drug- and crime-free. They include local residents in the design of programs, and they provide participants with an alternative form of group affiliation. They counteract geographic isolation by providing group travels outside the neighborhood. Restorers enlarge aspirations by providing alternative peer pressures and building confidence. They create higher ambitions by supplying tutoring and other education-enhancement initiatives so that college and a decent job can be seen as reasonable goals. They work to reweave atomized neighborhoods into communities by providing for volunteer organizations, recreational clubs, block clubs that build friendships among neighbors and set policies for the block (on such matters as noise and loitering), home rehabilitation and ownership initiatives, prayer marches, campaigns against crime and drugs, and places where neighbors can meet safely for mutual support and encouragement.

How to Become Restorers

Part Two of the book offers practical advice to churches on how to strengthen their outreach ministries. This involves (1) reinvigorating the church's vision for the biblical imperative to serve the poor and biblical teaching on ministries of mercy, (2) overcoming some common barriers to outreach, and (3) emphasizing relational, long-term ministries over "commodity-based" ones.

The essential foundation for ministries of restoration is the congregation's understanding of its reasons for taking such a step (because loving others, especially the poor, is central to the Christian life and God's great passion), what it hopes to accomplish (that those served develop a personal relationship with God and right relationships with others; that they walk in God's ways, be good stewards of their gifts, and engage in fruitful labor), and how to begin (e.g., with right motives and attitudes, and with respect for those served as fellow human beings capable of change).

After laying this foundation, a congregation will face barriers, both internal (fears of the unfamiliar, weariness, selfishness, time pressures) and external (class and cultural differences). Sherman navigates the difficult terrain between (a) reaching out to others in Christian love and (b) honestly confronting sin and expecting change when people's personal choices are harming others. New ministers of restoration need to get exposed to neighborhoods they might otherwise avoid, learn the experiences and histories of minority groups, face their own prejudices in prayer and repentance, make racial reconciliation personal and specific with real individuals, and fight the battle of their own busyness to make room for relationships of restoration.

Congregations will then be in a position to consider shifting to a relational ministry from a commodity-based one. People with long-term, complicated needs are often not effectively helped by food pantries or clothing exchanges; such ministries may entrench needy families in dependency, and generally don't foster personal relationships. However, some commodity-based ministries can be reformed to diminish the potential for abuse and to increase the opportunities they provide for relationship building. Sherman discusses many variations on this theme, using case reports of particular congregations' experiences. She describes at length three national movements that have worked out models for a transition to holistic, relational ministries, models that congregations can adapt by establishing local "chapters" of the organization.

Beginning a ministry is not merely a process of working through a checklist, and Sherman is careful not to imply this when she sets out ten practical steps a congregation can take: (1) assess the congregation's strengths and weaknesses, (2) learn about the community, (3) identify what others are already doing, (4) begin building relationships, (5) within the neighborhood of the ministry gather a core community team who embrace its vision, (6) determine the congregation's unique niche (vision and mission statements) and don't overextend, (7) learn from other models while defining goals and strategy, (8) determine basic organizational policies (e.g., administrative structure, hiring practices, fund-raising, relationship to governmental agencies, behavioral expectations), (9) establish a system for recruiting/training/placing/affirming volunteers, and (10) establish an evaluation system.

Public-Private Collaboration

In Part Three, Sherman considers the larger context in which churches conduct outreach efforts—public-policy issues and the possibility of public-private collaboration. Private institutions are perpetually in need of funds, and welfare-reform initiatives increasingly point to the possibility of collaboration. With characteristic evenhandedness, Sherman examines the potential benefits and pitfalls, and distills wisdom from existing examples of collaboration.

The potential benefits include: increased resources, cost-effective fundraising, predictability of funding, matching-grant approaches that encourage private donations, cross-learning from non-private organizational cultures, improved staff discipline through the process of writing proposals and reports, regulatory relief, influence on public policies, and seeing tax dollars reinvested in one's own community.

The pitfalls to collaboration spring in part from the nature of governmental institutions—inherently bureaucratic, sometimes overly process-minded. Some nonprofits report that the drive toward standardization and inflexibility stifles their creativity; unrealistic and expensive regulations may be imposed, sometimes putting ministries out of business; identifying the appropriate official to contact about a particular matter may be difficult; reimbursements can be delayed, with devastating cash-flow results for the private organization; some ministries suffer depersonalization through paperwork requirements or advanced-degree requirements; public funding may reduce private donations and, ultimately, the congregation's commitment to the vision; private organizations may then drift from the private donors who kept them accountable to their mission, as the state does not evaluate the transformation of lives in the qualitative way that a private supporter would; public financial support may even erode the credibility of the ministry in the eyes of the recipients; and church-based ministries may come to resemble secular welfare agencies rather than emphasizing what they uniquely offer—spiritual transformation and moral challenge. Sherman then examines several recent public-private collaborations as healthy, workable models.

She concludes with a look at how reaching out can affect the reachers. Among the possibilities: Whole churches are transformed, as financial stewardship improves and congregations become more diverse. Individuals and families are transformed as they encounter the spiritual richness of persons whom they might not otherwise have met and as they are driven to acknowledge their own prejudices and materialism. The witness of the Church is confirmed before a watching world. And civil society is reinvigorated as holistic, relation-based ministry sparks renovation of civil institutions like family and neighborhood.

There is much to commend about Sherman's work. She is modest in her claims and judicious in her proposals. *Restorers of Hope* is a strong resource for churches wanting to draw on the experiences of others for both a coherent vision and practical advice.

These four books, then, lay out differing approaches taken by influential American evangelicals to questions of poverty and welfare reform. Olasky's *Tragedy of American Compassion,* Sider's *Just Generosity,* and Schneider's *Godly Materialism* are broadly visionary, while Sherman's *Restorers of Hope* is highly practical. Together they constitute a condensed library of reflection and wisdom for evangelicals and others who want to pursue a Christian response to the problems of the poor.

CHAPTER NINE

Evangelicals and Charitable Choice

Amy L. Sherman

Faith-based social action is hot. Joe Klein praised the work of faith-based practitioners and researchers in no less prestigious a venue than the *New Yorker*.[1] *Newsweek* featured the Reverend Gene Rivers, an African-American Pentecostal trying to keep teenagers out of gangs in Boston, on its cover. In 1997 the *Wall Street Journal* highlighted the work of Good Samaritan Ministries in Holland, Michigan. That city was the first in the United States to move every able-bodied welfare recipient into a job—in large measure, said Governor Engler, because of all the mentors "Good Sam" mobilized from local churches to help people make the transition from welfare to work.[2] Stories from Chuck Colson's "InnerChange Freedom Initiative" to rehabilitate prisoners in Texas have also graced the pages of the *Journal*.[3] The *Washington Post*, *USA Today*, the *San Francisco Chronicle*, the *Boston Globe*, the *Dallas Morning News*, the *Atlanta Journal-Constitution*, and dozens of other major and minor newspapers have shone the spotlight on evangelicals laboring among the nation's poor. ABC "Nightly News," National Public Radio's "Morning Edition," the PBS "NewsHour with Jim Lehrer," and several other major television and radio programs have also joined in the acclaim.

Stories of faith-based organizations are everywhere, in part because they have been frequently referenced at the White House and in Congress since George W. Bush took office. The President unabashedly made the faith-based initiative a signature item in his domestic policy agenda. Over on Capitol Hill, Representative J. C. Watts and Senator Rick Santorum hosted more than 400 faith-community leaders for the National House-Senate Majority "Faith-based

Amy L. Sherman is a senior fellow at the Hudson Institute, where she directs the Faith in Communities project. She also serves as urban ministries advisor at Trinity Presbyterian Church in Charlottesville, Virginia.

Summit," aimed at showcasing successful models and giving a boost to legislation incorporating the President's proposals.

Evangelicals have been in the thick of all this. In fact, it was a brouhaha over government harassment of an evangelical drug-rehabilitation ministry in Texas that stimulated then Governor Bush to take aggressive action to promote faith-based charities. In 1995, Teen Challenge in San Antonio, which helps addicts get clean and sober by introducing them to Jesus Christ, was nearly shut down by an overzealous, process-loving state bureaucrat. Hundreds of grass-roots activists, religious leaders, and ex-addicts, the National Center for Neighborhood Enterprise, *World* magazine, and others whipped up fervent support for Teen Challenge—whose success rate dwarfs that of government-run rehabilitation programs in Texas—and Governor Bush agreed that state government ought to be praising the organization, not threatening to eliminate it.[4]

To avoid such debacles in the future, Bush convened a blue-ribbon panel to look at how state policies reined in Good Samaritans and to suggest how government could be more faith-friendly in the future. The resulting reforms earned Texas the only "A+" on a "national report card" sponsored by the Center for Public Justice, a Christian think tank that assesses government-faith collaboration nationwide. Governor Bush then became Candidate Bush and used his very first official speech, in Indianapolis, to highlight his support for the use of faith-based "armies of compassion" in the fight against poverty. After Candidate Bush became President Bush, evangelicals were at the center of crafting his faith-based proposals. Evangelicals such as Don Willett, Marvin Olasky, Stanley Carlson-Thies, Carl Esbeck, Ryan Streeter, Don Eberly, and I all played roles in designing the new White House Office of Faith-Based and Community Initiatives. Centers for Faith-Based and Community Initiatives were also established in five major cabinet departments (HUD, HHS, DOL, DOJ, DOE). Today, Willett, Esbeck, Streeter, and two other evangelicals, Lisa Cummins and Mark Scott, hold key positions in the Centers.

The scope of Bush's faith-based initiative is broad: stimulating private charitable giving to faith-based charities through new tax credits and deductions; identifying and eliminating government regulations that hamper faith-based organizations on the front lines; analyzing the proportion of government funding that supports specific arenas of faith-based social service relative to the faith community's actual work (total contribution) in those arenas; and advocating expansion of the "Charitable Choice" guidelines (adopted in 1996) to additional federal funding streams. This last item is by far the most controversial and debated.

What Is Charitable Choice?

"Charitable Choice" is the shorthand label for a series of guidelines regulating the way government does business with faith-based organizations (FBOs). The guidelines were written into the 1996 federal welfare-reform law. In brief,

Charitable Choice aims to: (1) create a level playing field between religious and secular social-service providers in the competition for public funding, and (2) safeguard, simultaneously, the religious integrity of FBOs and the civil rights of the needy persons they serve.

Government has long funded religiously affiliated social-service providers such as Catholic Charities and Lutheran Social Service. But these organizations are often distinct from what we might call "faith-filled" organizations where faith permeates the programming and animates the approach and ethos. Faith-filled organizations often consider personal religious commitments in their hiring decisions, to ensure that everyone working in the organization understands and attempts to live out its core values and doctrinal tenets. Faith-filled organizations are transparent and highly public about their religious identity: they do things like hanging religious artwork on the walls of their facilities, teaching classes from a biblical perspective, and praying with clients who are suffering. While these FBOs operate various programs that serve secular purposes (such as teaching English to immigrants and helping the unemployed find jobs), they typically accompany these services with "inherently religious" activities such as spiritual mentoring/counseling and Bible study. In short, these groups are "faith-based," not just because they have a religious-sounding name or a historical affiliation with a particular church, but because their faith is utterly central to and pervasive throughout their work.

In the past, rules governing the competition for public funding have sometimes shut out "pervasively sectarian" organizations. Or, though technically eligible to compete, FBOs have been discouraged from doing so by the "strings" attached to government money, strings they believe might secularize their work. Charitable Choice was crafted to address these problems. It gives faith-based organizations that choose to receive government funding important new rights: to retain authority over their mission and governing board; to maintain a religious atmosphere in their facilities; and to select only staff who agree with their religious beliefs (discrimination on other grounds, such as race or gender, is not permitted). Simultaneously, Charitable Choice guards the civil liberties of persons who receive social services from FBOs and congregations that collaborate with government. Religious groups must offer their services to all eligible participants regardless of their religious affiliation. If a client objects to receiving social services from a faith-based provider, under Charitable Choice the government must ensure that he or she obtains assistance from another organization. Moreover, FBOs must not use government funds for purposes of "sectarian worship, instruction, or proselytization," and they must not require service recipients to participate in religious practices.

Charitable Choice attempts to strike a delicate balance. FBOs are to be able to preserve their religious character when receiving government funds (while simultaneously protecting the civil liberties of clients) but are to refrain from using government funds for "sectarian" purposes. What is missing is a clear definition of what constitutes "sectarian worship, instruction, and proselytization," and this explains some of the disagreements among evangelicals about Charitable Choice. Those who worry that government monitors will define these activities very broadly fear that FBOs receiving government funding will be unable ever, for example, to offer prayer, to comment on scripture, or to allow volunteers to tell their testimonies.

Arguably, though, this section of the guidelines, read in conjunction with the statute's opening language about protecting the religious character of publicly funded FBOs, indicates a narrow definition. These restrictions should be interpreted in light of the overarching purpose of Charitable Choice: to facilitate collaboration with the faith community that does not require faith groups to secularize themselves. Using this approach, several other faith-based practitioners and I developed a "Code of Conduct" to help FBOs successfully navigate Charitable Choice, preserving their "religious character and autonomy" but not using public dollars for "sectarian worship, instruction, or proselytization."[5] For example, under the principle labeled "Autonomy/Preservation of Religious Character," the Code states:

> We celebrate our identity as a faith-based organization and affirm Charitable Choice's guarantee to protect our religious character. We agree to refrain from using government funds to underwrite instruction that seeks to convert people to our religious faith (e.g., confessional activities such as study of sacred texts or classes in religious doctrine). But we maintain our right to identify our faith perspective in our educational endeavors (for example, inculcating morals consistent with the Bible).

In the section labeled "Witness," the Code of Conduct commits signatories to "a gentle and winsome public witness and to the creation of an environment in which staff, volunteers, and program participants are free to speak autobiographically about their own lives, including their faith." It suggests that FBOs instruct their staff and volunteers "to welcome and lovingly respond to spiritual inquiry and discussion initiated by program participants" and to create an environment in which "the behavior and demeanor of [staff] and volunteers witnesses to [their] faith commitments." It goes on to say that FBOs should welcome the opportunity to explore "inherently religious topics like salvation, scripture interpretation, or worship" with program participants who so desire, but should arrange a time to do so outside the scheduled times of the government-funded program.

The Importance of Charitable Choice

Such guidelines are obviously relevant for evangelical groups working in the trenches in distressed communities, as they decide whether to compete for public dollars to underwrite their efforts. But why should evangelicals, more broadly, care about the faith-based initiative in general, or Charitable Choice specifically? Three reasons stand out. First, the ultimate goal behind the new initiative is to serve our society's most disadvantaged citizens. All evangelicals should share God's heart for the poor and be vitally concerned about public policies potentially affecting the needy. The President's plan seeks to strengthen the ability of the faith sector to help the downtrodden, an aim that should be embraced by all who proclaim allegiance to the One who came preaching good news to the poor.

Second, under welfare reform, government agencies are increasingly looking to private-sector organizations, including churches, for help in moving poor families from welfare to greater self-sufficiency. Close to a dozen states have convened statewide or regional conferences centered on educating the faith community about welfare reform and inviting FBOs and churches to join forces with them in serving low-income families. The National Association of Workforce Development Agencies prepared a "tool kit" that it planned to distribute to thousands of pastors, suggesting ways they can partner with their local One Stop Career Centers (which serve persons on welfare). Public officials may come knocking, and church leaders need to be prepared to respond.

Third, welfare reform set a five-year time limit on public assistance for the poor. As some families reach that limit but still are not financially self-sufficient, needy parents who can no longer expect help from Uncle Sam may also come calling. Congregations should be preparing for potentially increased demands. And part of preparing a strategy for church-based community outreach includes assessing the possibility of partnering with government.

A quick survey of evangelical publications and institutions suggests that while Charitable Choice is "on the radar screen" in the evangelical community, there still is not widespread lay understanding of it. *World* magazine and *Christianity Today* have run numerous articles on Charitable Choice. The magazine of Evangelicals for Social Action, *Prism*, has highlighted the issue, and its associated website, Network 9:35, includes links to detailed information. *Sojourners*, read by evangelicals more left-leaning in their politics, has reported on various faith-based conferences, carried a story on the ins and outs of Charitable Choice, and offered cover stories on "FBO Land" that included an interview with John DiIulio while he was the director of the White House Office of Faith-Based and Community Initiatives. Focus on the Family broadcast an interview with Don Eberly, formerly the number two man at the White House office. The Center for Public Justice has been in the forefront of the Charitable Choice debate from the beginning, publishing numerous articles and working papers and dedicating a major portion of its website to the issue.

I attempted to discover whether Christian campuses are attentive to Charitable Choice, but requests for information from most of the schools I contacted went unheeded. Jerry Falwell's Liberty University has published articles about Charitable Choice twice in the university's newsletter. Covenant College, Regent College, Seattle Pacific University, Dallas Baptist University, Wheaton College, and Grove City College have given at least minimal attention to the issue through forums and/or special lectures.

The North American Association of Christians in Social Work has sponsored several workshops on Charitable Choice and has covered the issue in its newsletter. The Christian Community Development Association, a network of more than 400 primarily evangelical community ministries, has for the past three years given education about Charitable Choice a prominent place on the agenda of its annual conference. The National Center for Neighborhood Enterprise and The Empowerment Network, which are not specifically Christian organizations but include numerous evangelical ministries in their constituencies, have given enormous attention to Charitable Choice and have sponsored major national and regional conferences on faith-based social action. All this activity suggests that, while perhaps the average evangelical in the pew may not be familiar with Charitable Choice, leading evangelical activists, communications vehicles, and institutions are.

The Supporters

As noted earlier, many evangelicals were part of the original design of Charitable Choice and the larger Bush initiative. Other evangelical leaders and institutions have also put their support behind it. Perhaps most importantly, the National Association of Evangelicals (NAE) passed a formal resolution at its March 2001 annual conference stating:

> The National Association of Evangelicals supports the concept of Charitable Choice, not only as effective public policy, but as a sound expression of faithful Christian discipleship. . . . NAE believes that institutions of Church and state can be confined to their respective spheres, without doing violence to the Establishment Clause, if the benefits of a governmental program, secular in purpose, are made available on a *neutral* basis to both religious and secular social providers. Such evenhandedness does not confer any imprimatur of government approval or endorsement of religion. For government to deny funds to faith-based charities would exhibit not neutrality, but hostility toward religion.[6]

Chuck Colson and Prison Fellowship are also firmly in the pro–Charitable Choice camp. Writing for the *Los Angeles Times*, Colson argued:

> Congress and the bureaucracy need to back the president's initiative for faith-based social services. Congress should provide tax incentives and increased deductions for specific areas of nonprofit social services. Re-

ligious organizations providing such services should be allowed to compete for government assistance on the same footing as other nonprofits and without having to sacrifice their faith identities.[7]

Legal commentator Terry Eastland wrote about Charitable Choice in the *Washington Times:*

> The point is to achieve a public purpose helping the poor and needy in the most effective and efficient ways possible. Government thus is not to ask "Who are you?" but "What can you do, and how will you do it?" [8]

The more conservative Family Resource Council (FRC) "likes the initiative so far," in the words of Susan Orr, point person on Charitable Choice. FRC sees a few problems with the legislation that Congressman J. C. Watts designed to advance the Bush plan but considers those problems "fixable."[9] FRC is also a member, along with NAE, of a new "Coalition for Compassion" that seeks to support the Administration's efforts.[10]

On the more liberal side of the political spectrum, both Evangelicals for Social Action (led by Ron Sider) and Call to Renewal (led by *Sojourners* editor Jim Wallis) are advocates for Charitable Choice. Ron Sider, in a thoughtful essay co-authored with Heidi Rolland Unruh, asserted the constitutional legitimacy of Charitable Choice with this argument:

> As long as participants in faith-based programs freely choose those programs over a "secular" provider and may opt out of particular religious activities within the program, no one is coerced to participate in religious activity, and freedom of religion is preserved. As long as government is equally open to funding programs rooted in any religious perspective—whether Islam, Christianity, philosophical naturalism, or no explicit faith perspective—government is not establishing or providing preferential benefits to any specific religion or to religion in general. As long as religious institutions maintain autonomy over such crucial areas as program content and staffing, the integrity of their identity and religious mission is maintained. As long as agencies are required to account for grant and contract funds in accordance with the ban on expenditures for inherently religious activities, no taxpayer need fear that taxes are paying for religion. While Charitable Choice may increase interactions between government and religious institutions, these interactions do not in themselves violate the First Amendment.[11]

Writing in *Sojourners* magazine, Jim Wallis urged his readers:

> First, we should support faith-based and other community initiatives at the grassroots level precisely because they have such great potential to help kids and families escape poverty. Second, we should do it in

ways that keep social services and religious activities separate. Third, we should insist on partnership between FBOs and government, rather than replacement of one by the other, and not allow anybody to abdicate their responsibilities. . . . [W]hether you trust Bush or not, the faith-based initiative can be supported and used to raise the most important issues of biblical justice to the very administration that has proposed the initiative.[12]

Supporters of Charitable Choice offer a variety of reasons for their enthusiasm. Some argue that the government funds being discussed are tax dollars from a citizenry that includes many evangelicals and that it is reasonable to hope some of this money will return to support charities working from an evangelical perspective. Others underscore the importance of the new protections afforded to evangelical FBOs by Charitable Choice and assert that these really have created a safer climate for government-faith partnerships. Still others note that, in the absence of Charitable Choice, government in effect discriminates against evangelical FBOs; Charitable Choice, they say, simply corrects this and creates an evenhandedness in government's interactions with social-service providers. And still others promote Charitable Choice because they believe that under it additional resources will flow to groups making effective progress against some of the social ills that plague America, including teen pregnancy, gangs, persistent poverty among the underclass, inner-city violence, and substance abuse.

The Critics

Not all evangelicals are enthusiastic about Charitable Choice. But both critics and supporters agree on some points: (1) Generally speaking, both groups are enthusiastic about increasing the use of vouchers in social-service programs. Under voucher programs, persons in need receive a certificate from government entitling them to a certain amount of funding to purchase a particular service for which they are eligible (e.g., child care or job training), and they may redeem their certificate at any approved provider—including faith-based providers. Under this mechanism, an FBO can be as "pervasively sectarian" as it wants without raising any church-state concerns, because persons with vouchers freely choose that provider and the government aid the provider ultimately gets is indirect. (2) Many in both camps also are enthusiastic about the President's plan to allow non-itemizers to deduct their charitable contributions; they believe such a step could dramatically increase private charitable giving in America. (3) Many in both groups agree that government regulations and procedures that hinder FBOs in their social-service efforts should be removed. (4) Many are supportive of plans to provide tax credits to individuals and businesses that contribute to faith-based, poverty-fighting charities.

Overall, then, evangelicals agree more than they disagree on the Bush faith-based plan. But the media have been slow to capture this reality and quick to report that conservative evangelicals oppose the President. Introducing an evening's program in March 2001, NPR's Juan Williams of "Talk of the Nation" began:

> Some of the generals in President Bush's army of compassionate conservatives have surprised him recently. When the president used an executive order at the end of January to open up an Office of Faith-Based Initiatives in the White House, he didn't expect criticism from people like Reverend Jerry Falwell and Pat Robertson. But even Marvin Olasky, the man who conceived of the idea of compassionate conservatism, has started to sound a little peeved.[13]

But after this introduction, Falwell's first words were: "Well, I think I've been misinterpreted. . . . I'm very supportive of President Bush's suggested faith-based initiatives program for the down and out, the disenfranchised, etc."[14] Similarly, Marvin Olasky emphasized that he favored the "general concept" and was "five-sixths in support of the president's initiative."[15]

Falwell's main concern with Charitable Choice was that the program might operate in a manner conducive to evangelical involvement under a friendly president like Mr. Bush but in the future, under a different administration, might be changed to place new restrictions or regulations on FBOs that accepted government funds. Falwell also said he would not support government funding for religious groups that lack a successful track record in providing social services:

> I would greatly object to providing funding for any group, evangelical or otherwise, to do something in the inner city, for example, if with private funds they had been doing nothing in the inner cities before public funds were available. Unless it's on their heart and it's a calling from God and they are greatly and deeply involved, I doubt they're going to be any more involved in heart after they have taxpayers' money to do their thing.[16]

Olasky's reservation is that he thinks FBOs unable to segment their programs into "secular" and "inherently religious" components would find it difficult to navigate Charitable Choice's prohibition on proselytizing with government money. As Olasky wrote in *World*:

> Evangelicals should never accept money unless evangelism is allowed. The government official at the top is particularly crucial: he needs to have made a commitment to defend faith-based groups against those who would suppress religious free speech.[17]

Olasky agrees with Falwell that "eternal vigilance" is required in this effort and says that even under a friendly president the "road is perilous." He has consistently counseled evangelical FBOs to refrain from accepting government funding for overhead expenses or for salaries of leaders,[18] but he is open to their acceptance of money to buy equipment, real estate, or facilities such as gymnasiums. Simultaneously, Olasky applauds Bush's proposals for tax credits and new tax deductions and his plan to root out regulatory barriers to effective FBO work on the ground.

Franklin Graham, son of evangelist Billy Graham and president of the relief and development ministry Samaritan's Purse, has taken a middle-of-the road stance. "People of faith must be cautious about receiving government aid for their work," Graham asserted in a Raleigh (N.C.) newspaper. "Federal funding can be most dangerous to the church because politicians inevitably will seek to use the connections for their own advantage. And . . . there are always forces seeking to use government entanglement to secularize."[19] Nonetheless, Graham expressed gratitude for President Bush's efforts to promote faith-based charities. "If the federal government wants to contribute by providing funds for cinder blocks and other building materials, we welcome the assistance," he said. "But if that same government requires us to put our faith in some kind of bureaucratic lock box as a condition of that assistance, we will respectfully decline."[20]

Richard Land, president of the Southern Baptist Convention's Ethics and Religious Liberty Commission, agrees. He believes that government money comes with government oversight; it will be difficult, in his view, for government to distinguish between "what is social service and what is ministry" in evangelical organizations, since for evangelicals "the gospel is woven into the roof of the entire ministry." For now, Land says he "wouldn't touch the money with the proverbial ten-foot pole."[21]

Pat Robertson has come out equally cautiously on Charitable Choice. On a "700 Club" broadcast, he expressed worry that government would fund religious groups that are outside the mainstream, such as the Church of Scientology, Hare Krishna, or the Unification Church. "This thing could be a real Pandora's box," Robertson said. "What seems to be such a great initiative can rise up to bite the organizations as well as the federal government."[22]

Joe Loconte, an evangelical commentator from the Heritage Foundation, has leveled pointed criticisms at government funding of FBOs. His primary concern is about secularization. "Ongoing, sustained, significant support by government cannot be good for faith-based providers. It sets up these groups for compromise."[23] Loconte has other worries also: that such support may displace private giving, if church members supporting outreach conclude their help is no longer needed; that government regulations, particularly those insisting on credentialing for staff, could lead to an increasing professionalization of ministries that formerly employed persons lacking in graduate degrees but abounding in street smarts; and that FBOs might fall into "mission creep," retooling their organizations to better position themselves for available grants.[24]

The most vehement criticism of Charitable Choice within the evangelical community, though, emerges from the Baptist Joint Committee on Public Affairs. According to testimony before a House subcommittee by BJC's executive director, J. Brent Walker,[25] Charitable Choice is "the wrong way to do right" for several reasons. Walker, a strict separationist, asserts flatly that Charitable Choice is unconstitutional, citing the Supreme Court's alleged prohibition on government aid to "pervasively sectarian" organizations. (Other constitutional scholars, such as Carl Esbeck and Douglas Laycock, assert that the Court has moved away from strict separationism to "neutrality theory," which allows public funding of FBOs, pervasively religious or not, to underwrite social-service programs.[26]) Walker also fears that Charitable Choice will bring about an excessive entanglement between government and religion, with government monitors making "razor-thin theological judgments about what amounts to worship, instruction, or proselytization" and churches having to spend more time reading the *Federal Register* (to comply with red tape) than studying the Bible. He is concerned also that receipt of government funds will dampen religious groups' prophetic voice, and that Charitable Choice will encourage an unhealthy rivalry and competition among religious groups.

What "Engaged Evangelicals" Think

What do evangelicals actually working on the front lines in places of poverty around think about Charitable Choice? Do leaders of churches engaged in community outreach, or staff at evangelical FBOs providing job training or mentoring or drug-rehabilitation services, have concerns about it?

I conducted an informal survey of "engaged evangelicals" over the course of a few weeks in spring 2001. The response rate was, not surprisingly, a very low 31 percent; persons busy rescuing kids from gangs and finding jobs for the unemployed are likely to have little time to fill out questionnaires. Nonetheless, the survey provides at least a window on the opinions of some on the front lines in a wide variety of ministries, such as medical outreach, prison ministry, drug and alcohol rehabilitation, economic development, housing, crisis assistance, counseling, teen mentoring, employment assistance, and instruction in English as a second language. I contacted 121 persons representing organizations that are members of the Christian Community Development Association, and 36 persons representing organizational members of the Presbyterian Church in America's "urban and mercy ministries network." Forty-nine of the 157 responded. Survey recipients were asked four questions:

1. Would you favor receiving government funds to provide services in your community if the law protected the religious character and mission of your organization?

2. Has your organization ever received government funds for programs offered?

3. Are you familiar with the "Charitable Choice" provision of the welfare reform act of 1996?

4. Do you support recent actions to create a national Office of Faith-based and Community Initiatives in an effort to give faith-based organizations equal access to government funding, protect their religious character, provide opportunity for increased involvement to solve community issues, and affirm their effectiveness in transforming lives?

There was significant openness to participating in financial relationships with government: 92 percent of respondents answered "yes" to question one. Support for the President's new Office of Faith-Based and Community Initiatives was just as high, 92 percent. Sixty-three percent of respondents had no experience in receiving government money, while 37 percent worked in organizations that had accepted public funds. Those open to government funding offered a variety of reasons for their position. One commented simply, "Funds alone cannot solve our social ailments, but funds can serve as a catalyst to strengthen ministries." A lay leader of a Michigan FBO explained that she favored government funding of FBOs because "tax dollars are given by Christians," while an evangelical Presbyterian from Atlanta said, "We'd love to get some of the tax money back to where it can be used effectively."

Some of the supporters, though, were cautious, encouraging Christian organizations to avoid depending on government for more than 20 percent of their budgets and to be sure to "have a strong stomach and lots of nerves." Another warned, "I share the concerns of many that we will sell our souls to get the money. The pressure to compromise when budgets are tight is substantial."

My informal survey did not turn up many opponents of Charitable Choice, but there certainly are some practitioners with serious concerns. One respondent critical of Charitable Choice wrote:

I believe that Christians have already given too many areas over to the government that have been their responsibility to Biblically fulfill. Having founded and continued to direct a faith-based nonprofit, it has always been my goal to demonstrate to the unbelieving world (especially the government) that Christians can support and carry out biblical mandates without outside intervention (financial support).

The extensive media coverage of Charitable Choice has identified other grass-roots practitioners critical of government funding of FBOs. Jeremy

Raynolds of Joy Junction, an evangelical drug-rehabilitation ministry, remained wary of Charitable Choice even after attending a small meeting with President-elect Bush in December 2000:

> We are honored by President-elect Bush's interest in faith-based ministries such as Joy Junction. However, it is important for these folks to realize that it is the "faith" in faith-based ministries that causes them to be so effective. While government bureaucrats and politicians say they want to partner with ministries such as ours, they appear to want to make the "faith" a casualty of that partnership.[27]

The Reverend Stephen Burger, executive director of the Union of Gospel Missions, shares the concern about secularization.[28] Other front-liners simply worry that government funding means endless red tape that will distract them from face-to-face ministry. Bob Cote, an ex-drunkard who runs a highly effective drug-rehabilitation program for the homeless in Denver, says government subsidies would complicate his program. "I'd have to have twenty counselors and eighteen therapists and thirty-five people to type everything in triplicate," Cote laments.[29]

Evangelical Experience with Government

In 1998, Professor Mark Chaves of the University of Arizona surveyed 1,236 religious congregations to learn how much interest there was in the new opportunities presented by Charitable Choice. Data were gathered through hour-long interviews with ministers, priests, rabbis, and other congregational leaders. Chaves found that conservative/evangelical Protestant congregations were less willing to apply for government funding than were Roman Catholic and liberal/moderate Protestant congregations.[30]

In light of these findings, it is interesting to note that according to the first major study of the implementation of Charitable Choice, evangelicals compose a significant minority of those organizations actually collaborating financially with government entities. My nine-state study, *The Growing Impact of Charitable Choice*, found as of late 1999 eighty-four examples of new (post-1996), Charitable Choice–regulated contracts between government agencies and FBOs. Of these, twenty were with FBOs labeling themselves evangelical.[31] Obviously, evangelicals are not completely reluctant to engage in government contracting. One potential explanation for the difference between the Chaves data and the Charitable Choice implementation study is that Chaves looked only at congregations, while my study looked at evangelical nonprofits as well as congregations. Nineteen of the twenty evangelical FBOs contracting with government were nonprofit organizations. (Many, though, had close ties to specific congregations.)

What has been the actual experience of evangelical groups that have engaged in government contracting under Charitable Choice? Have they had to compromise their religious identity? Do they find that government red tape hinders their on-the-ground efforts? In my nine-state study, I asked these and similar questions of staff at those evangelical organizations that were receiving government funds (most of them for the first time). These interviews were not exhaustive, and though I asked each person a standardized list of questions, I also allowed the conversation to meander with those interviewees willing to talk more broadly about their experiences. The study was not, in short, as formal as a number-crunching Gallup Poll, but it did reveal a lot about how these evangelicals (and their government counterparts) felt about their collaboration.

To summarize the main finding of the study: "So far, so good." Religious organizations contracting with government are not having to sell their souls in return for the funds, and the civil liberties of those participating in their programs are being respected. The study found virtually no instances of FBOs that felt "squelched" in their religious expression because of their collaboration with government. (Representatives of two evangelical FBOs did raise questions about the parameters of their activities; they were unsure just how far they could go with the spiritual content of their programs and expressed a desire for greater clarity from their government partners.)

Generally, church-state concerns were almost always reported as "nonissues" by both government and FBO. The four most common reasons were:

1. The FBO and government representatives had come to know and trust each other. The government staff felt it unnecessary to specify on paper what the ministry could or could not do; they assumed that the ministry would be respectful and responsible and not "cross boundaries."

2. The church/FBO staff did not think it necessary to be more specific in the government contract (or memorandum of understanding) because they felt they had been straightforward about their identity. The idea was that their government partner and the potential program participants were well aware of their religious identity. Since the clients' participation in their programs was voluntary, these FBOs/churches felt confident that they could "be religious." Clients were free *not* to participate in their programs.

3. An unofficial "gentlemen's agreement" existed between the church/FBO and its government partner that the ministry would not address spiritual concerns unless the client initiated interest in such matters.

4. The FBO did not see itself as particularly religious and had little desire to do explicitly spiritual ministry.

In February 2001 I re-contacted six evangelical organizations that I had interviewed for the nine-state study, to hear an update on their programming and learn whether they had experienced any problems with government since the original interview. One organization appears to have gone out of business; the other five reported that they had renewed and expanded their contractual relationship with government. For these, collaboration with the state has been positive. In Shasta County, California, for example, a group called FaithWORKS! received a $125,000 contract in 1998 to match families on welfare with mentors from the ministry's extensive network of churches who could provide emotional support and coaching. In February 2001, FaithWORKS! reported it was operating under a $227,000 contract to provide mentoring services to even more families. Executive Director Mike Evans reports that there have been no church-state problems. "Really, we are seen as a sort of 'chaplain' to the social-service community now," he says.[32] Dietrich Gruen of Middleton Outreach Ministry in Wisconsin was similarly enthusiastic about his organization's partnership with government. In an article in his local newspaper Gruen wrote:

> Church and state share mutual goals in wanting to serve the needy in tangible, financial and social ways. We do so as an extension of the love that God in Christ has for these people. Government seeks to help these same people because it is in our country's economic self-interest to do so, and because of certain inalienable rights that our Creator has endowed in all people. So my fellow citizens and Middleton Outreach Ministry supporters, let's take even more "no strings attached" federal funding for housing the homeless, government commodities to subsidize food programs, government subsidies for job creation and related support services to help people get off welfare and into the marketplace. . . . Separation of the Church and State is meant to keep the State from telling the Church what to do. It was never intended to restrict the faith-based community from effectively ministering to our neighbors in need.[33]

Concluding Observations

While evangelicals differ over the desirability of government funding of FBOs, their points of agreement outweigh their disagreement. Given two important realities—that some participants in the national policy conversations simply want to shut religion out from *any* role in the public square, and that we have a biblical responsibility to seek the peace of the Church—evangelicals would do well to follow the advice long offered by the Disciples of Christ: in essentials, unity; in non-essentials, liberty; in all things, charity.

Firm agreement should be sought on at least two essentials. First, evangelicals should vigorously promote an understanding of mercy ministry as a bedrock activity of the Church; we should steadfastly hold our community to the high calling of imitating Christ's compassion for the poor, the sick, the vulnerable, and the oppressed. Not every church needs to collaborate with government in caring for the poor, but every church ought to give high priority to ministry to its needy neighbors.

Second, evangelicals must insist on faithfulness to holistic ministry, addressing spiritual as well as physical needs. Jesus did not treat people as bodies without souls or as souls without bodies, and our ministry should similarly show care for the whole person. It is not possible to thoroughly integrate material and spiritual aid in every single instance of helping. But the overall thrust of church-based community ministry should be holistic. Benevolence aid should whenever possible be connected to opportunities for building sincere relationships with supplicants, relationships through which evangelism and discipleship are possible. Alongside efforts to build affordable houses or train people for better jobs or tutor at-risk kids should be activities like biblically based life-skills classes, mentoring by church volunteers through which "friendship evangelism" occurs naturally, and invitations to discipleship programs and prayer meetings. While these latter activities may not be funded with government dollars, they need not be extracted from a menu of programs simply because the ministry receives a portion of its support from government.

Evangelicals can agree to disagree, though, on how best to carry out a truly holistic ministry under both the protections and the restrictions of Charitable Choice. I've met almost no evangelicals thrilled with Charitable Choice's explicit restrictions on "sectarian instruction and proselytization"; most feel this section of the guidelines is unnecessary because persons in need are always free to choose a secular provider for services they require. The difference is that some evangelicals are devising ways to work within the current, B+ framework of faith-government collaboration created by Charitable Choice, while others want no part in receiving government funds until Charitable Choice earns an A+ by dropping these restrictions.

Diversity of opinion on this matter excuses no one from the duty of treating our brothers and sisters charitably. Those shunning involvement with government should not be accused of neglecting their duty to serve the needy, and those collaborating with the state should not be charged with compromising their religious integrity. Anything less than this approach fails to center our dialogue on the main point: getting on with the job of loving "the least" in America in Jesus' name.

CHAPTER TEN

The Loyal Opposition:
Evangelicals and Public Schools

David Sikkink

Americans have seen their public schools as pillars of the community and nation for most of the twentieth century. At least since World War II, public schools have been a primary locus of community identity, volunteering, and local politics. It was not surprising, then, that as the evangelical movement of the 1950s and 1960s attempted to counter the separatist trends of fundamentalism and to bring conservative traditions of Protestantism to bear on American culture, a commitment to public schools was a key part of their strategy. Evangelicals naturally looked to involvement in schools as a way to carry out their mission of engaging the world with Christian truth.[1]

For many evangelicals today, their view of how religion relates to public life is closely tied to their sense of Christian obligation to public schools. Is this likely to continue? Will public schools continue to provide a primary avenue through which evangelicals participate in public life? Or are changes in public schools, the rise of schooling alternatives, and the decoupling of community and school endangering this older evangelical tradition? If so, are evangelical parents who choose some form of non-public schooling becoming more isolated from public life?

There is reason to be concerned that the evangelical tradition of "witnessing to the world" through participation in public schools is indeed threatened. Robert Wuthnow has argued that the high demands of evangelical churches leave little time for civic engagement outside the church.[2] In addition, the expansion of school-choice plans and the explosive growth

David Sikkink is an associate professor of sociology and a fellow in the Center for Research on Educational Opportunity at the University of Notre Dame. His areas of research include religion and public life, private schooling and civil society, and quantitative methodology.

of home-schooling may leave church participation as the sole evangelical contribution to civic life. If this should occur, evangelical churches would provide for civil society strong *bonding* social capital—that is, dense and trustful networks within their religious group—but would not contribute to *bridging* social capital, the weak ties across broad social differences.[3] Yet it is also possible that evangelicals actually thrive on the existence of a clear boundary between the world and their religious community and will increase their resolve to take their faith into the world, especially within public schools.

One important obstacle to evangelical civic engagement within public schools is that schooling issues are lightning rods for "culture wars." Cultural conflict in which education professionals champion progressive reforms and are opposed by traditionalist parents may create a school environment that seems like hostile territory to evangelicals. The Christian Right and other political conservatives have fostered this feeling by construing public school issues in culture-war terms, using the schools as centerpieces for their broader lament about the direction of American society.

As public schools are increasingly perceived by conservatives as the cultural enemy, alternatives are increasingly available. School vouchers, charter schools, and magnet schools are multiplying, and there has been a revival of Catholic schools. The rapidly growing home-schooling option is attractive to those who have long emphasized the importance of moral training and "becoming a Christian" within the family. In addition, Christian-school options such as the Classical Christian school movement have proliferated.

In what follows I present an inventory of evangelical views of public schools and attempt to determine whether their involvement in schools, as well as their level of civic engagement outside of schools, is waning.

Trust in Public Schools

A key facilitator of civic engagement is trust—trust in strangers, in neighbors, and in public institutions. Evangelicals' higher tension with mainstream American society is likely to decrease their general levels of trust, and this may reduce the extent to which they are civically engaged. There is some evidence that evangelical Protestants, compared to mainline Protestants, have slightly lower levels of general trust in human beings,[4] and we would certainly expect them to have less trust in government institutions. Does this extend to public schools?

According to a 2000 national survey, evangelicals are right in the middle in their level of confidence in educational institutions; they register neither "great confidence" nor "hardly any confidence."[5] Religious differences here are not strong; for instance, evangelicals are little different from mainline Protestants on this measure. In attitudes toward funding for education, evangelicals are not quite as supportive of increased funding as mainliners, but they are not far behind, and they are not different from the average American.[6]

Yet other research has shown that evangelicals are alienated from public schools. A national survey of church-going Protestants reveals that Pentecostals are the most likely of all conservative Protestants to think that public schools are "hostile to their moral and spiritual values," but evangelicals are not far behind.[7] In part, this reflects the reaction of Pentecostal and other charismatic Protestants to changes toward more rational and bureaucratic organizational forms in public schools, and to the schools' increasing tendency to ground legitimate authority in efficiency, academic achievement, and the professionalism of teachers and administrators.[8] These trends may seem to downplay the importance of values and normative direction as essential to a good school and a good education.

Stephen Arons argues that parents' concerns with schooling are driven by the sense that children are growing up in a world of collapsed cultural meanings and dysfunctional social values.[9] Conservative Protestants see education as fundamentally an expression of *belief*, as an intimate form of communication, and thus as an extension of the normative sphere of the family. From the perspective of conservative Protestant parents, public schools are a world of shifting and arbitrary categories, insensitive to normative concerns—a place of bureaucratic order without ethical direction. Under these conditions, we might be surprised if evangelicals were *not* ready to abandon the public school ship.

Support for School Vouchers

Evangelicals' historical commitment to the public school as an expression of the community's and the nation's values would seem to reduce support for school vouchers, which would allow government money to go to any school that a parent chooses for a child. Certainly mainline Protestants' tradition of quiet support for the symbolic links among school, community, and nation explains the strong opposition to vouchers among mainline Protestants. But the evangelical custodial tradition may be muted on this issue, since we often assume that evangelicals strongly support voucher plans. Perhaps evangelicals' support of public schools is no longer seen as a commitment to a common democratic life in local communities; rather, it is limited to individual decisions by parents who feel "called" to keep their children in public school as a preserving presence in a sinful world. The schooling decision thus becomes less about the notion that public schools serve a public purpose—as places where the diversity of the neighborhood is melded into a common life—and more about individual choice. This choice, according to many evangelicals, should depend on the particular needs and strengths of the child and the particular condition of the local public school.

The evangelical emphasis on "being called" to public school, in contrast to the older evangelical tradition that made a religious principle out of public school attendance, is compatible with support for school vouchers. Further reducing evangelicals' qualm about vouchers is their strong opposition to a secular government's imposing on religious prerogative. Evangelicals may also see school vouchers as returning power to parents and helping to balance the tilt toward stronger government. In a national survey of Americans conducted in 2000, evangelical Protestants were surpassed only by Catholics in their support for a voucher plan "that would allow parents to use tax funds to send their children to the school of their choice, even if it were a private school."[10] While Pentecostals are slightly more supportive of vouchers than non-Pentecostal evangelical Protestants, the responses of both groups contrast sharply with mainline Protestant antagonism toward vouchers. The mainline tradition of support for public institutions that bring diverse Americans together leads these Protestants to oppose school vouchers to almost the same degree that evangelical Protestants support them—i.e., 60 percent. This contrast remains even after social and demographic differences between the two groups are taken into account.

General Support, Particular Differences

Even so, evangelicals actually support public schooling over the religious alternatives. When asked if they think Christians should work with the public schools, build strong Christian schools, or home-school their children, evangelicals—alone among conservative Protestants—tend to favor working with public schools.[11] Evangelical women are especially strong supporters of this.[12] This position is consistent with the older evangelical tradition that views their impact in society as primarily a matter of individual presence in public institutions, and this provides a religious motive for keeping students in public schools and keeping parents active in the public school mosaic. Some evidence of this lies in the fact that evangelicals are more likely than other churchgoing Protestants, including other conservative Protestants, to say that the best strategy for dealing with moral issues in public schools is one that focuses equally on electing school-board representatives and "trying through relationships to have a positive moral influence on students, teachers, and parents."[13]

Overall, then, I find evangelicals tenaciously holding on to their commitment to public schools—at least in the abstract—but sometimes in direct conflict with public schooling over both its general bureaucratic and professional direction and some specific programs and policies. For example, a national survey made in 2000 finds strong opposition among evangelicals to sex education in public schools.[14] This opposition holds up even after I control for the fact that evangelicals tend to be politically conservative, a characteristic that also increases opposition to sex education in schools. Still, evangelicals are well behind fundamentalists, who among religious groups show the highest level of opposition to sex education.

Evangelicals also favor some form of prayer in schools. In the same national survey in 2000, I find that they strongly disapprove of the Supreme Court decision that placed some limits on public prayer and Bible reading in schools. Evangelicals oppose this decision much more strongly than fundamentalists, who are more generally ambivalent about religion in the public square and who do not oppose the Court's decision any more than the average American does. But evangelicals are not nearly so opposed to the Court decision as Pentecostals. Catholics also oppose the Court's decision, but not as strongly as evangelicals.[15]

In another instance of opposition to the educational mainstream, evangelicals have a slightly different take on educational priorities than most Americans. For example, my analyses of a 1996 survey show that they tend not to favor an emphasis on "building self-esteem," something they may associate with progressive educators and with the watering down of academic standards.

My personal interviews with evangelicals on educational issues reveal that they are not in complete agreement on what they want from public schools.[16] One group holds that public schools should focus on the basics, the three "Rs," and should not get involved in social goals and teaching about religion. This group strongly opposes multicultural goals in education. Other evangelicals take the position that multicultural goals are valid if pursued fairly, That is, multiculturalism is fine if Christian perspectives have an equal place at the classroom table. Evangelicals in this camp probably see multiculturalism as an opportunity to engage difference with their religious perspective—a position of "engaged orthodoxy."[17] They feel obliged to understand cultural difference as part of their effort to "redeem" society. Active engagement with differences outside their own community helps them fulfill their calling to play a custodial role toward the culture and society.

This divide may explain why in my analyses of survey data, evangelicals on average are lukewarm—but not cold—toward multiculturalism. They exhibit about the same support for multicultural goals as mainliners, though somewhat less than liberals.[18] Partly explaining the disagreement is an underlying divide within evangelicalism on views of America. One segment of the evangelical community supports the view that America, despite its current religious and cultural diversity, is a Christian nation and needs to return to its Christian roots. Multiculturalism in the classroom does not fare well with these evangelicals. More importantly, many evangelicals are caught in a tension between "Christendom" and pluralism.[19] That is, they tend to think both that biblical truth should reign in all of life and should be imposed on non-believers, and that each person must come to the truth voluntarily and so Christian morality should not be imposed in public life. Most evangelicals draw on the "pluralism" side of this tension to support multiculturalism in the classroom, while others carrying the Christendom banner oppose it. Many other evangelicals are caught in the tension, and struggle to figure out how to live out their faith in relation to public schools.

Knowledge vs. Morality

While evangelicals see public schools as hostile arenas, they are on the whole willing to tolerate some secular trends within those schools. In personal interviews in 1996, I found that ordinary evangelicals tend to associate problems in the public schools with problems in home and family, and do not spend much time talking about an insidious force of "secular humanism" in the schools. They do not seem opposed fundamentally to the structural divide of knowledge vs. morality that is institutionalized in public schooling. Thus the changes they demand of public schools often sound little different from those of the average American: teach the "basics" well, avoid controversial "social" issues, make schools safer, and so on.

Beyond these concerns, there is a generally expressed wish for more student respect for authority, and more consistent and severe punishment for offenders. Often the loss of respect for authority is pinned on unsupportive parents who are "sue-happy," as one evangelical put it, and a legal system that encourages this. Evangelicals' understanding of these problems, however, does not appear much different from that of the average American parent who, in the time-honored way, bemoans a decline in respect for authority among youth. Although evangelicals' Christendom and pluralism sides do continue to battle, in the end most of the changes that evangelicals would like to see are framed in a way that at most calls for "equal time" rather than some kind of "Christian-izing" of public schools.

The strategies that evangelicals favor for changing public schools reflect their dual tradition of support for interpersonal methods of change, and unease with most organized attempts to change structures. Evangelical public engagement is seen primarily as a matter of the presence of Christians in public institutions, which is thought to have a preserving effect as "salt" and "light" in the culture. Efforts to transform public schools, in the view of most evangelicals, must be made through individual Christians. Almost by some kind of osmosis, the "presence" of Christians will have a positive effect on individual teachers, parents, and children, and therefore on the institution as a whole. In my interviews, evangelicals almost never explained the exact means by which this individual presence changes public schools, but they did emphasize that truly effective change comes through personal influence rather than stratagems.

Consequences for School Participation

This tradition of engagement through presence may continue to push evangelicals toward active engagement in schools. Moreover, evangelicals whom I interviewed showed a deep concern about the education of children, which may further increase their participation in schools compared with that of other Americans. My analysis of a national survey of Americans in 2000 showed that evangelical Protestants are more likely to participate in schools than are non-religious Americans.[20] When asked if they had participated in a "parents' association . . . or other school support or service group," evangelical Protestants showed higher levels of involvement than mainline Protestants, though mainliners were much more engaged than non-religious Americans. Evangelicals were second only to Mormons in this type of school participation. The same survey asked whether respondents had volunteered for a "school or youth group" in the last year. Evangelicals showed relatively strong commitment to this kind of volunteering at school compared to non-religious Americans, but less than mainline Protestants and significantly less than Mormons.

We can conclude from these data, then, that despite their sense of alienation from public schools, evangelicals on average maintain a relatively strong commitment to participating in civic life through involvement in schools. This provides some evidence that the evangelical tradition of engagement through the ubiquitous presence in public institutions of individual evangelicals has not completely withered away.

EVANGELICAL CHOICES IN EDUCATION

So how do these conflicting forces—a sense that public schools are hostile environments for faith, the partial support for a secular curriculum, the opposition to sex education and support for prayer in schools—affect the choices that evangelicals make for their children's education?

A national survey conducted in 2000 shows that evangelicals are significantly more likely than mainline Protestants—though less likely than fundamentalists—to take up home-schooling.[21] Pentecostals are slightly behind evangelicals in this. Catholics too are more likely than mainliners to use this option. But Pentecostals, while favorable toward home-schooling, tend not to use the alternative of Christian schools. Again, evangelicals and fundamentalists are the leaders in choosing Christian schools for their children.

While it is not surprising that the average evangelical is more likely to adopt home-schooling and other Christian alternatives than mainliners, the strength of this move seems to suggest that large cracks are emerging in the evangelical commitment to public schools as a form of engagement with the world. Yet it must be kept in mind that the home-school and Christian-school movements are still relatively small. A rough estimate puts conservative Christian families in home-schooling at about 1 million out of approximately 55 million elementary and secondary-school students, and families choosing Christian schools at about 2.5 million.[22]

Consequences for Civic Engagement

Although evangelicals are using alternatives to the neighborhood public school, this may not reduce their overall level of civic engagement. In part, the reason is that private schools can, like public schools, serve the important function of generating civic participation outside the school.

Some prominent scholars have argued that democracy is weakened by the fact that Americans are withdrawing from public life. And there is concern that private schools, especially fundamentalist Christian schools, tend to isolate religious families in "total worlds" that create a wall of separation from public life.[23] But there are still unanswered questions about how different types of schools contribute to or stem the trend toward disengagement. Do public schools still create an important link between parents and the broader community? Do parents of children in private schools tend to become disconnected from public life, focused on private gains through education? How, then, would school-choice plans affect parents' civic participation?

My analysis of data from a 1996 government survey shows that families who exercise choice in schooling are more likely to participate in civic activities—especially political activities.[24] This survey identified six schooling options: (1) home, (2) Catholic, (3) non-Catholic church-related, (4) private non-religious, (5) assigned neighborhood public school, and (6) public school of choice. Interestingly, parents who *choose* a public school—such as a magnet school, charter school, or a non-assigned public school under an open-enrollment plan—are more likely to participate in political life than are parents whose children attend the neighborhood public school. They may have become active in politics in order to change schooling policies that limited choice. And they may continue to be politically engaged because the school-choice plan itself and the operation of the schools it makes available depend on policies and decisions made within the political sphere.

As for families who choose private schools, there are differences across the various types. Compared with parents whose children attend the neighborhood public school, those who choose a private *non-religious* school are *not* more likely to participate in politics, and those who choose non-Catholic religious schools are *less* likely to do so. Parents who choose Catholic schools, however, show much higher levels of involvement in political activities—such as voting, attending public meetings, working for or giving money to a political cause—than parents of children in any other school sector.

These findings raise some concern that evangelicals' choice of Christian schools—though not other school choices, such as magnet and charter schools—may reduce their civic engagement outside of schools. But there are social trends that may both (a) reduce civic participation generated through public schools and (b) increase it among parents in religious schools.

Americans often view public schools as the first institution of democracy. Public schools contribute greatly, we believe, to the social bonds of the community. We expect that parents who are not involved in civic life before their children go off to school will cut their political teeth through involvement in parent/teacher organizations and school-board elections. Public schools have been important sites for building relationships among parents.

Trends in society and schools, however, make it much more difficult for public schools to fulfill this traditional role as centers of community social life. Geographic mobility, the loss of neighborhood and community ties, the development of "bedroom communities" that separate community and workplace—such trends make it more difficult for community to form through geographically based public schools. Further, control of a local school is much less in the hands of the community and much more subject to outside pressures, such as state and federal regulations. Public school teachers may be oriented less to the local community than to national professional organizations.[25] And public schools are usually run according to bureaucratic models that make it difficult to create a community within the school.[26]

Religious schools, in comparison, are more successful at creating a community of learning that involves parents in the school, and, in the case of Catholic schools, this facilitates involvement in local and national politics. A shared moral culture, a common mission, local governance, and the overlapping networks of church and school increase opportunities for creating strong communities of parents through the religious school. Private non-religious schools are not able to do this as well as religious schools.

Two characteristics that differentiate Catholic schools from many conservative Protestant schools also help to generate strong communities. Compared to fundamentalist schools, Catholic schools are oriented less toward walling out the outside world and more toward service in the community. Also, Catholic churches do more than conservative Protestant ones to encourage religiously motivated involvement in political life. The organizational links among Catholic schools, churches, service organizations, and political groups ensure that parents' involvement in Catholic schools facilitates their involvement in public life, especially political life. Catholic schools, then, have the unique combination of a culture that encourages involvement in public life and links to outside organizations that create a path from private schools to public life.

Do evangelical Christian schools do the same? We would expect so; evangelical traditions of engaged orthodoxy should lead to a difference between evangelical and fundamentalist schools in fostering outside civic engagement. Although survey data are not available to answer this question, we do know that "Christian schools"—conservative Protestant schools—are not all cut from the same cloth.

Conservative Protestant schools fall into at least three groups: fundamentalist, Lutheran, and evangelical.[27] Of these, the evangelical schools are most likely to mirror the civic-participation strength of Catholic schools. Fundamentalist schools—the whipping boy of Christian schools both within the movement and in the popular press—tend to be closely affiliated with a particular church, often a fundamentalist Baptist church. They focus on developing personal character and discipline, and they teach fundamentalist doctrines such as the literal interpretation of the Bible and six-day creationism. The Christian schools positioned more centrally within the evangelical movement—some Southern Baptist schools, nearly all Christian Reformed schools, and many independent Christian schools—tend to be more focused on an academic mission and more open to seeing Christian education as including engagement in the world.[28] We would also expect these evangelical schools to have connections to churches that are active within the community and to other political and nonpolitical organizations. While perhaps not rivaling the Catholic schools, evangelical schools are likely to have well-worn pathways from school and church to civic life. They at least provide the foundation for bringing parents into the school and perhaps for sending them out into the community as well.

Interestingly, under forms of school choice, public schools still provide an important avenue for encouraging parents to participate in public life. From the evidence available in the 1996 government survey, it appears that when parents are actively involved in choosing a public school for their children, they are more likely to participate in political life. In this way, school choice is empowering for parents and fosters greater political participation.

HOME-SCHOOLING AND POLITICAL PARTICIPATION

Many evangelicals are active in the home-schooling movement, and that movement has grown very rapidly over the last twenty years. We might expect a corresponding decline in evangelical civic engagement. But there are some encouraging signs that the home-schooling movement is an important vehicle for civic engagement, though it slightly alters the style of that engagement.

One highly visible form is home-schoolers' recent success in influencing Congress. The movement has undoubtedly been effective in grass-roots mobilization. But beyond telephone and writing campaigns to safeguard home-schooling interests, are these parents generally withdrawn from political life? How does home-schooling affect the types of political activities that parents take up? It seems likely that home education creates barriers to conventional political involvement, and thus pushes home-schooling parents toward unconventional political action. In addition, we would expect that the tasks of home-schooling increase the civic skills of parents, which in turn increases civic engagement.

One important reason why home-schooling may reduce political participation is simply that home-schoolers are not connected to the one institution that generates political engagement for most parents—the local public school. Local political struggles over the institutional resources of public schools encourage participation in a way that national political issues and elections may not.

Building Network Ties

But home-schoolers are creating new organizations that may make up for this lack of connection. Strong home-schooling organizations link home-schoolers and foster the network ties marked by trust and mutual obligation, what Robert Putnam calls "bonding social capital." This organizational involvement has many of the strengths that Sidney Verba and colleagues have attributed to nonpolitical organizations, including opportunities for (1) generating civic skills, (2) facilitating network recruitment, and, as a result, (3) fostering political participation.[29]

First, the relatively democratic and horizontal ties of these groups may make them more effective than parent associations within public schools in generating civic skills. Home-schooling parents are likely to hone these skills as they do things like organize visits to museums and coordinate science classes for the home-schooling group. The organization may increase their opportunities to speak in front of groups and to exercise other leadership skills. Also, civic skills learned through teaching may translate into the political sphere. Teaching history and government to children may increase parents' political knowledge. And efforts to provide "real world" learning experiences for home-schooled children—using the community as a classroom—may increase parents' awareness of local issues and organizations.

Second, the dense home-schooling networks become natural recruitment networks for political organizers; parents hear about opportunities for political involvement, and through the social bonds they have formed they encourage one another to participate.

And third, home-schooling parents are likely to gain political cues through their organizations as they discuss education issues and the political climate for home-schooling. These local networks disseminate information from national organizations such as the Home Schooling Legal Defense Association. In fact, the combination of (a) dense cells that generate identities and social control and (b) links between these cells through national home-schooling organizations and publications may mean that home-schooling rivals Catholic schooling in providing the best organizational environment for generating civic engagement.

To understand the political participation of home-schooling parents, we must also take into account the fact that the decision to educate children at home places the family relatively outside mainstream political concerns and in opposition to the dominant norms in schooling. And so home-schooling fosters a more general countercultural orientation. The cultural orientation of home-schooling may include, for example, opposition to dating among teens, unhurried learning and a challenge to academic achievement norms, and unconventional lifestyles—such as a self-sufficiency that includes milking goats and raising nearly all the family's food.

One result may be that home-schoolers are not attracted to conventional politics. A political minority as small and distinctive as this one may find few openings to pursue its interests through, say, the local party caucus. It is generally true that conventional politics in a majoritarian political system impedes the representation of small political minorities. This pushes home-schoolers toward a form of political participation common to highly motivated special-interest groups.

Home-schooling may also influence political participation by the demands it places on the family's time. The time commitment for home-schooling reduces free time available for political participation. Parents' time with children has to include not just the regular instruction at home but library visits, field trips, and home-schooling group activities. There is also an investment of time in building home-schooling networks, informal and formal. The effect on civic participation may be like the effect of being part of a conservative Protestant church. As Robert Wuthnow has argued, investing one's time, intellect, and emotion in a tight-knit group reduces opportunities for outside involvement.[30]

Parents' Political Knowledge

But in my analysis of a national survey of parents with children in the sixth through twelfth grade, home-schooling parents showed fairly high levels of political engagement, and evidence of higher civic skills.[31] They measure significantly higher than local-public-school parents on various indicators of political efficacy and knowledge. For instance, they strongly disagree with the statement that their family has little say in government. They report high levels of confidence that they could express an opinion clearly in a letter to a government official. They are likely to give correct answers to questions about how government works and who the major political players are.

Despite their knowledge of the political system, however, there is no evidence that home-schooling families are very attentive to national news media. While parents of children in Catholic and private non-religious schools are significantly *more* likely than local-public-school parents to read the news often, home-schooling families are not significantly different in this regard from local-public-schoolers. And they are significantly *less* likely than local-public-schoolers to watch or listen to the national news. These findings on use of national media may reflect the tendency of home-schoolers to find alternative media sources for their news, and may also reflect the boundaries that home-schooling parents tend to create with mainstream American culture—which may include disapproval of watching television.

Home-schooling parents stand out when it comes to boycotts or public protest activities. This may in part reflect time flexibility: home-schooling mothers can perhaps more easily arrange schedules to participate in protests. Also, the home-schooling networks increase opportunities for recruitment and mobilization. And to a somewhat marginalized and relatively small group, perhaps the avenue of political protest seems the most open and effective. Home-schooling parents are also significantly more likely than local-public-school parents to have contacted elected officials or news editors by telephone or letter. The only other schooling group that is close to them on this score is the public-schoolers who have chosen their schools. Again, this type of political involvement may be enhanced as home-schooling families attempt to defend their interests against the claims of government and outside social pressures. It is also possible that parents use these opportunities for protesting and grassroots lobbying as a learning experience for their children.

Findings for the other measures of political and civic participation show that home-schooling families do not differ significantly from local-public-schoolers. They are no more likely to give money to political candidates and parties, to attend a public meeting, to participate in a community-service organization, or to vote.

For the most part, these findings apply to all types of home-schoolers. While the survey does not ask any detailed questions about religion, it does ask how often the respondent attends church services. We can be reasonably certain that the home-schoolers reporting high church attendance are evangelical Protestants. Across most types of political participation, the high-attending home-schoolers do not differ from low-attending home-schoolers, which supports the claim that the effects of home-schooling on civic participation do not vary by the religion of the parents. There are a couple of exceptions. One is that the high-attending home-schoolers are *more* likely to report membership in a community-service organization and giving money to a political candidate; they are *less* likely to watch or listen to the news.

Concluding Observations

Evangelicals find themselves torn between a religious tradition of engagement in public schools through individual presence—as student and parent "witnesses"—and a public school system that has drifted away from its earlier moorings in Protestant establishment culture. They are faced with strong alternatives to the neighborhood public school, such as charter and magnet schools, Christian schools, and home-schooling. But on the whole, evangelicals remain committed to the public school system, even though the school environment seems hostile to their moral and spiritual values.

Since evangelicals are both supportive and skeptical of public schools, it is not surprising that many are choosing Christian schools or home-schooling as a stopgap measure in these "troubled times." But these moves are not likely to isolate them in religious cocoons. Instead, both Christian schools and home-schooling provide a social context that draws parents into networks marked by trust and solidarity, and sends them out into political and nonpolitical forms of civic life. Their movement into private schools has the unintended outcome of generating engagement in public life. Rather than withdrawing, evangelicals continue their engagement with the world through schools.

CHAPTER ELEVEN

Faith That Separates: Evangelicals and Black-White Race Relations

Michael Emerson

Ask non-evangelicals what they think about white evangelicals and racial issues and most will tell you that white evangelicals (whom they usually call fundamentalists) are highly prejudiced against blacks and are indeed racial bigots. Ask white evangelicals what they think about evangelicals and race and most will tell you that the Church is the only place where racism can be overcome: the world is full of sin, and so those outside the Church have no hope of overcoming racial bigotry—but Christians can be and are different.

After studying evangelicalism and race, a study that culminated in the book *Divided by Faith: Evangelical Religion and the Problem of Race in America*, I believe the story is not quite so simple as either of these views suggests.[1] My goal here is to tell the story of evangelicalism and black-white relations. White evangelicals are generally well intentioned and are being honest when they say they desire a nation free from racial problems. Indeed, in recent years, their engagement with race issues has increased greatly, so much so that in 1997 the *Wall Street Journal* called evangelicals "the most energetic element of society addressing racial divisions" (June 23, 1997). Yet despite this well-intended activity, I argue in the book that white evangelical theology and practice actually frustrate racial healing and justice.

"Racism" is one of the most overused and least understood terms in current usage. Definitions vary widely; people apply the label to a dizzying array of situations, actions, and thoughts. And people are highly defensive

---

Michael Emerson is an associate professor of sociology at Rice University. He is the co-author, with Christian Smith, of *Divided by Faith: Evangelical Religion and the Problem of Race in America* (Oxford, 2000), and, with Curtiss DeYoung, George Yancey, and Karen Chai, of *United by Faith: Multiracial Congregations as a Response to the Racial Divide* (Oxford, 2003).

187

about the charge. Almost no one wants to be called a racist, or to have an organization he or she cares about labeled racist. The term produces conflict and anger, and often shuts down social interaction.

For many, racism is best exemplified by the Ku Klux Klan, with its overt doctrine of racial superiority and hatred and the resultant discriminatory actions. From this perspective, racism is seen as irrational and as a fault that lies in individuals. The racist is filled with racial hatred and intentionally behaves in a racist way.

This definition presents problems. Take a slave owner, for example: was he racist if he was born into a society where for the past hundred years his ancestors and peers all owned slaves, and he simply did what everyone else in his social circle was doing? Was he racist if he viewed his slaves as part of his family, treated them with care, saw them as equal to himself before God, yet needed slaves to raise and harvest his crops and learned in his church that slave-owning was God-ordained? According to the Ku Klux Klan model, not at all. This slave owner was not filled with hate, his actions were not irrational, and he viewed himself not as inherently superior to the slaves but simply as occupying a different position in the God-ordained social order.

The Ku Klux Klan model of racism is not a sufficient way to understand race relations and inequality in our society, because it focuses on the individual perpetrators, rather than on the system generating the inequality and on those who bear the brunt of it. Using this model pulls us away from the real problems. Certainly racist people are part of the problem, but they are only part.

In attempting to understand race issues, I use the term "racialized society." A racialized society is one wherein race matters profoundly, creating differences in life experiences, life opportunities, and social relationships. A racialized society allocates society's goods—income, wealth, health, status, psychological well-being—unequally along racial lines. Society creates the racial lines (which often change over time) and the form of racialization (for example, slavery, Jim Crow segregation, de facto segregation, and inequality), but its unchanging essence is that race matters considerably for who people are, whom they know, and what their chances in life are.

This perspective leads us to a different definition. From the racialized perspective, racism is not individual, overt prejudice, but *the collective misuse of power that that leads to inequality in the distribution of society's goods*. It is a changing ideology with the constant and rational purpose of *perpetuating and justifying a racialized social system*. This justification *may* include individual, overt prejudice, but it need not; a legal system or a system of religious beliefs can be just as effective. Racism, then, is a concept that helps us understand how racialized systems are maintained, but it is not the primary way of understanding racial problems.

Is the United States Racialized?

Slavery is long over, and the segregation of the South was outlawed in the 1960s. Programs such as affirmative action have been instituted to help blacks succeed. Is the United States then still racialized? Let us look at some comparative evidence for blacks and whites.

- Less than 2 percent of white and blacks marry outside their own race.[2]
- Regardless of the state of the economy, for as long as records have been kept, blacks have been twice as likely to be unemployed as whites. The disparity in unemployment rates in the last few decades is actually larger than it was in the 1940s and 1950s.[3]
- For every dollar earned by whites, blacks make just two-thirds of that.[4]
- Black Americans are three times as likely to be poor as white Americans.[5]
- Black Americans have just *8 percent* of the wealth (assets minus debts) that white Americans do. This gap in wealth remains even when we look at blacks and whites with similar levels of education or in similar occupations.[6]
- Residential segregation is far higher between whites and blacks than between any other two other groups. That level remained constant from 1990 to 2000 in places that are more than 3 percent black. Residential segregation, scholars have shown, produces artificial gains for whites and isolates blacks, concentrating poverty and social problems in their neighborhoods.[7]
- Three-quarters of white adults own their own homes; fewer than half of black adults do.
- Blacks who own their own homes pay, on average, higher interest rates and greater closing costs for houses that appreciate at a substantially slower rate than white-owned houses.[8]
- Of senior-level managers—vice presidents and above—in the Fortune 1,000 industrial and Fortune 500 services companies, 97 percent are white.[9]
- If blacks were equally represented among the Fortune 500 companies, sixty black Americans would be CEOs. The actual number at the time of writing was 0.
- Infant mortality is twice as high among blacks as among whites, and black women are three times as likely to die in childbirth.[10]
- For the last half-century, black Americans have been at least five times as likely to be murdered as white Americans.[11]
- People who kill whites are punished far more severely than people who kill blacks.[12]
- The average life expectancy for blacks is five to ten years less than for whites.
- Prejudice and discrimination remain at the social level—such as the criminal justice system (for example, profiling by police)—and at the individual level. While I was writing this chapter, a white friend called, distressed that her

adopted African-American daughter had come home crying from school because she had been called a "big monkey" and a "dirty ape." Nearly every family I interviewed that had a school-age cross-racial child conveyed similar experiences.

■ In over 90 percent of the Christian churches in the United States, the congregation is at least 90 percent of one race.

Based on our definition of a racialized society—that it is one in which race creates profound differences in life experiences, life opportunities, and social relationships, and that it is characterized by inequality—the United States in the early twenty-first century is racialized.

The Crusade for Racial Reconciliation

Since the late 1980s, a flood of books, seminars, college courses, study groups, magazine articles, speeches, movements, apologies, concerts, rallies, new organizations, and even an occasional merger of once racially separate organizations has rolled across the evangelical sector of the nation. This activity has been truly remarkable.

But not all is well. Promise Keepers head Bill McCartney, in his book *Sold Out*, gives us a glimpse of the problem.[13] Through his experiences with the variety of backgrounds of his football players at the University of Colorado, McCartney came to see the powerful ways in which race affects our culture and people. Moved by this realization, he went on a national tour of churches and, speaking from his experiences as football coach and from biblical imperatives, called for racial reconciliation. But always when he finished, he says, "there was no response—nothing. . . . In city after city, in church after church, it was the same story—wild enthusiasm while I was being introduced, followed by a morgue-like chill as I stepped away from the microphone." McCartney goes on to speculate that a major factor in the decline in the attendance at Promise Keepers stadium events was the group's teachings on race.

Why the "morgue-like" responses? Why do evangelicals, seemingly so active on issues of race, react in this way? To find out, my colleagues and I interviewed thousands of Americans—both evangelical and non-evangelical—and traveled to twenty-three states to interview evangelicals in their homes.

How Evangelicals Think about the Race Problem

Debbie, 27, was raised in an evangelical home, is "born again," holds firmly to the authority of the Bible, is active in her church, graduated from an evangelical college, shares the message of Christ with others, and gives money for missions. Raised in a "wheat belt" state in a small community, she has had limited contact with non-whites.

Sitting down to hot tea on a cold morning, I interviewed her about a number of subjects. Finally I arrived at racial issues. When I asked whether she thought our country has a race problem, she told me that we *make* it a problem. How, I asked. She replied:

Well, to me, people have problems. I mean, two white guys working together are gonna have arguments once in a while. . . . It happens between men and women, between two white guys [or] two white women. It's just people. . . . I feel like once in a while, when an argument happens, say between a black guy and a white guy, instead of saying, "Hey, there's two guys having an argument," we say it's a race issue.

The race problem for Debbie is basically one of misinterpretation. People disagree, and when they happen to be of different races, we incorrectly interpret their disagreement as racially based. When I asked her if she saw a race problem beyond misinterpretation, she said that there are cases in which people think or act in negative ways simply because of the race of another person, but that such cases are rare and are inexcusable for Christians.

Her view was typical of those I heard from many white evangelicals: the race problem is (a) minimal and (b) caused by the misinterpretation of relational problems between individuals. "I think our country has a *perceived* race-relations problem," a Presbyterian man said. "We have individuals who have race-relations problems. I don't think our country in its current form has a race problem." A Baptist woman told me, "Race has very little influence on life in America. It's a shame that there are still some who struggle to get along with each other because of skin color, but such people are a tiny minority."

I found that other white evangelicals viewed the race problem in one of two ways: (1) groups try to make race problems a group issue when the problems are merely problems among a few individuals, or (2) the race problem is a creation of the self-interested, such as representative individuals of minority groups, the media, or a liberal government. For most white evangelicals, then, the race problem ultimately came down to the personal defects of some people as, lacking Christ-like love and understanding, they attempted to relate to one another.

Cultural Tools

To understand evangelicals' rejection of the racialized character of the United States in favor of this individual-level assessment of the race problem, I use the concept of cultural tools. Culture creates ways for people and groups to organize experiences and evaluate reality. It does so by providing a "tool kit" of ideas, interpretations, skills, and habits.[14] For many Americans, including evangelical Christians, religion plays a major role in shaping their cultural tools. Such tools must be generalizable, i.e., usable not just in the situation in which they were first learned but also in new and different situations.[15] For example, certain cultural tools may be learned in a religious context but then used to interpret the race problem.

White American evangelicalism is rooted in an individualized theology. People are saved "one heart at a time," and the Christian life means a personal relationship with Christ. A maturing Christian nurtures this individual relationship with Christ through Bible study and prayer and also through relationships with other maturing Christians. This foundational understanding of the Christian life helps to create three cultural tools: accountable individualism, relationalism (a high valuation of interpersonal relationships), and anti-structuralism (the inability to see or unwillingness to accept social-structural influences).

1. Accountable individualism. Many Americans are individualists to some degree, but evangelicals are *accountable* individualists. They believe they must account for their choices to themselves, to others, and to God. The threads of faith, individual choice, and accountability are tightly interwoven and constitute a singular garment for interpreting life. Human beings are free actors, unfettered by social circumstances, personally responsible for their thoughts and actions. But human nature is fallen, and so individuals are separated from God. God seeks to reconcile them to him through the atoning work of Christ. Apart from this relationship with Christ, human beings will make sinful, destructive choices and are condemned.

2. Relationalism. The fundamental importance of this person-Christ relationship leads evangelicals to place strong emphasis on human relationships also, with family, friends, and other believers. The state of these relationships, whether they are sick or healthy, is of great importance to them.

These cultural tools help to account for the belief we commonly heard expressed in our research, that "we don't have a race problem, we have a *sin* problem." An evangelical man attending a Congregational church, when asked why we have a race problem, said it was "an issue of original sin." A Wesleyan man responded, "It's human nature to be a sinner . . . to not be accepting of a black person." A Baptist woman assessed the root of the race problem as a deficiency of love: "We don't love our neighbors as ourselves. That is the primary commandment of the Bible, to love our neighbor as our self." The human problem is that of an individual's broken relationship with God, and the race problem consists of broken relationships between individuals.

3. Anti-structuralism. Absent from white evangelical accounts of the race problem is the idea that relationships and individual actions might be subject to social-structural influences, such as laws, institutional operating practices, and employment patterns. White evangelicals not only interpret the world in individual and relational terms but also find other types of explanations irrelevant or wrong-headed. This anti-structuralism—the inability

to see or unwillingness to accept explanations not based on individual behavior—is thus a corollary to accountable free-will individualism and relationalism. Although much in Christian scripture and tradition suggests the vital influence of social structures on individuals, the stress on individualism and relationalism is so dominant among white American evangelicals that structure are nearly ignored. To talk about anything beyond individual choice and relationships is interpreted as an attempt by fallen human beings to pass the buck, to wrongly blame something other than the responsible individual.

Many white evangelicals we interviewed expressed frustration with black Americans, especially black Christians, for shifting blame away from individuals. An evangelical woman attending a Nazarene church gave a common response: "[Blacks] will attribute any problem to race where it may not be a racial issue at all. It may be a personal conflict and not have anything to do with race." Even when explicitly asked, white evangelicals found it difficult to see the race problem as anything other than an individual and relational problem.

But I did find a few evangelicals who did not interpret the race problem solely in individual and relational terms. What made the difference?

Racial Homogeneity and Racial Views

In traveling to interview white evangelicals, I was repeatedly struck by the racial homogeneity of their worlds. Their friends, neighborhoods, churches, schools, supermarkets, television shows—all were overwhelmingly white. Many brought this up in the interviews; they told me they were insulated from racial diversity and racial issues.

Such homogeneity has important implications. These evangelicals do not experience cross-racial issues directly, and so they think such issues simply cannot be much of a problem. The problems of which others speak must be a matter of minorities' being unable to let go of the past, or trying to shift blame elsewhere, or being tricked into misinterpretation by self-serving others. The view that race is essentially a problem of poor individual relationships or involves only a few bigots is reinforced by nearly every part of white evangelicals' experience and social contacts.

But less isolated white evangelicals interpret the world quite differently. When asked if there is a race problem in this country, they were likely to suggest that the answer was quite obvious—so obvious that what I asked was not really a question. (This was a common response among the African-Americans I interviewed as well.) According to "contact theory," contact not meeting specific conditions (such as equal status among those in contact) can lead to greater conflict and prejudice. This was evidenced by responses from relatively non-isolated people. Jane, a Lutheran woman, lives in a Midwestern town of about 25,000 that, while formerly all-white, had recently become about one-third non-white. When I asked her whether there was a race problem, she had this to say:

> It's hard in this neck of the woods because we've never really been exposed to it. Even as Christians we say, "Well, I don't have a problem with that." But all of a sudden, when your town is about a third other cultural groups, you find out that it's a little bit harder to mix than you thought it was. It seems our crime has increased, and I can't help but think it is because of the new arrivals. The people from the different cultures clash, and I can feel the tension in this town. We are like clashing groups. Yes, we have a serious race problem.

Jane still uses her cultural tools, but she modifies them and applies them differently than most white evangelicals. Though she interprets what she is seeing with her individualist and relational cultural tools, she does not limit her interpretations to those levels, nor does she believe the race problem has been artificially created or overblown. For her it is now quite real.

Those few white evangelicals who had had extensive interracial contact modified their cultural tools even more, and came to different interpretations of the race problem and its severity. Carol is one example. She grew up in a typically racially isolated milieu, but her life changed dramatically when she married an African-American man. Now she lives and works in an all-black community in a large city, and her social relationships are almost wholly with black Americans. When asked if our country has a race problem, she answered, "Oh yeah . . . it really is scary." I asked if she was adjusting to living in a black neighborhood, and she replied:

> I'm adjusting to it. I think my daughter finds it hard because she's mixed. They call her cracker. Crackers are white. They call her Puerto Rican because she doesn't look like she's totally black, you know, and people resent her. But I do think that I'm probably better off in a black neighborhood. I'm more openly accepted than if my husband were to move in an all-white neighborhood. I think there'd be hell to pay there.

For white evangelicals like Carol, the race problem is something beyond individuals and bad relationships. It involves these, to be sure, but as Carol suggests, it also involves group issues, such as where mixed-marriage couples can live and the experience of being a racially mixed child.

What Causes Racial Inequality?

Recall that a racialized society is one wherein race matters profoundly for life experiences, life opportunities, and social relationships. It is characterized by unequal access to and possession of society's goods and status markers. But nearly all white evangelicals made no reference to material inequality in their explanations of the race problem. Because inequality is so fundamental to what race means in the United States, and because it was not part of white evangelicals' definitions of the race problem, I sought to understand how evangelicals explained inequality between blacks and whites.

First, I examined data from a national telephone survey.[16] After pointing out that "on average blacks have worse jobs, income, and housing than white people," the researchers asked:

Do you think these differences are

1. because most blacks have less inborn ability to learn?

2. because most blacks just don't have the motivation or willpower to pull themselves up out of poverty?

3. because most blacks don't have the chance for education that it takes to rise out of poverty?

4. mainly due to discrimination?

For each of these four options, the interviewee could say yes or no.

These options fall into important categories for our study. The first explanation—that blacks and whites are inherently unequal—does not fit evangelicals' belief that all human beings are created equal and all are equal in Christ. The second explanation—lack of motivation or willpower—attributes the responsibility for inequality to blacks and what they do or do not do. This option aligns well with the cultural tools of white evangelicals, especially accountable free-will individualism. The latter two explanations are structural: they say there is something about the way society is arranged that produces unequal outcomes. They therefore do not align well with white evangelicals' cultural tools.

If white evangelicals' understandings of race stem from their theologically driven cultural tools, we can make some clear predictions and then test them with comparable data from a random sample of Americans. Compared to other white Americans, white evangelicals: should not be more likely to say that blacks are biologically inferior; should be more likely to support the individual-level explanation of lack of motivation; and should be less likely to support the structural explanations. Furthermore, if I am correct in suspecting that the theological tools and social contexts of white and black evangelicals drive them in opposite directions in their explanations, then the individualist-structuralist gap ought to be greater between white evangelicals and black evangelicals than between whites and blacks in general.

To test these predictions, I first had to pin down the term *evangelical*. I combined self-identified fundamentalists and evangelicals into a category called "conservative Protestants." Conservative Protestants gave their religious identity as evangelical or fundamentalist and said they believe in the afterlife and believe that the Bible is the literal or inspired word of God. Here are some of my findings:

■ If conservative Protestants are more individually prejudiced than other whites, they ought to be more likely to say there is inequality because blacks *lack the inborn ability to achieve*. This is not the case. Ten percent of each group agrees with this explanation. And for both, this is easily the least chosen explanation.

■ Are white conservative Protestants more likely to explain black-white inequality in individual terms, and less likely to explain it in structural terms, than other whites? Yes. They are more than twice as likely to cite *lack of motivation* as to cite *discrimination* as the reason for inequality—a gap of 33 percentage points for white evangelicals versus 15 percentage points for other whites. And compared with other whites, they are six times as likely to cite *lack of motivation* as to cite *unequal access to education*—a gap of 30 percentage points versus 5 percentage points. These large gaps in explanations between conservative Protestants and other whites remain even when we control for other factors, such as educational level and overall prejudice.[17] What is more, the individualist-structuralist explanation gap is even larger when conservative Protestants are compared with theologically liberal white Protestants.

■ How do white conservative Protestants compare to black conservative Protestants, and how does the gap between these two groups compare to that between other whites and blacks? The data suggest that conservative Christians are divided by race. The gap between other white and other black Americans who cite *lack of motivation* by blacks as a reason for black inequality is 9 percentage points (51 percent of other whites, 42 percent of other blacks), but that gap more than triples to 31 percentage points for conservative Protestants (62 percent of whites, 31 percent of blacks). We find similar discrepancies when examining the structural explanations. With the percentages citing *unequal access to education* as a reason for inequality, the gap between other whites and other blacks gap is 7 percentage points (46 percent of whites, 53 percent of blacks), but between white and black conservative Protestants it is 22 (32 percent of whites, 54 percent of blacks). For the *discrimination* explanation, the "other" white-black gap is 27 percentage points (36 percent of whites, 63 percent of blacks); that swells to 45 for conservative Protestants (27 percent of whites, 72 percent of blacks). In short, blacks and whites holding an evangelical faith are considerably more divided in their explanations of why we have racial inequality than are non-evangelical blacks and whites.

These large gaps shrink considerably when we consider less racially isolated white evangelicals (always a small percentage). The longer and more complete the contact with African-Americans, the less likely the respondents are to give primacy to individual-level explanations of racial inequality, and the more likely they are to choose to structural-level explanations.

These findings are evidence that theologically rooted cultural tools within the context of racial isolation are driving the explanations for inequality given by conservative Protestants. They are also part of the explanation for why isolated white evangelicals, unlike black evangelicals, did not discuss inequality unless asked. In short, in regard to the perception of race and racial inequality, conservative religion, when practiced in racially homogeneous social contexts, appears to intensify the different values and experiences of each racial group, sharpening the racial divide.

Christian Solutions to the Race Problem

Having asked evangelicals about the race problem and racial inequality, I then went on to ask what they saw as Christian solutions to the problems of race relations. Given that white evangelicals did not cite racial inequality or systematic, institutional injustice as part of the race problem, I did not expect them to address these as part of the Christian answer. And they rarely did.

Hal, a forty-something white evangelical living in a nearly all-white suburb of a large southern city, gave an explanation that is representative of what I often heard. As people become Christians, he said, the race problem disappears. "How so?" I asked.

> There's a top-down approach. At the top is our personal experience of love and forgiveness. Then we combine that with Jesus' commands to love God with all your heart, soul, and mind, and love your neighbor as yourself. So, as we experience His love and forgiveness firsthand, we respond back to Him in praise and thankfulness, allowing his love and respect for us to flow. That love and respect then overflows into our love and respect for our neighbors. When that outpouring is experienced at a personal level and applied to others, then that's of great benefit, and it is the great problem solver. It's at a one-on-one, friendship level. As a Christian, if it circumvents the personal level, then it's missed the mark, the Christian mark.

Every major component of what white evangelicals said were the Christian solutions to the race problem is present in Hal's response. Hal uses what other scholars have called the "miracle motif."[18] The miracle motif is the theologically rooted understanding that as more and more people become Christians, problems—whether individual or social—are automatically solved. The answer to any problem—whether crime, divorce, drug use, corporate price gouging, or racial profiling—is for large numbers of people to become Christians. As a nondenominational woman from Illinois expressed it, "Christianity has the answers to everything if individuals become Christians."

Derived in part from the cultural tools of accountable free-will individual-ism and relationalism, the miracle motif holds that society is improved by the improving of individuals, one at a time. Hal calls this the top-down approach, but most would call it the bottom-up or grass-roots approach. At least for race relations, the miracle motif is rooted in the Christian building block of univer-salism.[19] This principle is encapsulated in Galatians 3:28, that in Christ there is no distinction between Jew and Greek, slave and free, male and female. All are one in Christ Jesus. All are equal.

The principle of universalism underlies Hal's solution to race problems. It helps us understand why he and most other white evangelicals believe that the race problem dissipates as more people become Christians. Hal told me that as people become Christians, they are overwhelmed by the forgive-ness, acceptance, love, and respect given to them by God, and this over-flows to others. Thus, given the cultural tools of white evangelicals, the principle of universalism with its emphasis on equality before God helps us see why the miracle motif is a logical and commonly cited solution to social problems.

But the cultural tools also shape how universalism is interpreted and ap-plied. Equality before Christ does not mean working for fair access to equally good schooling, fighting unjust laws, or other structural approaches. Rather, universalism is applied interpersonally, in the one-on-one relationships Hal says are *the* marks of a Christian solution. Anything else is superficial and non-Christian. According to one Assemblies of God man, the main reason for the persistence of race problems is that "we are dealing with it up here [holding his hand above his head] on the superficial level with programs and laws. It's only with Christianity that you can change people's hearts."

These views of course have implications for what people will support and act upon to combat racism. To examine this, I turned to a random, nationally representative survey of Americans that my colleagues and I conducted, the 1996 Pew Survey of Religious Identity and Influence. We asked the following: "[Christians/people] disagree about the best way to work against racism. For each of the following possible ways, please tell me if you think it's a very important way that [Christians/people] should work against racism." Four ac-tions were offered:

1. Try to get to know people of another race.
2. Work against discrimination in the job market and legal system.
3. Work to racially integrate congregations.
4. Work to racially integrate residential neighborhoods.

Knowing what I did about white evangelicals' cultural tools, I expected that support for these racism-reducing alternatives would decline as we moved from action *one* to action *four*. Clearly, *one* captures the personal-influence strategy, and is consistent with individualism, relationalism, and anti-structuralism. Action *two* should also garner much support, because the wording of the question invokes the equality and freedom-of-opportunity aspects of universalism so important to evangelicals, and because it clearly resonates with the American values of equality, fairness, and opportunity. The least support should be given to *four*, integrating neighborhoods, because this solution is structural; it suggests reorganizing the very structure of metropolitan America, moving people as groups rather than individuals, perhaps against their will.

The *third* action, integrating congregations, has some elements that resonate with evangelicals' cultural tools and some that do not. On the one hand, congregations represent a more micro-level, relational institution than neighborhoods, and integrating them suggests a greater degree of voluntarism than does residential integration. On the other hand, integrating congregations connotes structural change, moving groups rather than individuals. Action *three*, then, should garner less support than *one* and *two*, but more than *four*.

I define *evangelicals* as Kellstedt and Smidt do in their extensive work in this area.[20] Evangelicals are those who say they are evangelical and display the doctrinal hallmarks: they claim Christ as their Savior and Lord, say Jesus is the only way to salvation, view the Bible as true in all ways, and actively evangelize or give money for evangelizing. Based on these measures, I classified strength of evangelical identity as follows: (1) "not evangelical"—those who did not assent to any of the doctrinal hallmarks and did not call themselves evangelical; (2) "strong evangelical"—those who assented to all the hallmarks and said their main or only religious identity was evangelical; and (3) "moderate evangelical"—all others.

For "strong evangelicals," the survey confirms my expectations about the ordering of support for the solutions to racism. Nine out of 10 *white* strong evangelicals say that getting to know people of another race is a very important way to deal with racism; about 8 in 10 say working against discrimination in jobs or courts is very important; slightly fewer than 6 in 10 say racially integrating congregations is very important; and fewer than 4 in 10 say racially integrating neighborhoods is very important. White strong evangelicals, then, are 2⅓ times as likely to choose getting to know people of another race as to choose integrating neighborhoods as the solution to racism.

How does this compare with the views of *black* strong evangelicals? For the option that best resonates with evangelical cultural tools—getting to know people of another race—there is no difference between whites and blacks. For the next closest match—fairness in jobs and the legal system—black strong evangelicals are somewhat more supportive than white strong evangelicals (93 percent compared to 83 percent). For the two remaining options, which have more structural elements, the gap between white and black strong evangelicals grows. Nearly 90 percent of black strong evangelicals support integrating congregations as a very important way to address racism, compared with 58 percent of white strong evangelicals. And 64 percent of black strong evangelicals support integrating neighborhoods, compared with just 38 percent of white.

Just as we found when examining explanations for racial inequality, the racial division concerning solutions to race problems is greater among strong evangelicals than among others. Indeed, between black and white *non*-evangelicals there are no significant differences in this area. Again, faith, via theologically rooted cultural tools and in the context of racial isolation, works to divide black and white evangelical Christians. Given the strong support and belief in the miracle motif—i.e., that as people become Christians, social problems dissipate—this finding is ironical. The very opposite appears to occur.

Overcoming Racialization?

At the beginning of this essay, I mentioned that evangelicals have recently begun to address racial division and strife with characteristic vigor. But I shall now argue that their perspectives and activity actually buttress the racialized society.

For most white evangelicals, though there are some prejudiced individuals and broken relationships, America is not racialized. Their cultural tools of individualism, relationalism, and anti-structuralism made it hard for them to conceive of the problem in any other way. Any person, group, or program that challenges their perspective comes to be seen as part of the race problem.

Racial inequality is substantial and widespread, and is a powerful shaper of life experiences, life chances, and the ability to maximize children's life chances; yet evangelicals do not see it as part of the race problem. In their assessment, the plight of black and other minorities is largely of their own making: members of these groups lack the vision of what can be, fail to see the opportunities available to them, lack motivation and willpower, and engage in such unwise practices as having children out of wedlock.

What these white evangelicals see as the Christian solution to the race problem has almost nothing to do with addressing the core of racialization. Instead, they focus on improving individuals and relationships. Specifically, they often say that the solution lies in conversion to Christianity. And nearly all evangelicals support making a friend across racial lines.

White evangelicals make these assessments with the best of intentions. They desire a "colorblind" society, and often oppose color-conscious actions for that reason. Their cultural tools and their racial isolation curtail their ability to perceive why people of different races do not get along, the lack of equal opportunity, and the extent to which race matters in the United States. And although their intentions are good, their perspective is a powerful means of reinforcing racialization. Because reality is socially constructed—that is, created by people's beliefs and actions—a most effective way to maintain a racialized society is simply to deny its existence. Just as alcoholism cannot be overcome until the drinker first recognizes that she or he is an alcoholic, so the necessary first step in overcoming the devastating racialized character of America is to recognize it.

Failing to recognize the racialized character of the United States, white evangelicals do nothing to diminish it, and can act in ways that buttress it. They may resist attempts at corrective action, perhaps by black Christians, viewing it as misguided. Why check me into an alcohol treatment center if I am not an alcoholic? Overcoming racialization depends in part on social programs and policies, and evangelicals' opposition to such programs and policies can heighten racialization.

Research suggests, on the positive side, that those whites who use individualistic explanations to account for racial inequality are more receptive to helping black Americans whom they perceive to be trying hard.[21] But they are also more likely to oppose government assistance tailored to blacks.[22] According to Martin Gilens, the factors that most strongly predict opposition to aid to the poor are, in increasing order of importance, (1) blaming blacks for racial inequality, (2) an individualistic perspective, and (3) blaming the poor for their poverty.[23] These are the very factors white evangelicals offer and operate from to explain why we have racial inequality.

By missing the vast disparities in environments in which people are raised, or dismissing them as unimportant, white evangelicals fail to see that the correlation between individual initiative and outcome is far from exact. Because of structural differences in our society, it takes far more effort by blacks to succeed. Given the positive environments most whites experience—with such elements as good schools, neighborhoods where poverty is low and the expectation of opportunity and success is high, and substantially more access to wealth and connections within their social networks—it takes far less effort by whites to succeed.

Cornel West writes that those with an individualistic perspective "rarely, if ever, examine the innumerable cases in which black people do act on the Protestant ethic and still remain at the bottom of the social ladder."[24] They fail to notice "the incessant assaults on black intelligence, beauty, character, and possibility."[25]

West says that a serious discussion of race in America "must begin not with the problems of black people, but with the flaws of American society—flaws rooted in historic inequalities and longstanding cultural stereotypes"; we must "acknowledge that structures and behavior are inseparable, that institutions and values go hand in hand."[26] But white evangelicals do not acknowledge this. Their solutions have to do with changing individuals, and establishing cross-race friendships. By themselves, these solutions, however desirable, do not and cannot work. If a building is collapsing because of a faulty design, merely improving the quality of the bricks or cementing a few more tightly together will not save it.

Consider the understanding that race problems will disappear as people convert to Christianity. As we have seen, ironically it is the converted who are most divided on issues of race. This is due, not to a lack of power of the Christian faith, but to the cultural constructions of that faith in the context of racial isolation. Faith is linked to social and cultural contexts, and if these contexts are divided—as they are, given the racialized character of the United States—then applications of that faith to racial problems will also be divided.

Or consider the solution of making friends across racial lines: research fails to support the assumption that this alleviates racial problems. In fact, white Americans often use such limited friendships as a license to be even more confident in their assessments of the minimal and individualized character of race problems.[27] But even if making friends across racial divides were the answer, the massive extent of segregation and racial inequality characteristic of the American racialized society continually works against the successful formation of friendships, and precludes the possibility that enough people will ever form enough friendships to make a real difference. Friendships are formed primarily under two conditions: similarity and proximity. Those two conditions are much more unlikely with structures of inequality and segregation than under conditions of equality and integration.

White evangelical solutions are laudable for bringing to the discussion components often missing from public discussion, moral and spiritual aspects such as personal responsibility, repentance, and forgiveness. But they fail to address major issues of racialization. They do not address structural disparities in such areas as employment opportunities, health care, treatment by police and courts, housing availability, mortgages, educational opportunities, political power, and environmental protection.

Concluding Observations

I have painted a rather dismal portrait of the realities and prospects for positive race relations among American Christians. It is not the picture I had hoped to paint, but it is the one true to the evidence. Although in recent years white evangelicals have devoted considerable time and energy to addressing problems of racial division, their efforts, I fear, do more to perpetuate the racialized society than to reduce it.

Shortly after the release of the book I mentioned at the beginning (*Divided by Faith*), *Christianity Today*, the flagship magazine of (white) evangelicalism, devoted a special section to its conclusions.[28] In a letter of reply printed in a subsequent issue, an evangelical woman in Missouri unintentionally reinforced those conclusions:

I really believe that the black community needs to take it upon itself to improve its own conditions. If this makes me racist and means I'm hindering the healing, so be it. . . . There comes a time in the life of well-meaning individual whites when we realize that whatever we do for the blacks, it really is not our problem and we cannot solve it. Therefore, the best and healthiest thing for us to do is to mind our own business. For myself, my business includes being friend and sister to the blacks I meet.[29]

Her response, representative of the views of many white evangelicals, suggests that merely pointing out the limits of their understandings about racial issues will not be enough to change their perspectives. And it shouldn't be, given that those perspectives are rooted in the very faith they hold so dear. To address racial division within the American church, much work lies ahead for evangelical leaders and the people in the pews. Perhaps they will find that the Bible has something to say that goes beyond individualism.

CHAPTER TWELVE

Creating a Diverse
Urban Evangelicalism:
Youth Ministry as a Model

Rhys H. Williams and *R. Stephen Warner*

Two propositions are so well accepted in our society that they seem to qualify as "facts." First is the idea that young people today face a huge number of social problems—substance abuse, sexually transmitted diseases, crime and violence in society and in schools, uncertain economic futures, and others—that make growing into a healthy adulthood a challenge. The second is that religiousness is positively correlated with desirable behaviors and attitudes such as achieving success at school, and negatively correlated with undesirable behaviors such as substance abuse and suicide attempts. Much recent research on religion and adolescent well-being seems to show this.[1] These correlations withstand controls for self-rated educational ability, gender, and household type; they also seem to apply across ethnic groups and religious traditions.

These two facts lead many parents to be particularly concerned with the religious upbringing of their children. And in addition to the social benefits of religious involvement, many parents believe their religion holds truths that are important to their children's salvation. Furthermore, people from many religious traditions also feel a "calling" to spread their faith to others as part of

Rhys H. Williams is associate professor of sociology at the University of Cincinnati. His research has centered on the involvement of religious groups in American politics. He is the editor of *Promise Keepers and the New Masculinity* (2001) and of *Cultural Wars in American Politics* (1997). **R. Stephen Warner** is professor of sociology at the University of Illinois, Chicago. He is the author of *New Wine in Old Wineskins: Evangelicals and Liberals in a Small Town Church* (1988) and co-editor (with Judith G. Wittner) of *Gatherings in Diaspora: Religious Communities and the New Immigration* (1998).

their religious duty. They are likely to believe that spreading their faith in this way will help to ameliorate wider social problems.

In this essay we are focusing on evangelical Protestants, and we will report on some research concerned with youth programs in evangelical churches. We will look at how these programs reach out to young people, trying to encourage in them the growth of healthy religious and social identities and to prepare them to play a positive role in society.

Evangelical Protestant parents may feel that passing on their religious tradition is a particular challenge. They often represent "conservative" religious traditions in a society known for its liberalness. Evangelicals often infuse the whole world with religious significance but live in a culture that has come to compartmentalize religion. Many therefore regard themselves and their religious commitments as "embattled."[2] And of course their children, like other American young people, are likely to go through a period of adolescent rebellion; with or without secular influences from the wider culture, they may resist parents' attempts to mold their lives.

Young people express their religion and their spirituality in varying ways, often in non-organizational settings. Particularly if they leave home for college or a first job, they may stay away from religious organizations, claiming that "you don't need a church to be a good Christian" or that they find spiritual nourishment in nature, or with friends, or in other non-church settings. Nonetheless, churches and parachurches are particularly significant sites for developing and passing on religious commitments, and are often key to the social benefits religion has for youth. The networks young adults develop in these settings are likely to provide role models, self-esteem, emotional support, even material support. True, many other types of associational activities do this, not just church-related ones. But all associations have a particular content, and religious organizations give this content a specific moral character. They can link that moral content to a community and its past, present, and future. Both explicitly and implicitly, they offer a vision of how a moral person should live in the world.

In our research we are asking organizational-level questions in part because organizations are so central to the formation of individual, group, and social identity. We live in an organizational society, and we are shaped by institutions in many ways, some of which we can only dimly perceive. If we as a society are to have informed, engaged, and compassionate citizens, we must have institutions that foster those qualities.

By looking at the involvement of young people in organizations, we are looking at the development of "collective identity" as much as individual identity. Collective identity gives shape and content to the "we" with whom we identify and the "they" from whom we distinguish ourselves. Such distinctions take place through "boundary markers" that are likely to be embodied in the organizations with which we associate. Religion often plays a role in establishing those boundaries. The boundaries it encourages can be discriminatory and narrowly sectarian. However, religion can also provide leverage for negotiating and transcending boundaries: when the "we" is securely held, a potential universalism can encompass the "they." Identities and boundaries are of course being actively negotiated in late adolescence. The intersection between young adults and their religious organizations is therefore a particularly useful site for exploring questions of both individual identity and institutional and societal health.

In sum, we are looking at two areas: (1) how religious organizations and institutions (which we will generically call "churches") are reaching out to young people, attracting them to church programs and keeping them involved in the institution; and (2) what types of individual and collective identities these programs are fostering, and how those identities are oriented to society and public life. In this essay we will focus on evangelical Protestant churches.

The Data

We will draw upon data gathered in the Chicago area by the Youth and Religion Project, which we co-direct. We have divided youth who are involved with religious organizations into two categories: (1) "emancipated" young people, organizationally involved in what we call "young adult ministries," and (2) young people still living with their families and involved in what we call "family ministries." These categories are neither mutually exclusive nor exhaustive. We have also studied ministries in which many of the high-school-age participants are not attending the same church as their parents; their parents either do not attend church at all or attend a different church, often in a different faith tradition. This latter group includes some of the young people we are most interested in. They are often from poorer neighborhoods and are more at risk from aspects of life "on the street." In organizational terms they are more like emancipated youth in that they are making autonomous decisions about religious involvement, but they are not living separately from their families.[3]

We recognize that we have been in touch with the young people most connected to their religion and to religious communities, and we make no assumptions about young people generally, especially about those who have shed their religion. We assume, in fact, that a religious identity is important to the young people with whom we are concerned. Our data come from a variety of sources: individual in-depth interviews; focus group interviews; site visits to religious organizations for worship services, lectures, and classes; and analysis of literature and periodicals available at our investigative sites. We have also interviewed adult religious leaders of young adult, youth, and family ministries. We have not done in-depth interviews with anyone under 18 (although informal conversations at a youth group meeting often appear in our field notes). Finally, we have done "family ethnographies" in which we spend a day with a family, observing and participating in their religious practices, whether at church or at home, and asking parents and children what their religious activities mean to them.

ASPECTS OF VIBRANT YOUTH MINISTRIES

The Youth and Religion Project has been visiting and gathering data from Christian (Protestant and Catholic), Hindu, and Muslim youth groups that work with white, black, Latino, Asian, South Asian, and Arab youth. The data presented here are from the evangelical Protestant groups we have observed, in particular those that minister primarily to Latino and to white, non-Hispanic youth. Several of our sites are African-American churches that could be classified as "evangelical"; however, as those who are familiar with the black church will recognize, we find a much different dynamic among black churches and black youth than among the other groups.

We will report here particularly on several programs that operate in Chicago with a very "urban" constituency. Some are in churches that serve working-class neighborhoods, often in ethnically diverse neighborhoods. Most of these programs have an "edge" to them, in part attributable to the sense of danger—both potential and manifest—that exists outside the church walls. We are also looking at a few suburban evangelical youth ministries, but our focus in this essay is on urban ones.

We have come to a number of conclusions about the youth programs we have studied, all of which we judge to be successful in attracting and keeping youth. Since we have not studied unsuccessful programs, we cannot say for certain that the aspects we have identified "cause" success. We are just describing some similarities we have seen among vibrant, active programs. We are interested in how these elements of youth programs affect their capacity to help young people develop healthy personal identities and public selves.

Autonomous Space and a Culture of Responsibility

First, the youth programs we have observed provide autonomous space for young people and their peer groups, while at the same time they foster a culture of personal responsibility. As Tocqueville noted about religious congregations in the nineteenth century, they can function as "mini-democracies," giving people practice in governing themselves, engaging in social actions that require cooperation, and taking responsibility for making decisions and performing tasks. Most of the groups we have seen have their own space in the church building, their own meeting times, and their own adult leaders. These leaders are generally younger that the overall church leadership, and many of them are part-time, volunteer, or seminarians. Thus, while the youth are supervised, often reasonably tightly, the monitoring comes from people who are a bit more like peers than parents, and are thus perceived by the kids as having some experiences in common with them. The leaders are usually male, and are young enough that occasionally girls in the group develop crushes. But an age gap is necessary; the acceptable range seems to be from a six-year to a twenty-year age difference.

The autonomous space provides a setting for what is often intensely personal disclosure, made with a great deal of candor. In periods of testifying, young adults may reveal pasts with drug use, sexual activity, harrowing encounters with gangs or crime, intensely painful relationships with parents. The response to these revelations that we have observed combines support with an emphasis on the need to "get right with God" and act in a morally responsible manner.

A program that is particularly popular now is called "True Love Waits," in which young people pledge sexual abstinence until marriage. One room we visited had dozens of signed "true love waits" pledge cards plastered to the walls, in the shape of a fish and a cross. While this is a very traditional kind of sexual morality in that it emphasizes a complete ban on non-marital sex (and in several cases seems more directed at females than at males), for modern young people particularly threatened by sexually transmitted diseases and teenage pregnancy, that message offers an important form of liberating support.[4]

One area in which the African-American churches we have studied are distinctly different from the white and Latino ones is that the autonomous youth ministry is not practiced in the same way. We have concluded that in the black church, religion is inherently intergenerational. We went to "youth nights" at several black churches, and found them all attended by as many adults as young people. Youth may be on stage—in essence performing for their elders in a way that shows they have learned their religious lessons well. But remarkably little that they do in the church is free from substantial adult involvement. When we asked adults about their attendance at "youth night," they invariably responded that they needed to be there to "support our young people." Along with this support, we note, there is a monitoring function. But it makes a certain amount of sense. In a community where growing up is a risky business, lack of supervision and monitoring can be dangerous, even deadly, and African-Americans may well feel that they do not want the church to serve as another autonomous space for youth.

Safe Havens and Positive Alternatives

Youth ministries provide safe spaces for young people who are often facing very real risks in the wider society. Adult leaders of the groups we observed could often name off very quickly the young people who had brothers in gangs, or who had family members with drug or alcohol problems. Part of the way religious involvement protects kids from risk is by inculcating values and ideals that urge them away from substance abuse, crime, and other risky behavior. But more important, in our view, is the creation of an "alternative community" for young people who see a lot of problematic or self-destructive behavior in other parts of their lives. It is crucially important that they have contact with groups of people who do not engage in such behavior. Wesley Perkins's research with college students shows that the single biggest contributor to students' refraining from binge drinking is the realization that *not* "everybody does it."[5] Knowing that particular behaviors are not mandatory for social acceptance seems to be pivotally important to young people, given the centrality of peer groups.

Urban youth ministries also help relieve some of the turf pressures that are part of life in a multi-ethnic urban environment. This is in part a "gang" issue, and we have reports of religious involvement helping kids resist gang recruitment. But even for those not involved with formal gangs, there are pressures of solidarity that go with neighborhood and ethnic identity. Several of the programs we studied had participants from several different neighborhoods and from a variety of ethnic groups. The kids crossed neighborhood lines to attend the group, and found there a way to transcend the turf-based divisions outside.

Moral Boundaries and Social Diversity

Many of the programs we have observed offer, as a formal ideology, a conservative theology of biblical literalism and traditional morality (often focused on abstinence from "sins of the flesh"). From one perspective, conservative theology might well be the reason for their success. In a version of economic reasoning, many scholars maintain that people value most that which is costliest.[6] Therefore, they argue, strict moral controls on behavior, which are more demanding, will be more valued.

But a simple economic metaphor does not capture the variety of things going on in these programs. Young people we saw do indeed seem to be responding enthusiastically to conservative theology. One reason for this may be that in a period of intense growth and personal exploration, adolescents actually want some limits and constraints. This may be particularly true for those whose families do not offer much supervision. Furthermore, young people are often attracted to something that seems new, different, or alternative, even if it is in fact a more "traditional" behavioral code. And of course some young people may be attracted only by the social scene of the youth programs and may put up with the conservative theology and morality as "the price of admission."

However, while these youth ministries may be ideologically conservative, socially they are generally liberal. The social divisions that have historically marked white evangelical Protestantism are notably absent. The programs we observed are informal in dress and demeanor, stress a certain amount of egalitarianism among congregants and between laity and leaders (often making the point that God is "no respecter of persons," a phrase from Romans 1), and are generally comfortable with such aspects of contemporary culture as youth music. The programs we observed were full of teenagers with baggy hip-hop clothing styles, multiple body piercings, tattoos, heavy jewelry, and so on.

We were most struck by this pattern of social inclusion and diversity at youth programs that had as their base a Latino population. They may have Hispanics, Anglos, and African-Americans all in one ministry, but it is more common to have African-American and Latino, or Anglo-American and Latino, than to have black and white. (This type of integration seemed more common among Puerto Rican populations than among other Latino groups, perhaps because Puerto Rican culture is more racially mixed historically, or because Puerto Rico has been more Protestant than Mexico or much of Central America. Or it may just be a feature of Chicago, where there are so many Mexicans and Mexican-Americans that they can have their own churches and need not intermingle with other groups.) While we saw some African-Americans in white churches, and some Euro-Americans in black churches (though this was less common), the truly integrated programs were Latino based.[7]

Given Chicago's residential patterns, such mixing means that these young people probably were crossing neighborhood boundaries, as well as ethnic divisions, in order to participate in the same church. The music they play tends to reflect that diversity, featuring a variety of styles as long as they are up-to-date and funky. The music also reflects the gospel, although with our middle-aged ears we often found it hard to pick up the words that do that. We had no trouble discerning that the music had a beat that makes kids want to move and dance.

Several of the adult leaders we spoke to did not make much of this ethnic integration, saying that the young people tend to be "blended" before arriving at the church by growing up in diverse neighborhoods. We noted, however, that these ethnically integrated youth programs were not always connected to ethnically integrated churches. A leader of perhaps the most diverse group we observed believed that most of the kids in her program came to the church on their own, not as members of church families; but another leader thought most of the kids were indeed from church families. Whatever the actual ratio, the important point for us was that the youth program was reaching out to the neighborhood and beyond, and attracting a variety of people.

Sacralizing the Secular

While there is a debate among many evangelical Protestants about whether certain forms of contemporary culture (such as rap), even when their words express Christian thoughts, can truly be considered "Christian," there does not appear to be this kind of cultural conservatism in the programs we have studied. Culture and religion appear to be separable; the medium is not necessarily the message. The youth programs applied this conceptual separation to forms of urban culture that are often considered representative of the very threats the involved young people are trying to escape.

Of course, the leaders of these groups in one sense "use" popular cultural forms to attract kids to their programs. This is neither surprising nor new; evangelicals have been adapting popular culture to their own ends at least since the 1740s. We have heard youth pastors discuss among themselves the dangers of relying too heavily on "entertainment" to draw youth in. One leader said he had never known a church-sponsored basketball tournament to be successful as a spiritual exercise; winning or losing, not the Christian message, he said, becomes the thing that sticks with the young people. Another warned that "entertainment-oriented youth ministries" tend to have two outcomes: (1) there is high turnover—the group you have this year will not be the one you had last year; and (2) the kids will fall apart when they go off to college because they haven't been properly "discipled." There is no staying power in entertainment-oriented youth programs, say these leaders.

Nonetheless, the programs we observed did not shy away from contemporary cultural forms, provided they were imbued with the right content. In fact, the concept of mission that animates these urban evangelical programs understands its purpose in part as transforming—or at least reforming—secular culture. These programs work at "domesticating" urban youth culture so it becomes an ally in their work rather than a threat. In the end, part of their work is "sacralizing" the secular world. They are trying to create a "counterculture" to what they perceive as a culture that stresses hedonism, instant gratification, personal license, and secularism, and they adapt elements of that culture to serve their ends. This is a version of the Apostle Paul's strategy of becoming "all things to all men, that I might by all means save some" (1 Cor. 9:22). This form of outreach allows unchurched or disaffected youth to come to faith and a new lifestyle gradually. And it makes going to the youth group "cool," a necessary factor in creating the peer-group culture for a vibrant gathering.

Rather than shunning the city as a site of corruption and moral decay, the churches we have observed deliberately choose it as a place for mission, a place to reform, a society in need. They are not merely "stuck" in the city, unable to respond to demographic changes. Many of the adult leaders we have encountered have a seminary background with a specific focus on urban ministry. They are not just trying to save individual kids; they also have a wider agenda. These Chicago-area youth leaders meet regularly in an ethnoracially diverse group they call "Urban and Youth Pastors" (UYP). Help from denominational agencies is often viewed warily, as many denominations are perceived as too rural, small-town, or suburban to have much to say to urban youth ministers (one respondent dismissed some denominational literature on youth ministry as something that "may work in Iowa, but not in the city."). Similarly, programs by suburban evangelical churches may be assessed insufficiently sensitive to urban culture.

The political sympathies of the people who run these programs seem to be quite mixed. They are generally conservative, particularly on issues of personal morality. However, they certainly do not worship the free market, and they have an almost "countercultural" critique of the materialistic ethos of American society. The "urban evangelicalism" they are creating is not something that would be easily recognized by ideologues on either side of our society's so-called culture wars.

CREATING A DIVERSE URBAN EVANGELICALISM

The social diversity was perhaps the most striking aspect of the urban evangelical youth programs we observed. This type of diversity is not found in most mainline Protestant or Catholic youth programs, and we had to wonder how these evangelical ministries managed it. We offer here a tentative two-part answer, one part related to the dynamics of theology and outreach, the other to our understanding of the sociological dimensions of symbolic boundaries and collective identities.

First, ideology matters, and these youth ministries take the shape they do in part as an expression of theology. Evangelical Protestantism has a theology with elements of universal perfectionism. No human being lies beyond the power of redemption. And the power of true faith can transcend the divisions among people, creating a new person that—in the Apostle Paul's words—is neither Jew nor Gentile, male nor female. Evangelicals are called to bring their faith to all populations, regardless of their social status, their societal location, their cultural differences.

This missionary mentality is facilitated by structure. Evangelical Protestantism has never been organized either ethnically or geographically in the same way that Catholicism has. Its organizational form is the congregation rather than the parish, and this has made it adaptable, mobile, and potentially available to a variety of people and purposes.

Sociologically, however, we know that crossing emotionally laden and socially significant boundaries is a difficult process. Divisions of race, ethnicity, and neighborhood can be daunting to even the best-intentioned attempts to bring people together. And historically, U.S. evangelical Protestantism was often not hospitable to social diversity. We speculate, consistent with much recent theorizing about the importance of symbolic boundaries for ordering social life,[8] that one way to facilitate the crossing of such significant boundaries is to offer another boundary—perhaps equally emotionally laden—as a rival organizing scheme. Perhaps these urban ministries are offering just such a replacement boundary in their rigorous codes of personal morality. Moral rigor separates people into good/bad, saved/unsaved, righteous/fallen. This may offer a set of emotionally satisfying distinctions that can replace ethnoracial divisions as a collective identity, a way for people to identify "we" and "they."

For instance, young people in these groups may learn that being Latino or Anglo is a less important distinguishing feature than practicing sexual chastity or abstaining from alcohol. This kind of reordering of the social world allows youth to cross ethnic or neighborhood lines, and to forsake old ways of thinking (as well as old social networks) that held potential peril for them. With this shift in organizing the social world, there can be an accompanying shift in personal identity. "I" statements begin to revolve around actions connected with personal morality—"I am not a person who has premarital sex"—rather than around ascribed characteristics. Further, the moral code also makes concrete the more abstract dimensions of a developing religious identity. That is, it gives practical, daily meaning to the idea that "I am a Christian," postponing more difficult issues of theology and belief until behavioral dimensions of the identity are more secure.

In sum, we think that these stricter, more traditional moral codes may indeed be one of the reasons why the youth groups we studied functioned so well. Such codes give the participants (a) an immediate and practical way to demonstrate their commitments and (b) the beginnings of both a personal and a collective identity that can help them move beyond the life circumstances in which they find themselves.

In this essay we have been considering some urban youth ministries run by evangelical Protestant churches. In addition to the role these groups often play in helping young people as individuals develop into healthy, self-sufficient adults, their social diversity across racial and ethnic lines could provide some hope for the larger society. If congregations are anything close to what Tocqueville called them, the "first institutions of American politics," then this voluntary diversity may bode well for our national public life. Increased diversity will not happen without work and perseverance; it is not a "natural" by-product of conservative religion or traditional morality. And it will be hard-pressed to occur in exurban megachurches that flee transition neighborhoods. But within the dynamics of these urban evangelical youth ministries, there may be models for a more inclusive public sphere.

CHAPTER THIRTEEN

Evangelicals and International Engagement

Allen D. Hertzke

The post–Cold War challenge of defining America's global role is recasting ideological alignments and producing strange bedfellows. Because of this, the press has largely missed a signal story of the changing face of international human-rights advocacy. The conventional image, of course, pitted "idealistic" liberals pressing human rights in foreign affairs against conservative "realists" who accept an imperfect world where niceties give way to hardheaded calculations. Though the reality was never quite that simple, the image contained some truth.

It is now clearly obsolete. Evangelicals, propelled initially by the suffering of fellow believers, have become the grass-roots vanguard of efforts to elevate human rights as a key aim of America's global leadership. Few in elite circles have noticed, because evangelical Christianity remains widely caricatured in the news rooms and faculty clubs of the literati. To capture what is happening, I propose the following headlines:

■ Evangelicals Work with Catholics, Jews, and Episcopalians to Enact Landmark International Religious-Freedom Legislation;

■ Conservative Evangelical Churches Join Black Congregations in Campaign against Slavery and Genocide in Sudan;

■ Evangelical Leaders Team Up with Leading Feminists to Champion Legislation Curbing Global Sex Traffic in Vulnerable Women and Children.

A look at the stories behind these rather startling headlines reveals a lot about how the new engagement by evangelicals is transforming the politics of

Allen D. Hertzke is professor of political science and director of religious studies at the University of Oklahoma. He is the author of several books, including *Representing God in Washington*, an analysis of religious lobbies, and he is completing a book on global religious persecution and U.S. foreign policy called *Freeing God's Children*.

215

international human rights. Evangelicals provided the main grass-roots energy that led to the passage of the International Religious Freedom Act of 1998, and they are among those pushing for vigorous implementation. Their confidence buoyed, evangelical leaders have moved beyond what some might consider self-interested religious concerns to attack such abuses as the sex trafficking in persons by global crime syndicates, or to support the Jubilee campaign of debt forgiveness for poor nations.

While this chapter deals primarily with human-rights advocacy, it is crucial to note that evangelical development groups have also moved increasingly into public-policy advocacy. The realization that small changes in U.S. policy can sometimes dwarf the impact of private development initiatives abroad has led groups like World Vision to take a more active lobbying role. This advocacy intersects the parallel human-rights movement in complex ways, sometimes complementing and sometimes in tension with the faith-based alliance on religious freedom.

Engagement in these specific issues, as I will show, points toward broader trends in evangelical civic life: (1) evangelical witness on the international stage is not restricted to, or even predominantly driven by, "Christian Right" impulses as those are generally understood; (2) a cadre of evangelical leaders inside and outside government is demonstrating strategic sophistication in translating religious values into concrete political aims; (3) evangelical leaders seem increasingly comfortable forging unusual alliances, sometimes with groups they oppose on the domestic front; (4) international engagement has awakened a new sense of citizenship among many evangelicals in the pews, providing a crucial constituency for the human-rights thrust in U.S. foreign policy; and (5) this new engagement is gaining respect in circles outside the evangelical orbit, helping to break down the negative stereotypes of theologically traditional Christians.

To understand the significance of these developments, it will be helpful first to trace the roots of international involvement by evangelical Christian persons and organizations and then to look at the broader context of this effort.

THE ROOTS AND CONTEXT OF CONTEMPORARY ENGAGEMENT

In one sense, evangelical Christians have always been internationally engaged because of the Great Commission given by Jesus to "make disciples of all nations." Today the World Evangelical Alliance, the main umbrella organization for missionary outreach, encompasses nearly 150 separate missionary organizations, and there are a host of other independent groups. This engagement reaches deeply into the pews as congregations contribute money, develop sister-church programs, and hear from missionaries returning from the field. Of course, human-rights activists have often viewed this missionary activity as self-serving and even harmful to indigenous cultures; the colonial image captured by the depiction of the missionary in James Michener's *Hawaii* exercises a powerful hold on liberal and secular imaginations. But as Richard Land of the Southern Baptist Convention argues, this caricature does not capture the dramatic indigenous growth of evangelical churches in the developing world. Evangelical churches have also been heavily involved in relief and development work through such agencies as World Relief, Mercy Crops, Samaritan's Purse, and World Vision. The largest of these enterprises, World Vision, represents the more "liberal" impulse within the international evangelical orbit. In its statement of core values, for example, World Vision speaks of "identification with the poor, the afflicted, the oppressed, the marginalized," God's "challenge to unjust attitudes and systems," and "his call to share resources with each other"—language we associate with the more progressive churches. This similarity is more than rhetorical, as World Vision has sometimes joined with liberal churches in lobbying on issues of foreign aid, Third World debt relief, and the like. Serge Duss, head of governmental affairs for World Vision, argued that these initiatives flow from his organization's increasing focus on advancing justice for the oppressed. Such a focus led the organization to take the lead in successfully challenging the marketing of "conflict diamonds," gems seized by rebels in the African nation of Sierra Leone that have fueled a brutal civil war there.

The changing posture of World Vision has also led it to take exception to the approaches employed by other evangelical groups in the campaign against religious persecution. For example, while such groups as Samaritan's Purse were stepping up their support of the predominantly Christian population in southern Sudan, World Vision refused to accept conditions dictated by the Sudanese rebels and dropped out of the relief consortium for a time in the spring of 2000.[1]

The extent of evangelical missionary and development work demonstrates the engagement of evangelicals *as members of religious congregations.* What is noteworthy about the new international engagement is how it has awakened awareness of their role *as citizens* of the world's most powerful nation. Engagement in international issues represents an enhanced civic role for a religious community known more for domestic focus. Moreover, given the size of the evangelical population, this international engagement may serve as a counterweight to isolationist tendencies in the citizenry and heighten support for U.S. foreign-policy initiatives on human rights. Such a possibility would have seemed inconceivable to human-rights advocates as recently as a few years ago.

These two roles—members of congregations and citizens—can interact. World evangelization puts denominations in touch with believers who live under harsh conditions, while the status of the United States as the world's sole superpower provides a unique political opportunity to champion those believers. As a result, the current foray of evangelicals into foreign policy reaches into the pews, enlisting many average churchgoers to contact members of Congress and other officials. Moreover, the positive experience gained by evangelical leaders in the legislative effort against persecution has led them to become involved in other areas of human-rights advocacy. Thus, contrary to the often distorted images that appear in the media, devoutly religious Americans are now leading the way in championing this vital thrust in international relations.

Broader Context of Engagement

This international advocacy should be seen in the context of broader forces at play in the world. One is the resurgence of religious faith around the globe. Since the Enlightenment, the West's great thinkers have predicted that as rationalism and science advanced, religious commitments and enthusiasms would wane. But secularizing trends in Western Europe and among a thin (if influential) stratum of global intellectual elites now stand out as the exception to more general trends. Around the globe, religion is resurgent, dynamic, and increasingly political.[2]

The abandonment of traditional evangelizing by "mainline" churches is another important piece of this picture. As mainline church leaders embraced more liberal theology and engaged in "worldly" ecumenical enterprises, they left the missionary field to theologically traditional Protestants, who quietly went about the business of spreading the good news in Asia, Africa, and Latin America. Paul Pierson's exhaustive missionary history shows a dramatic reversal since World War I, when over 80 percent of the 10,800 Protestant missionaries from the United States were sponsored by the historically mainline churches. By 1996, those same oldline churches mustered only 2,600 missionaries out of a total of 43,600 sent abroad. Evangelicals dominate the mission field today. Notably, the Southern Baptist Convention, by fielding some 3,500 missionaries annually, dwarfs the *combined* missionary effort of the oldline denominations.[3] To be sure, around the globe there are still many congregations of the historic mainline; but, having been formed in an earlier age of missionary effort, they are likely to be more orthodox in their religious commitments than their current U.S. counterparts..

The crucial story is not primarily about missionary activity, however, but about the indigenization of Christianity outside the West. Harvard political scientist Samuel Huntington has argued that the forces of modernity—mass communication, technology, and global markets—uproot people and weaken traditional faiths tied to village or place. This produces a space into which proselytizing and cosmopolitan religions, such as Christianity and Islam, can move.[4] Thus, an unheralded demographic revolution has occurred in the last half century, a tectonic shift of Christianity toward the developing and non-democratic world. While in 1950 only 25 percent of all Christians lived in Asia, Africa and Latin America, today that figure is around 60 percent and rising. Christianity has become a major indigenous faith of the post-Communist and Third World.[5] And the most dramatic growth is probably from evangelicalism. Since 1970, according to estimates by church demographer David Barrett, the evangelical population has grown more than 200 percent in Africa and Latin America, and more than 300 percent in Asia, so that perhaps 70 percent of all Protestant evangelicals now live in Asia, Africa, and Latin America.[6]

This shift of Christianity toward the developing and non-democratic world was epitomized by a gathering of 10,000 church leaders from some 190 countries in Amsterdam in the summer of 2000. The meeting was sponsored by the Billy Graham Evangelistic Association, and its flavor was captured in the story of a pastor from Papua New Guinea who had personally founded more than 300 churches in the past two decades. Given the credibility and reach of Graham's work in the religious heartland of America, it is no surprise that this constituency would be the most likely to identify with evangelical developments abroad.

One of the most rapidly growing branches of evangelicalism abroad is Pentecostalism, which is particularly appealing in the Third World because it provides a vivid emotional experience, makes the church the center of community life, and teaches a strict code of personal morality that especially appeals to women. Although it was introduced by missionaries, its emphasis on lay involvement, along with the few formal requirements it imposed on ministers, helped it to become an indigenous movement quickly.[7] Huntington argues that the growth of Pentecostalism in Latin America actually represents a net increase in faith practice, as "nominal and passive Catholics become active and devout Evangelicals." Thus while only 20 percent of Brazil's population is Protestant and 70 percent is Catholic, on Sundays more than 20 million attend Protestant churches compared to 12 million in Catholic parishes.[8]

Christianity often elevates the status of women in traditional societies (as it did in ancient Rome), and faith communities in non-Western societies are disproportionately female. Contrary to the secular or left-wing image of Christendom as affluent, Western, and male, the majority of the world's Christians are women of the developing world.[9]

Often these indigenous Christians are agents of democratization and human rights. Such prominent scholars as Seymour Martin Lipset and Samuel Huntington have documented the strong relation between Western Christianity—both Protestant and Roman Catholic—and democracy.[10] The Christian teachings of the equality of all souls before God, the dignity of the individual, and allegiance to authority beyond the state (with the attendant separating of church and state institutions) contribute to the democratic ethos. Remarkably, of the countries that Freedom House classifies as "free," more than eight out of ten are majority Christian, while others (such as South Korea and Taiwan) have substantial Christian populations and notable Christian leaders who contributed to democratization.

Because of its tendency to nurture independent civil society, Christianity threatens despotic regimes. This is particularly evident in the Communist remnant, where in various ways regimes clamp down on its presence. The rise of militant forms of Islam presents a further threat to vulnerable Christian minorities. From Asia and the Middle East to Nigeria, Ethiopia, and Sudan, Christians are under pressure by regimes purporting to represent Islam or exploiting Islamic symbols for secular purposes.

The Suffering Church

Christians in the West, especially evangelicals, are naturally drawn to these besieged believers. Moreover, the growth of this "suffering church" abroad appears to be transforming the relationship between American churches and their counterparts outside the West. In their approach to Christian communities abroad, American evangelicals increasingly see themselves less as "leaders" sending missionaries and more as "servants" providing support to heroic indigenous believers.

Vivid models of courage and fidelity among modern martyrs and "Christians in catacombs" serve evangelical aims, a potential not lost on church leaders. As one parishioner observed, "It's done me a world of good in my commitment to see the examples of these people who have joy and strength in their faith while they daily face the threat of personal disaster."[11] Indeed, at some evangelical events the featured speakers are likely to be foreign Christians, often treated like celebrities and role models, who share poignant testimony of how God sustained them in prison and of how the Christian community has increased despite persecution.

Voice of the Martyrs is among the largest of the advocacy groups, and at one of its annual conferences I saw huge maps of the world, displays featuring Christian communities in Africa, the Middle East, and Asia, and rooms brimming with related books, tapes, and videos. The atmosphere of the conference, while thoroughly evangelical, also had an international flavor. Featured performers were a Hmong choir from Laos and some Persian musicians from Iran. The attendees (mostly from North America) were, in their own way, globalists who had come to hear and meet leaders of the persecuted church abroad. Among those leaders were:

Getaneh Getaneh, a gentle man whose radiant ebony face belies the horrors he experienced during the red terror of the Mengistu regime in Ethiopia. Arrested by the Communist authorities for preaching, he spent years in prison where he was repeatedly interrogated, was denied food, water, and sleep for days, had boiling oil poured on his feet, and was whipped with metal cable. Through it all, his faith in Jesus Christ endured. **Pastor Wally**, who was imprisoned and beaten, and nearly died at the hands of authorities in Saudi Arabia for leading Christian worship services for Filipinos, which is against the law. **Thuong Tram**, a sophisticated young Christian woman from Vietnam, who could pass for a political-science graduate student or a representative at a feminist conference. She fled for her life from a regime that sees religion as a threat to its hold on power. **Noble Alexander**, who spent over two decades in Cuban jails. He testified with amazing humor about the "power and love of the Holy Spirit" that sustained his missionary work despite excruciating torture. In one of his vignettes he told of being placed waste deep in a pool of raw sewage; but God provided a sign, he said, a fragrant blossom that bloomed during the night to overcome the stench. **Bob Fu**, a Christian from China who told about the two lives he led: an English instructor for top party officials during weekdays, an illegal evangelist in off hours. **Brother Robak**, who ministered at great peril to Persian Christians on the front lines of the Iran-Iraq war. **Brother Kim** and **Sister Lee**, who work to penetrate North Korea with the Christian message. **Dr. Vang**, a refugee from Communist Laos who led a team to produce the first Hmong Bible translation.

It would take the most hardened skeptic to resist being touched and inspired by these believers, who seem to radiate good humor as well as deep conviction. And it is not hard to envision the potential political clout of channeling concern for such people into a coordinated campaign to influence America's foreign policy. Without realizing it, therefore, a number of American Christians are becoming internationalists, translating their relationships abroad into resources for foreign-policy influence.

One indication is the rapid growth of "Shatter the Silence," the annual International Day of Prayer for the Persecuted Church. The event is planned by a permanent organization that provides congregations with information about religious persecution and suggested activities of solidarity. Spurred by the World Evangelical Alliance, the International Day of Prayer began in 1996 with around 5,000 participating congregations; by 2001 it claimed to have enlisted some 300,000 congregations, a third of them in the United States. Even allowing for some exaggeration, this would mean that between a fourth and a fifth of U.S. houses of worship (estimated total between 350 thousand and 500 thousand) participate in this event, which is an enormous grass-roots reach. Leading the effort has been the Southern Baptist Convention, which allocated funds to send packets to all 40,000 of its member congregations. In reporting on this phenomenon, the *New York Times* suggested that "a wide swath of Americans who admit they never before paid much attention to foreign affairs or human rights is beginning to exert its influence on American foreign policy," lobbying cities to stop doing business with nations that persecute Christians, and writing letters to foreign governments demanding the release of Christian prisoners. As Richard Cizik of the National Association of Evangelicals put it, human rights is "no longer . . . the prerogative of the left."[12]

Competing Impulses

Clearly, American evangelicalism has become an important new player in human-rights advocacy. But there are obstacles to unified engagement within the evangelical community itself. Despite the popular media image of a disciplined "Christian Right" drawing millions into its fold, Bible-believers exhibit a number of competing impulses toward politics in general and international engagement in particular.

One impulse is to withdraw into personal piety or communal devotions detached from the wider world. Robert Putnam argues that evangelical congregations tend to produce strong "bonding" among members but do less "bridging" outward.[13] And contrary to their "fundamentalist" image, most evangelicals, as Christian Smith demonstrates, are neither militant nor overly focused on politics.[14] Indeed, the catalyst for the international religious-freedom legislation, Michael Horowitz, found evangelicals often apologetic about the past sins of Christendom and sheepish about advocating for their fellow believers abroad. Furthermore, some evangelical leaders persist in castigating politics as too focused on this world.[15] Thus it takes a lot of effort to mobilize the faithful for unified political action.

A second impulse is to devote all their attention to domestic issues. Intensely concerned about their children, civic-minded evangelicals invest heavily in battles over such matters as education, trash TV, and religious rights at home. With popular culture seemingly inhospitable to "people of faith," they spend enormous energies either fighting rear-guard actions against degradation of the moral ecology or carving out space for religiously grounded education.

Even persecution against Christian believers abroad does not necessarily result in political action, because a third impulse sees persecution and martyrdom as biblically foretold, even necessary for the faith. Some evangelicals use Tertullian's famous dictum—"The blood of the martyrs is the seed of the Church"—to justify political quiescence. One can pray for the persecuted, feel inspired by their stories, even prepare for a similar fate. But to expect politics to make things better may be fruitless or even counterproductive to God's plan of using martyrdom to build the global church.

Finally, there are spirited disagreements among civic-minded evangelicals about how best to approach international engagement. One view, reminiscent of "Fortress America," would eschew international entanglements entirely in the interest of maintaining national sovereignty. Driven by fear of the "new world order," some evangelicals suspect that international engagement will end up ceding American sovereignty to the United Nations and, ultimately, to a world government hostile to Christianity. As Duane Oldfield's research has shown, several notable Christian Right leaders chose not to support the International Religious Freedom Act (backed vigorously by other evangelicals) precisely because it invoked United Nations covenants.[16]

If the preceding view tends toward paranoia, another civic impulse may err on the side of hope. It advocates quieter negotiation with foreign governments to create space for Christian witness, to free particular prisoners, and ultimately to change the hearts of leaders. Those who counsel these quieter approaches fear the unintended consequences—such as reprisals against vulnerable believers—that might flow from confrontation or sanctions. Their reasoning also involves a pragmatic calculus: the need for workable relations with non-democratic governments to keep avenues of ministry open. Thus Billy Graham supported the normalization of trade relations with China because he believes it will foster channels for religious contact and evangelizing. This view is especially compelling to those evangelicals in business and education who have quietly witnessed to their faith while engaged in more secular, officially sanctioned pursuits abroad.

But there is also an Augustinian theological impulse that justifies non-confrontational engagement. Governments, as St. Paul proclaimed, are instituted by God. Who are we to claim that God is not working through, say, Chinese leaders as they struggle to maintain stability amidst forces that could plunge their nation into chaos? And the Bible is replete with stories of God's working through kings and princes who were quite unaware of their providential role. Thus some evangelicals counsel humility, oppose "demonizing" countries, and work to develop relationships that may bear fruit decades hence in God's unfolding plan.

This approach is exemplified by Advocates International, founded and headed by Sam Ericsson, former director of the Christian Legal Society. Unlike such groups as Open Doors or International Christian Concern, Advocates International does not expose or criticize. It nurtures relationships with leaders abroad as the means to help build legal infrastructures that protect religious freedom. It seeks to build trust by appeals to common moral principles, especially the Golden Rule. Ericsson draws support for this approach from the Bible, especially from Old Testament figures—such as Esther, Daniel, Joseph, Nehemiah, and Obadiah—whose faithful service to worldly leaders built a relationship that enabled them at critical junctures to advance justice for God's people.[17]

The two quite different approaches are vividly illustrated by attitudes toward a top Chinese official. Sam Ericsson believes that his cordial personal relationship with Ye Xiaowen, head of China's Religious Affairs Bureau, fostered a key policy clarification in 1997 regarding the legality of Bible studies in homes. In contrast, Voice of the Martyrs director Tom White has castigated Ye Xiaowen as "China's Caiaphas," a reference to the high priest who brought charges against Jesus.[18]

A final impulse in the evangelical camp, often allied with liberal skeptics of the new human-rights movement, sees the focus on religious persecution as too self-serving, overly focused on Christians, and not sufficiently attentive to such broader "justice" concerns as crushing poverty and economic exploitation. This is a view increasingly characteristic of the general posture of World Vision. Its leaders do not dismiss concerns for persecution, but they tend to emphasize other problems and issues. Take, for example, the Summer 2001 issue of *World Vision Today* magazine, which focused on refugees. Though a short review article noted that Sudan has the world's largest number of internally displaced persons, the Sudanese were not among those profiled in the issue, which featured Palestinians, Colombians, and Africans from Sierra Leone and the Congo. The seeming de-emphasis of Sudan contrasts markedly with the stance of *World* magazine, which made the Sudan tragedy a major focus of its reporting in 2000–2001. In a sense, a real debate is emerging within the evangelical camp over the priorities of international engagement.

Given these competing impulses, how has the evangelical community gained such prominence in the new international human-rights movement? As we will see in the examples that follow, several factors have contributed to this seemingly sudden prominence. First, the potential for such witness had been growing for years and awaited a spark. Second, evangelicals (a) were nudged by Jews and (b) joined the crucial institutional work of Catholics and other religionists. Third, the most widely respected, theologically sophisticated, and politically astute evangelical leaders chose the more assertive route.

INTERNATIONAL RELIGIOUS FREEDOM ACT OF 1998

Religious liberty was the "first freedom" in the American constitutional system—the first itemized in the Bill of Rights—and is deeply instrumental to other human rights. Vaclav Havel and other heroes of the revolutions in Eastern Europe attest to this fact. When religious communities there gained more latitude for worship—through the efforts of Pope John Paul II and Jewish and Protestant leaders—cracks began to develop in the walls that the Communist system had also built around labor organizers, political dissidents, artists, and intellectuals. Freedom for Jews in the Soviet Union represented the beginning of the end for the gulags. Freedom for Catholics in Poland was a key force in bringing down the Iron Curtain.

Yet despite this pattern, the response of the U.S. government to the growing evidence of severe religious persecution around the globe had been anemic or sporadic. Some U.S. diplomats serving abroad did not even cultivate contacts with religious leaders.

That began to change when in 1998 Congress passed the International Religious Freedom Act, making the promotion of religious freedom a "basic aim" of U.S. foreign policy. This comprehensive human-rights statute created high-level government offices to promote international religious freedom. It requires the State Department to issue an annual report on the status of religious freedom around the world—which sets in motion presidential action against violating countries. It reaches into the daily routines of foreign policy by providing better training for diplomatic personnel and fostering their contacts with vulnerable religious communities.

The law also created an independent commission, with staff and budget, to monitor violations and hold our policy-makers accountable for their response. The U.S. Commission on International Religious Freedom, whose members constitute a distinguished cross section of religious America, has made its presence felt.

Finally, the law established an Ambassador-at-Large for International Religious Freedom. The first person named to the position was Bob Seiple, former director of the Christian development organization World Vision, who in his first report to Congress had this to say:

> We share a common vision—a simple but profound vision. It is to help people who suffer because of their religious faith. Such people live literally around the globe, and they number in the millions. . . . They worship "underground" in 21st century catacombs, lest authorities discover and punish their devotion to an authority beyond the state. They languish in prisons, and suffer torture, simply because they love God in their own way. They are children, stolen from their parents, sold into slavery and forced to convert to another religion. They are Christian mothers, searching for their missing sons. They are Buddhist monks in "re-education camps," Jews imprisoned on trumped-up charges of "espionage," Muslims butchered for being the wrong kinds of Muslims. They hail from every region and race, and their blood cries out to us. Not for vengeance, but for help, and for redress.[19]

Seiple's testimony illustrates how the supposedly parochial concern of evangelicals for fellow believers now embraces the broader goal of religious liberty.

The roots of evangelical engagement on this issue can be traced to the Cold War, when such organizations as Voice of the Martyrs and Open Doors with Brother Andrew formed to succor besieged Christians in Communist countries. What has given the contemporary movement its bite and reach is the growing number and sophistication of these advocacy groups, and their ability to tap into vibrant local organizations and rich social networks of the evangelical world. From the mid-1990s onward, evangelical presses, broadcast networks, and para-church organs increasingly publicized the plight of believers abroad. Though much of this activity occurred beneath the radar of mainstream media, politicians with antennas finely tuned to their local constituencies detected the buzz.

A Jewish-Evangelical Alliance

Surprisingly, it was a Jew who seemed to understand better than anyone else the nascent potential of this religious community. Michael Horowitz is credited, even by critics, with being a major catalyst for evangelical activism on issues of religious freedom and sex trafficking. Horowitz also helped to enlist other prominent Jewish leaders to take up the cause of persecuted Christians. Journalist Abe Rosenthal dramatically raised the profile of the issue through repeated columns in the *New York Times*. Mainstream Jewish organizations, from the Union of American Hebrew Congregations to the Anti-Defamation League, were pivotal backers of legislation. The first two chairs of the newly created Commission on International Religious Freedom were Jews: David Saperstein, the top lobbyist for Reform Judaism, and Elliott Abrams, then president of the Ethics and Public Policy Center.[20]

The Jewish-evangelical alliance is not the only example of how profoundly the issue of international religious freedom transcends traditional ideological lines. The institutional support of the National Conference of Catholic Bishops helped legitimate the issue outside the evangelical world, especially among Democratic legislators, as did backing by the liberal Episcopal lobby. In the lobby campaign, conservative evangelicals joined with such religious minorities as Tibetan Buddhists and Iranian Baha'is, clearly signifying a move beyond the "parochial concern" for fellow believers.

Evangelicals, newly awakened to their citizenship potential and responsibility, have unquestionably provided most of the grass-roots support behind efforts to elevate human rights in U.S. foreign policy. Influential in mobilizing these constituents are Christian broadcasting and direct-mail ministries such as Focus on the Family and the Family Research Council, and denominational or church-affiliated organizations such as the Christian Life Commission of the Southern Baptist Convention and the National Association of Evangelicals. During the lobby campaign, congressional staff members reported waves of letters after Christian radio broadcasts by Charles Colson and James Dobson. Unquestionably, Charles Colson, who enjoys both universal respect in the evangelical world and credibility beyond, has been the most important figure in this emerging engagement. He not only mobilized lay evangelicals on religious persecution but also planned strategy and personally lobbied members of Congress. Equally important, through prolific writings, speeches, and radio commentary, Colson articulates a clear theological rationale for public engagement. He remonstrates vigorously against quietism and inaction, labeling "self-indulgent" and unscriptural the view that because martyrdom is good for the Church, evangelicals should not support political attempts to ameliorate persecution abroad.[21] It is important to note that evangelical actors disagreed among themselves, sometimes fiercely, about the proper way to combat international religious persecution. A number of groups backed the bill sponsored by Frank Wolf, which passed the House in the spring of 1998. Other groups favored the more calibrated Senate legislation, which was initially drafted by a cadre of evangelical staff members who objected to the "harder edge" of the Wolf bill. That the two rival bills both had strong evangelical sponsorship and backing speaks volumes about the importance of the Bible-believing community on the issue.

Still, questions remain about how deep into the pews lay concern for international issues reaches, and how enduring it is. Certainly the issue is salient among the evangelical elite. In the Pew-sponsored survey conducted in 2000 by John Green and his colleagues (see chapter 1), over three-quarters of the evangelical leaders surveyed said they strongly agreed that fighting religious persecution should be a major goal of U.S. foreign policy. At the lay level, awareness and interest have probably not reached levels found among Jews during the campaign for Soviet Jewry in the 1980s. But if constituent pressure has not been persistently high, it has not just been a one-shot affair either. Two years after passage of the International Religious Freedom Act, a constellation of international concerns—general religious freedom, Sudan, relations with China—was generating a fairly constant religious buzz on Capitol Hill.[22] Senator Brownback, for example, noted how at town-hall meetings across Kansas he continually hears "heartfelt" concern about international human rights from constituents who are members of faith communities.

Major Issues: Sudan, Sex Trafficking

An emerging example of this human-rights engagement concerns Sudan, where the National Islamic Front government has pursued a brutal civil war against its largely Christian and animist black African population. The measures employed—wholesale killing of civilians, crop destruction and forced famine, indiscriminate bombings, abduction, enslavement, and forced conversions—amount to genocide. Nearly two million people have lost their lives, more than in the conflicts in Rwanda, Bosnia, and Kosovo combined, and five million others have been displaced.

Critics charge that the Western response to these atrocities has been woefully inadequate, even craven. The hope for breakthrough, they argue, lies with U.S. leadership. But though the United States labeled the Islamic Front a terrorist regime and even bombed a pharmaceutical plant in Khartoum, response to this genocide has been uneven. This may be due in part to peacekeeping fatigue, along with the view, expressed in 1999 by then Secretary of

State Madeleine Albright, that "the human rights situation in Sudan is not marketable to the American people."[23] That context changed as evangelical groups joined with black churches, civil-rights leaders, and anti-slavery organizations to bring international pressure on the regime. Here, too, we see the maturing of an advocacy infrastructure in the evangelical community, which includes members of Congress, Christian lobbies, NGOs, college students, and even television producers. Since the early 1990s, evangelical Christian groups such as Christian Solidarity International, Christian Solidarity Worldwide, Voice of the Martyrs, and Samaritan's Purse have publicized the atrocities committed in Sudan. This material has been increasingly picked up by a variety of activists: from the celebrated grade-school class of Denver teacher Barbara Vogel; to New York City pastor Jim Geist, who held a series of well-publicized hunger strikes aimed at pressuring the city to take divestment action similar to that during the South Africa sanctions campaign;[24] to producers of the popular TV show "Touched by an Angel," who focused a powerful episode on the slave traffic in Sudan that featured actual exiles from that land.[25]

In the spring of 1999, some 400 Christian students, attending schools that ranged from Christian institutions like Wheaton and Calvin to Harvard and Berkeley, landed with backpacks and sleeping bags at Georgetown University for a conference on Sudan sponsored by Freedom House and supported by the Coalition for Christian Colleges and Universities. The format was distinctly 1960s, with rousing speakers such as the Baroness Caroline Cox of Christian Solidarity Worldwide, slide shows highlighting the brutality of the regime, testimonies by escaped Sudanese Christians, and breakout sessions on organizing strategies for a largely e-mail campaign of techno-friendly students. But those who might have experienced time warp would also have noted some characteristically evangelical moments, as when a young man stood up to implore his fellow students to join him in prayer. The effort sparked a number of creative tactics. For instance, students at Southern Wesleyan University constructed a mock slave pit on Lincoln's birthday, while on another campus a student braved the cold in a makeshift slave pen for several days until at least 75 percent of his fellow students had contacted Congress.[26]

In the wake of the successful campaign to enact the International Religious Freedom Act, the emerging religious-freedom coalition sought to focus these growing if disparate initiatives on Sudan into a more unified effort for government sanctions, capital market pressure on the oil interests abetting the regime, and tangible support for those Sudanese suffering from manmade famine. With the election of George W. Bush, whose electoral base was heavily evangelical, the born-again constituency became even more pivotal to this Sudan campaign. And there were indications that, contrary to certain "realist" impulses among his foreign-policy advisors, Bush was being influenced by concerns from the evangelical camp to elevate Sudan's human-rights crisis to a higher priority. Several advisors spoke of atrocities being committed there, and Bush himself singled out Sudan's genocide in a speech delivered on May 3, 2001, before the American Jewish Committee. Crucial to this heightened attention is the fact that some major evangelical leaders who have personal relationships with the President—such as Charles Colson and Franklin Graham—are deeply committed to the Sudan cause. Graham's Samaritan's Purse organization is heavily invested in relief and development work in Sudan, and his projects have been directly hit by Khartoum's bombs and raids. This gives him a remarkable credibility on the issue.

What is striking about the Sudan issue is the emerging alliance of liberal African-American groups and conservative evangelical organizations. Ironically, the American civil-rights establishment largely ignored the plight of black Africans in southern Sudan for much of the 1990s. As the Sudan campaign heated up, evangelical and Catholic groups were joined by several prominent black preachers and by disparate activists such as Samuel Cotton of the modern anti-slavery movement. Not until the turn of the century, however, did civil-rights leaders, whether spurred by the efforts of the evangelical groups or shamed by other activists, join the campaign against the Sudanese regime. This engagement produced one of the most striking coalitions in recent history, as such black leaders as Kweisi Mfume, Eleanor Holmes Norton, Walter Fauntroy, and Al Sharpton joined conservative evangelical leaders in calling for demonstrations, divestment, and presidential action against the National Islamic Front regime. Those members of Congress most responsive to this coalition were heavily weighted from the evangelical Christian community, including such figures as Congressmen Frank Wolf and Tom Tancredo and Senators Sam Brownback and Bill Frist. In April 2001, a prominent black radio personality in Washington, D.C., testifying before the Human Rights Caucus of the House of Representatives about his trip to Sudan, even lauded Senator Jesse Helms for his work on Sudan. As of this writing, the national press has yet to fully capture the nature of this emerging alliance.

Sex Trafficking

Another subject of faith-based international involvement is the international sex traffic. According to the Protection Project at the Nitze School at Johns Hopkins University, more than one million women and children each year are trafficked across international boundaries into prostitution, many bought and sold until they die of disease and abuse. Impoverished young girls from Asia, Russia, Eastern Europe, and Latin America are either targeted with misleading appeals or sold outright by families, ending up virtual slaves of their pimps. This is a lucrative business, according to Laura Lederer, director of the Protection Project, because "unlike drugs, which are sold only once, a human being can be sold over and over again." Landmark legislation aimed at cutting this grotesque trade passed Congress in 2000, sponsored by Chris Smith and Sam Gejdenson in the House and Sam Brownback and Paul Wellstone in the Senate. This legislation provides harsher penalties for international traffickers, equips enforcement agencies with new tools to deal with organized crime syndicates that run the traffic, and provides for penalizing countries that fail to criminalize and punish international sex trafficking.

This not only has involved an interfaith alliance but has brought evangelicals and feminist leaders together in the legislative effort. Evangelical leaders have actively plotted strategy with such feminist groups as Equality Now. Even in a town known for strange bedfellows, this coalition was unusual. At the pivotal last stage of the legislative campaign, members of Congress were receiving a letter from Gloria Steinem and other prominent feminist leaders just when they were being lobbied by such evangelical figures as Charles Colson, Richard Land of the Southern Baptist Convention, Richard Cizik of the National Association of Evangelicals, and John Busby of the Salvation Army.

In one sense, this issue helps to connect contemporary evangelicalism with models of religiously inspired political leadership of the past. Charles Colson in particular views his efforts to end the sex traffic as inspired by the leadership of William Wilberforce, the English parliamentarian who led the effort to abolish the slave trade. No secular human-rights group can approach the potential of evangelical leaders to reach average citizens, to create an actual human-rights constituency. This reality, Colson believes, means evangelicals have both an opportunity and a moral obligation to play a major role in shaping America's response to the human-rights challenges of the twenty-first century.

This view is echoed by another evangelical activist, Gary Haugen, president of the International Justice Mission. A former Justice Department lawyer and U.N. genocide investigator in Rwanda, Haugen felt called to reclaim the vocabulary of justice for the evangelical Christian community and to offer practical guidance about how Christian believers could promote it in a hurting world. Working around the world, his International Justice Mission intervenes in cases of child prostitution and exploitation, sexual bondage, religious persecution, and torture, assisting legal authorities where feasible and providing succor to the victims. The "good news about injustice," Haugen has written, is that God is against it.[27]

The Governmental Presence

National policy-makers are not just "dependent variables" pushed about by constituent and interest-group pressures. Cynics might not think so, but religious commitments and worldviews do shape the work of many members of Congress.[28] My own investigation confirms a thriving religious life on the Hill, including weekly faith-sharing sessions across party and denominational lines. Given the exceptional vibrancy of religious life in the United States, it should not surprise us that the people's representatives generally reflect that, and that some consciously link their faith and human-rights advocacy. Evangelical members of Congress—such as Senators Sam Brownback (R.-Kans.) and Bill Frist (R.-Tenn.), former Senator Dan Coats (R.-Ind.), and Representatives Frank Wolf (R.-Va.), Tony Hall (D.-Ohio), Tom Tancredo (R.-Colo.), and Joseph Pitts (R.-Pa.)—were among the crucial leaders of Congress on the initiatives discussed in this chapter, conducting fact-finding missions, documenting abuses, and sponsoring legislation.

Universally admired for his human-rights work, Frank Wolf stands out as Washington's first "bleeding heart conservative." For years this devout Presbyterian has "traveled the world in search of famine, death and war, trying to find ways to help," said *Washington Post* writer Lori Montgomery.[29] Some pastors in Eastern Europe were said to carry dog-eared letters from Wolf to use when harassed by authorities.[30] Wolf is respected by colleagues across the aisle; the liberal San Francisco Democrat Nancy Pelosi, for instance, referred to him as "my leader" on religious freedom issues.

Often joining Wolf are two congressional friends and prayer partners, Chris Smith (R.-N.J.) (a Catholic) and Tony Hall (D.-Ohio), who have traveled the world to meet with a panoply of Jewish *refuseniks,* Chinese dissidents, imprisoned pastors, Sudanese refugees, tortured believers, war refugees, and victimized women. Hall, a Democrat from Dayton, defies stereotypes. A devout Christian, he participates in a weekly Bible-study group on Capitol Hill and is strongly opposed to abortion. But he is most renowned as a liberal crusader on international hunger issues, activity that he sees as flowing from his Christian calling. When he learned that the House Select Committee on Hunger was to be abolished he led a highly publicized hunger strike, shaming his colleagues into giving more attention to the issue.[31]

Other House champions are Joseph Pitts, who created the Religious Prisoners Congressional Task Force, a group that provides a mechanism for using congressional clout to gain the release of pastors and others held in jails for practicing their faith, and Tom Tancredo, who emerged as a leader of the Sudan campaign. House leaders Tom DeLay (R.-Tex.) and Dick Armey (R.-Tex.) have invested serious capital in shepherding legislation sponsored by others. Armey is an especially intriguing example of evangelical witness. Known primarily as a fiscal conservative and flat-tax advocate, the Texas Republican experienced a religious conversion, and Hill observers have noticed his new tendency to speak in faith-based terms. He has backed this rhetoric with action, using his position as Majority Leader to ensure favorable floor consideration of bills against religious persecution and sex trafficking.[32]

In the Senate, Sam Brownback not only sponsored the sex-traffic legislation but has become the central figure on the Sudan issue. He has traveled to Sudan, spoken at conferences, and sponsored congressional initiatives, including an amendment allowing food aid to rebel areas that he has pressed the executive branch to use vigorously. Brownback traces his activism on Sudan to his roots in Pottawotamie County, the hotbed of often evangelically inspired anti-slavery agitation in the Kansas territory of the 1850s. Senator Bill Frist is another member who links his faith and his political leadership. A physician, he has gone to Sudan twice under the auspices of the evangelical relief ministry Samaritan's Purse to provide medical services, which included performing surgery in a hospital that had no electricity.

The prominence in human-rights advocacy of such figures as Frist, Pitts, Brownback, and Tancredo, all elected as part of the supposed Christian Right surge in Congress, suggests that the evangelical community is not as predictable as some journalists might have expected.

The emerging advocacy infrastructure also includes a growing cadre of evangelical staff members with ties to international church groups and respect in the religious community. Some bring experience in foreign missions, other (such as Sharon Payt on Senator Brownback's staff) in human-rights advocacy abroad; still others serve as Fellows sponsored by religious groups. Two such staff fellows, John Hanford in the office of Senator Richard Lugar (R.-Ind.) and Laura Bryant Hanford in the office of Congressman Bob Clement (D.-Tenn.), were intensely involved in the process that hammered out what ultimately became the Nickles-Lieberman bill, enacted as the International Religious Freedom Act.

The maturing of the evangelical presence in politics is also reflected in its executive presence in implementing the religious-freedom legislation. The first Ambassador for International Religious Freedom was former World Vision head Robert Seiple, who was succeeded by another evangelical, John Hanford; and Steve McFarland, formerly of the Christian Legal Society, was the first executive director of the U.S. Commission on International Religious Freedom.

Concluding Observations

Bible-believing Protestants, approaching a third of the population, have been the sleeping giant of American foreign policy. They have traditionally invested their energy in church-based activities and domestic political issues. Now, inspired by the suffering church abroad, the sleeping giant has awakened to international concern, at least for the moment.

Whether this concern can endure the setbacks of realpolitik is another matter entirely. Even the most successful foreign-policy initiatives aimed at ameliorating suffering abroad tend to produce modest and incremental advances, which may seem like small reward for prodigious effort. Such small victories, over time, can bring about major progress, but persistent constituent pressure is required to sustain the effort.

Given its size and passion, the evangelical constituency is certain to be pivotal to the fate of the human-rights thrust in American foreign policy. But saying this does not automatically tell us the direction that evangelical advocacy will take. For example, on the eve of the House vote in May 2000 over granting permanent normalized trade relations (PNTR) with China, evangelicals were strong, though certainly not unified, voices. Continuing the legacy of Gary Bauer, the Family Research Council took a vigorous stance against PNTR. It hosted Chinese dissident Wei Jingsheng and co-sponsored (with the AFL-CIO) an anti-PNTR rally. Other evangelicals backed normalized trade relations, either in public statements or in testimony before Congress. An engaged evangelical community does not necessarily mean a unified one.

Nonetheless, an internationally engaged evangelicalism probably will mean that negative stereotypes of theologically traditional Christians will dissolve somewhat as votaries of religious freedom and human rights find in them potential allies. The fact that liberal Jews and conservative evangelicals worked deeply and cordially together on several congressional lobby campaigns testifies to the power of international witness to foster new relationships and alter perceptions. Eventually we may even see in the news rooms, faculty clubs, and salons of the literati a positive reassessment of the role of revived Christianity in the modern world—a profound outcome indeed.

APPENDIX

Who's Who in Evangelical International Engagement

■ **Charles Colson**, the former Nixon counsel who founded Prison Fellowship, a widely praised global ministry for prisoners and prison reform. His support became pivotal to the religious-freedom campaign, both for grassroots mobilization and for bringing other leaders to the table. Colson credits Michael Horowitz with showing him the scope of the problem and sparking his commitment.

■ **Paul Marshall**, a human-rights scholar and political theorist who wrote *Their Blood Cries Out*, a polemical account of Christian faith under siege. An evangelically oriented Anglican, Marshall offered trenchant explanations for the inadequate response of Western Christians to the persecution of their counterparts abroad. He now is working for Freedom House to produce reports scaling the status of religious freedom around the globe.

■ **Evangelical members of Congress**, especially Senators Sam Brownback and Bill Frist and Congressmen Frank Wolf, Tony Hall, Tom Tancredo, and

Joseph Pitts, who have conducted fact-finding trips documenting international human-rights abuses and have championed legislation. They are aided by a cadre of evangelical staff, who in the case of the International Religious Freedom Act spent months drafting competing bills and working out compromises that smoothed passage.

■ **Journalists** such as David Aikman, formerly of *Time* and later head of a fellowship of Christian journalists, and Kim Lawton of the PBS program "Religion & Ethics Newsweekly," whose foreign reportage often illuminates religious dynamics hidden from secular journalists.

■ **Evangelical scholars and activists** working in such think tanks as the Ethics and Public Policy Center and the Institute for Religion and Democracy, who have sponsored symposiums and published reports on international religious-freedom issues.

■ **Advocates International**, a U.S.-based group headed by Sam Ericsson, which takes a non-confrontational approach in working with foreign leaders to build legal institutions that protect religious rights. Staffed primarily by attorneys, it trains lawyers, judges, and legislators around the world in principles of religious freedom. It identifies and works with professionals who are, or might be, in positions to advance religious liberty.

■ **Christian Solidarity International**, an interdenominational organization founded in 1977 and headquartered in Switzerland. It has been the most heavily involved of all the groups in the controversial practice of slave redemption in Sudan and has helped sponsor the campaign against the Khartoum regime.

■ **Christian Solidarity Worldwide,** headed by Baroness Caroline Cox of the British House of Lords, a fervent Christian who describes herself as "a nurse and social scientist by intention, and a baroness by surprise." Lady Caroline has personally taken on the cause of besieged believers in Sudan, who have become victims of some of the worst human-rights abuses in the world today. She traveled to Sudan more than two dozen times in four years, flying into unsecured landing strips, sleeping in tents, and hiking for miles to redeem African Christian and animist slaves from Arab traders.

■ **International Christian Concern,** headed by Steve Snyder in Washington, D.C., an organization with links to underground churches in a number of countries and credibility for early reports of persecution in such places as China, Pakistan, Saudi Arabia, and Algeria.

■ **Open Doors with Brother Andrew,** an international organization that was begun in 1955 to support the efforts of a Dutch pastor, Andrew Vanderbijl, who smuggled Bibles and other Christian materials behind the Iron Curtain during the Cold War. With offices in seventeen countries, including the United States, Open Doors now focuses broadly on persecution of Christians under Communist, Islamic, and authoritarian governments. Its Compass Direct News

Service, out of Santa Ana, California, publishes credible monthly reports of incidents around the globe.

- **Prayer for the Persecuted Church,** which sponsors the annual "Shatter the Silence" International Day of Prayer. In 2001 it enlisted an estimated 300,000 congregations around the world (100,000 in the United States) in a Sunday devoted to learning about and praying for the persecuted.

- **Voice of the Martyrs,** a missionary organization begun by a Romanian pastor and his wife, Richard and Sabina Wurmbrand, who endured brutal treatment at the hands of Nazis and Communists in their native land. In exile, the Wurmbrands began a ministry to countries behind the Iron Curtain that now offers assistance to persecuted churches in some eighty countries. The organization, headquartered in Bartlesville, Oklahoma, has grown rapidly to over a hundred thousand members. Current director Tom White spent seventeen months in a Cuban jail for smuggling Christian literature into the country.

- **Specialized groups,** such as Iranian Christians International, which documents persecution of Christians inside Iran, assists refugees, and engages in government advocacy.

- **Para-church Christian broadcasting and direct-mail ministries,** such as Focus on the Family, the Family Research Council, and the Christian Coalition, which help activate millions of American citizens on international issues of concern.

- **Denominational or church-affiliated organizations,** such as the Christian Life Commission of the Southern Baptist Convention, the National Association of Evangelicals, the Religious Liberty Commission of the World Evangelical Alliance, and the Salvation Army, which maintain grass-roots constituencies at home and contacts with communities abroad.

- **Church mission organizations,** numbering by the scores, which serve the missionary impulse in evangelicalism. To maintain workable relations with foreign governments—and thus access for evangelical work—mission boards sometimes take issue with other evangelical advocates and counsel against public criticism or sanctions against persecuting countries.

- **Evangelical relief and development organizations,** such as Mercy Corps, Samaritan's Purse (directed by Franklin Graham), World Relief, and the largest, World Vision, which has a major presence not only among the international NGOs but in policy circles as well. World Vision's leaders have sometimes taken issue with the "harder-edge advocacy" of other evangelical groups.

Notes

Introduction: CORRECTING MISCONCEPTIONS
John Wilson

1. Stephen Macedo, *Diversity and Distrust: Education in a Multicultural Democracy* (Cambridge: Harvard University Press, 2000), xi.
2. Ibid., ix.
3. Ibid., 201–11.
4. Ibid., x.
5. Ibid.
6. Ibid., 142.
7. See Ethics and Public Policy Center, "Conflict on Campus: Religious Liberty versus Gay Rights?" *Center Conversation* #6 (August 2000).
8. See also French's presentation in "Conflict on Campus."
9. John G. West Jr., *The Politics of Revelation and Reason: Religion and Civic Life in the New Nation* (Lawrence: University Press of Kansas, 1996).
10. Macedo, *Diversity and Distrust*, 231.
11. Robert D. Putnam, *Bowling Alone: The Collapse and Revival of American Community* (New York: Simon & Schuster, 2000).
12. Ibid., 65–69.
13. Ibid., 77.
14. Ibid., 409–10.
15. Robert N. Bellah, Richard Madsen, William M. Sullivan, Ann Swidler, and Steven M. Tipton, *Habits of the Heart: Individualism and Commitment in American Life*, updated ed. (Berkeley: University of California Press, 1996).
16. Ibid., 295–96.
17. Ibid., 231.

Chapter 1: CIVIC ENGAGEMENT OVERVIEW
John C. Green

1. See Christian Smith, *American Evangelicalism: Embattled and Thriving* (Chicago: University of Chicago Press, 1998); and Sara Diamond, *Not by Politics Alone: The Enduring Influence of the Christian Right* (New York: The Guilford Press, 1998).
2. See David P. Gushee, ed., *Christians and Politics Beyond the Culture Wars: An Agenda for Engagement* (Grand Rapids: Baker Books, 2000).
3. See Robert D. Putnam, *Bowling Alone: The Collapse and Revival of American Community* (New York: Simon & Schuster, 2000); Martin E. Marty, *Politics, Religion, and the Common Good* (San Francisco: Jossey-Bass Publishers); E. J. Dionne, ed., *Community Works: The Revival of Civil Society* (Washington, DC: Brookings Institution Press, 1998).

4. Lyman A. Kellstedt et al., "Grasping the Essentials: The Social Embodiment of Religion and Social Behavior," in John C. Green et al., eds., *Religion and the Culture Wars: Dispatches from the Front* (Lanham, MD: Rowman & Littlefield, 1996), 174–92.

5. See Mark A. Noll, ed., *Religion and American Politics: From the Colonial Period to the 1980s* (New York: Oxford University Press, 1990).

6. See Michael Cromartie, "The Evangelical Kaleidoscope: A Survey of Recent Evangelical Political Engagement," in Gushee, *Christians and Politics*, 15–28; and James W. Skillen, *The Scattered Voice: Christians at Odds in the Public Square* (Grand Rapids: Zondervan, 1990).

7. See Marty, *Righteous Empire: The Protestant Experience in America* (New York: Dial Press, 1970); and Joel A. Carpenter, *Revive Us Again: The Reawakening of American Fundamentalism* (New York: Oxford University Press, 1997).

8. See George M. Marsden, *Fundamentalism and American Culture* (New York: Oxford University Press, 1980).

9. See David O. Moberg, *The Great Reversal* (New York: Lippincott, 1977).

10. See Carpenter, *Revive Us Again*.

11. See David P. Gushee, "From Despair to Mission: Toward a Christian Public Theology for the New Millennium," in Gushee, *Christians and Politics,* 29–44.

12. See Michael Lienesch, *Redeeming America: Piety and Politics in the New Christian Right* (Chapel Hill: University of North Carolina Press, 1993).

13. See, e.g., Cal Thomas and Ed Dobson, *Blinded by Might* (Grand Rapids: Zondervan, 1999).

14. See Timothy Smith, *Revivalism and Social Reform* (Baltimore: Johns Hopkins University Press, 1980); and Robert D. Linder, "The Resurgence of Evangelical Social Concern," in David F. Wells and John D. Woodbridge, eds., *The Evangelicals: What They Believe, Who They Are, Where They Are Changing* (Nashville: Abingdon Press, 1975).

15. See Mark A. Noll, *Adding Cross to Crown: The Political Significance of Christ's Passion* (Grand Rapids: Baker Books, 1996).

16. See Robert Wuthnow, *The Struggle for America's Soul: Evangelicals, Liberals, and Secularism* (Grand Rapids: Eerdmans, 1989).

17. See, e.g., Thomas W. Heilke and Ashley Woodiwiss, *The Re-Enchantment of Political Science* (Lanham, MD: Lexington Books, 2001).

18. Mark D. Regnerus and Christian Smith, "Selective Deprivatization among American Religious Traditions: The Reversal of the Great Reversal," *Social Forces* 76 (1998): 11347–72.

19. Cromartie, "Evangelical Kaleidoscope."

20. James W. Skillen, "Christian Faith and Public Policy: A Reformed Perspective," in Gushee, *Christians and Politics*, 45–56.

21. See Ralph Reed, *Active Faith* (New York: The Free Press, 1996).

22. See, e.g., from a center-left perspective, Randall L. Frame and Alan Tharpe, *How Right Is the Right?* (Grand Rapids: Zondervan, 1996), and from the right, Ronald H. Nash, *Why the Left Is Not Right* (Grand Rapids: Zondervan, 1996); also Christian Smith, *Christian America? What Evangelicals Really Want* (Berkeley: University of California Press, 2000).

23. See J. Philip Wogaman, *Christian Perspectives on Politics* (Louisville, KY: Westminster John Knox Press, 2000).

24. Robert N. Bellah et al., *The Good Society* (New York: Knopf, 1991), 179–219.

25. For a review of the evidence on all these question see David E. Campbell, "Acts of Faith: Strict Churches and Political Mobilization" (paper presented at the annual meeting of the American Political Science Association, 2000, San Francisco); see also Robert Wuthnow, "Mobilizing Civic Engagement: The Changing Impact of Religious Involvement," in Theda Skocpol and Morris P. Fiorina, eds., *Civic Engagement in American Democracy* (Washington, DC: Brookings Institution Press, 1999).

26. See E. J. Dionne and John J. DiIulio, eds., *What's God Got to Do with the American Experiment?* (Washington, DC: Brookings Institution Press, 2000).

27. Corwin Smidt et al., "The Characteristics of Religious Group Activists: An Interest Group Analysis," in William Stevenson, ed., *Christian Political Activism at the Crossroads* (Lanham, MD: University Press of America, 1994), 133–71.

28. See Robert H. Gundry, *Jesus the Word According to John the Sectarian: A Paleofundamentalist Manifesto for Contemporary Evangelicalism, Especially Its Elites, in North America* (Grand Rapids: Eerdmans, 2001).

29. See Fredrick C. Harris, *Something Within: Religion in African-American Political Activism* (New York: Oxford University Press, 1999).

30. We did not ask this particular question of the evangelical elites; however, it is abundantly clear from other items that their religion strongly influences their politics.

31. See James L. Guth et al., "The Political Relevance of Religion," in Green, *Religion and the Culture Wars*, 300–329.

32. This index was calculated from the five items in Table 2. Respondents with the strongest public responses received a "2" for each item, and less strong responses received a "1." For example, in the first item, individuals who chose engagement in politics received a "2" and those who chose helping individual non-believers received a "1." All these responses were summed, with the highest score (most in favor of engagement) "10" and the lowest score (least in favor of engagement) "0." The mean for the sample was 4.20, and for evangelicals 4.70.

33. See James L. Guth et al., "Onward Christian Soldiers: Religious Interest Group Activists," in Green, *Religion and the Culture Wars*, 62–85.

34. Lyman A. Kellstedt et al., "The Puzzle of Evangelical Protestantism: Core, Periphery, and Political Behavior," in Green, *Religion and the Culture Wars*, 240–65.

35. This index was calculated from the ten items in Table 3 by counting each response in the table as a "1" and summing all the responses. Thus the highest score (highest religious engagement) was "10" and the lowest score "0." The mean for the sample was 3.53, and for evangelicals 4.79.

36. We were able to ask more detailed questions of the evangelical elites than of the evangelical public.

37. See Nancy Ammerman, "Connecting Mainline Protestant Churches with Public Life" and Mark Chaves, Helen Giesel, and William Tsitos, "Religious Variations in Public Presence: Evidence from the National Congregations Study" (papers presented at conference, "The Public Role of Mainline Protestantism," Princeton University, April 7, 2000).

38. This index was calculated from the ten items in Table 5 by counting each response in the table as a "1" and summing all the responses. All the responses were

summed for the overall index, and for just the religious and secular responses. Thus the highest score (highest engagement) was "10" and the lowest score "0." The means for the sample were 3.41 for overall engagement, 1.17 for religious engagement, and 2.20 for secular engagement; the comparable means for evangelicals were 3.24 overall, 1.33 religious, and 1.90 secular.

39. We also asked about these activities in 2000, and the results were very similar. As might be expected, the percentage of individuals reporting political activity in a single year was less than what was reported for the four-year period.

40. This index was calculated from the ten items in Table 6 by counting each response in the table as a "1" and summing all the responses. Thus the highest score (highest political engagement) was "10" and the lowest score "0." The means for the sample was 2.88, and for evangelicals 2.80.

41. See Wuthnow, "Mobilizing Civic Engagement" (in note 25)

42. The categories in Table 7 were developed in two steps. First, four summary indexes (religious engagement, support for social programs in religious venues, support for social programs in secular venues, and political engagement) were subjected to factor analysis, which produced two significant factors, one a religious dimension (religious engagement and support for social programs in religious venues), and the other a secular dimension (political engagement and support for social programs in secular venues). These two separate dimensions of civic engagement were then cross-tabulated at their means to produce the four categories: full engagement (above the means on both dimensions); faith-based engagement (above the mean on the religious dimension and below the mean on the secular dimension); secular engagement (below the mean on the religious dimension and above the mean on the secular dimension); and low engagement (below the means on both).

43. See Sidney Verba, Kay Lehman Schlozman, and Henry E. Brady,. *Voice and Equality* (Cambridge: Harvard University Press, 1995).

44. The full-engagement and faith-based-engagement categories were on balance conservative on the political issues, especially social issues, in all the traditions. However, there were significant groups of moderates and liberals in all these groups as well.

Chapter 2: THE CHRISTIAN RIGHT
Mark J. Rozell

1. Mark J. Rozell and Clyde Wilcox, eds., *God at the Grass Roots: The Christian Right in the 1994 Elections* (Lanham, MD: Rowman & Littlefield, 1995); Rozell and Wilcox, *Second Coming: The New Christian Right in Virginia Politics* (Baltimore: Johns Hopkins University Press, 1996); Rozell and Wilcox, *God at the Grass Roots 1996: The Christian Right in American Elections* (Lanham, MD: Rowman & Littlefield, 1997).

2. John C. Green, Mark J. Rozell, and Clyde Wilcox, eds., *Prayers in the Precincts: The Christian Right in the 1998 Elections* (Washington, DC: Georgetown University Press, 2000).

3. Kenneth D. Wald, *Religion and Politics in the United States*, 3rd ed. (Washington, DC: Congressional Quarterly, 1997); Rozell and Wilcox, *Second Coming*.

4. Matthew Moen, *The Transformation of the Christian Right* (Tuscaloosa: University of Alabama Press, 1992); "The First Generation of Christ-Right Activism," in Corwin Smidt and James Penning, eds., *Sojourners in the Wilderness: The Christian Right in Comparative Perspective* (Lanham, MD: Rowman & Littlefield, 1997).

5. Steve Bruce, *The Rise and Fall of the New Christian Right* (Oxford: Oxford University Press, 1988).

6. Clyde Wilcox, Mark J. Rozell, and Roland Gunn, "Religious Coalitions in the New Christian Right," *Social Science Quarterly* 77 (1996): 543–58.

7. Joe Taylor, "Christian Coalition Revamping Image," *Richmond Times-Dispatch*, December 7, 1992, B4.

8. See Moen, "First Generation"; Mark J. Rozell, "Growing up Politically: The New Politics of the New Christian Right," in Smidt and Penning, *Sojourners in the Wilderness*, 235–48; Rozell and Wilcox, *Second Coming*; and Clyde Wilcox, *Onward Christian Soldiers: The Religious Right in American Politics* (Boulder, CO: Westview Press, 1996).

9. Rozell and Wilcox, *Second Coming* and *God at the Grass Roots*.

10. Cal Thomas, "Which Way for the Religious Right and the GOP?" *Washington Times*, October 23, 1996, A14.

11. See, for example, the analysis in Liz Szabo, "Christian Coalition Losing Clout," *Virginian Pilot*, February 19, 2000; and Hanna Rosin, "Christian Right's Fervor Has Fizzled," *Washington Post*, February 16, 2000, A1.

12. Mark J. Rozell, " . . . Or, Influential as Ever?" *Washington Post*, March 1, 2000, A17.

13. It is surprising that Bauer staked his candidacy early on a state with a very small Christian Right population rather than save his resources for primary states with more voters likely to be hospitable to his views.

14. Exit polling data from http://cnn.com/ELECTION/2000/primaries/NH/results.html.

15. Exit polling data from http://cnn.com/ELECTION/2000/primaries/NH/poll.rep.html.

16. McCain had made it clear that his support for softened platform language did not lessen his own commitment to the pro-life agenda. Rather, he thought a softened platform position would signal that the GOP was a broad-based party. The issue of his support for fetal tissue research is more complicated. He had long opposed it until his close friend, former Arizona senator Morris Udall, who had been suffering from Parkinson's disease, urged McCain to rethink the issue. As for his statement about the *Roe* decision, McCain said that he had simply misspoken. He stood by his statement about letting his own daughter decide the abortion issue for herself. When asked the same hypothetical question about his daughter's being pregnant and considering abortion, Bush too replied, "It would be up to her." Of all the GOP candidates, only Keyes and Bauer said that answer was unacceptable for a pro-life advocate.

17. Thomas B. Edsall and Terry M. Neal, "Bush, Allies Hit McCain's Conservative Credentials," *Washington Post*, February 15, 2000, A1.

18. Text of Bush letter quoted in "Bush Regrets Visit to Anti-Catholic School," *Washington Times*, February 8, 2000, A8.

19. C-SPAN broadcast of February 16, 2000, McCain campaign rally at Furman University. Watching this speech on television, I thought McCain appeared truly embarrassed by this statement.

20. http://cnn.com/ELECTION/2000/primaries/SC/poll.rep.html

21. http://cnn.com/ELECTION/2000/primaries/MI/poll.rep.html

22. From McCain's standpoint, the attack on Robertson is perfectly understandable, given the vitriol that Robertson directed at him and at former senator Warren Rudman. But it is curious that McCain would include Falwell in the same denunciation, since Falwell had been silent about the GOP contest in 2000. In his anger at being treated unfairly by Robertson and some other Christian Right leaders not mentioned in the Virginia speech, McCain unfairly tarred Falwell as one of the chief offenders.

23. http://cnn.com/ELECTION/2000/primaries/VA/poll.rep.html

24. Nancy Gibbs, "Fire and Brimstone," *Time*, March 13, 2000, 33.

25. George Lardner Jr., "Abortion Foes Spend $200,000 to Beat McCain," *Washington Post*, March 7, 2000, A8.

26. Ibid.

27. Ralph Z. Hallow, "McCain's Religion Gambit Draws Quick Backlash in New York," *Washington Post*, March 1, 2000, A1.

28. Associated Press, "GOP Conservatives Give Bush the Edge," *Washington Times*, March 8, 2000, A12.

29. http://cnn.com/ELECTION/2000/primaries/NY/poll.rep.html

30. Quoted in Tom Curry, "Christian Coalition Rates McCain Highly," http://www.msnbc.com/news/412356.asp?cp1+1.

31. Ibid.

32. See Gary Langer, "Perception vs. Reality," abcnews.go.com/onair/Nightline/poll0000225.html.

33. See the various essays in Green, Rozell, and Wilcox, *Prayers in the Precincts*.

34. Clyde Wilcox, "Whither the Christian Right? The 2000 Elections and Beyond" (paper presented at Reflections of the Elections conference, Rice University, Houston, February 2001).

35. Lorie Slass, "Spending on Issue Advocacy in the 2000 Cycle" (Washington, DC: Annenberg Public Policy Center, 2001).

36. Wilcox, "Whither the Christian Right?"

37. FEC data; Wilcox, "Whither the Christian Right?"

Chapter 3: CONSERVATIVE PROTESTANTS AND THE FAMILY
W. Bradford Wilcox

1. "Conservative Protestantism" refers to Protestant Christians in the United States who are members of denominations that subscribe to a literal view of the Bible, stress a personal relationship with Jesus Christ, and emphasize the importance of personal evangelism. This category includes evangelical, fundamentalist, and Pentecostal Protestants in denominations like the Southern Baptist Convention, Assemblies of God, and Christian and Missionary Alliance, as well as nondenominational evangelicals and independent Baptists.

2. Robert Wuthnow and Matthew P. Lawson, "Sources of Christian Fundamentalism in the United States," in Martin Marty and Scott Appleby, eds., *Accounting for Fundamentalisms: The Dynamic Character of Movements* (Chicago: University of Chicago Press, 1994).

3. Christian Smith, *American Evangelicalism: Embattled and Thriving* (Chicago: University of Chicago Press, 1998), 102.

4. James Davison Hunter, *Evangelicalism: The Coming Generation* (Chicago: University of Chicago Press, 1987).

5. Hunter, *Evangelicalism*; and Edward Shorter, *The Making of the Modern Family* (New York: Basic Books, 1977).

6. Smith, *American Evangelicalism*.

7. James Davison Hunter, *American Evangelicalism: Conservative Religion and the Quandary of Modernity* (New Brunswick, NJ: Rutgers University Press, 1983).

8. Hunter, *Evangelicalism*.

9. W. Bradford Wilcox and Mark Chaves, "The Family Programming of American Religious Groups" (Princeton: Princeton University, Department of Sociology, 1999).

10. Rus Walton, *One Nation under God* (Nashville, TN: Thomas Nelson, 1987), 45.

11. Beverly LaHaye, *How to Develop Your Child's Temperament* (Irvine, CA: Harvest House Publishers, 1977), 69.

12. Gary Smalley and John Trent, *The Blessing* (Nashville, TN: Thomas Nelson, 1986), 15.

13. James C. Dobson, *The New Dare to Discipline* (Wheaton, IL: Tyndale House, 1992 [1970]).

14. Richard J. Fugate, *What the Bible Says about Child Training* (Tempe, AZ: Alpha Omega, 1980), 154.

15. Hunter, *Evangelicalism*.

16. Dobson, *New Dare to Discipline*, 94.

17. W. Bradford Wilcox, "Conservative Protestant Childrearing: Authoritarian or Authoritative?" *American Sociological Review* 63 (1998): 769–809.

18. Dobson, *New Dare to Discipline*, 36.

19. Anthony L. Jordan et al., *Report of the Baptist Faith and Message Study Committee to the Southern Baptist Convention* (Salt Lake City, UT: Southern Baptist Convention, 1998), 2.

20. James C. Dobson, *Love Must Be Tough* (Nashville, TN: Word Publishing, 1983), 235.

21. James C. Dobson, *Straight Talk: What Men Need to Know, What Women Should Understand* (Nashville, TN: Word Publishing, 1991), 129.

22. Gary Smalley, *If Only He Knew: What No Woman Can Resist* (New York: Harper, 1988), 25.

23. Ibid., 16.

24. Ibid., 13–14.

25. W. Bradford Wilcox, *Soft Patriarchs and New Men: Religion, Ideology and Male Familial Involvement* (dissertation, Princeton University, 2001).

26. Diana Garland, *Family Ministry: A Comprehensive Guide* (Downer's Grove, IL: InterVarsity Press, 1999), 556–57.

27. Wilcox, *Soft Patriarchs and New Men*.

28. Christian Smith and Melinda Lundquist, "Male Headship and Gender Equality," in Christian Smith, *Christian America? What Evangelicals Really Want* (Berkeley: University of California Press, 2000).

29. Smalley, *If Only He Knew*, 27, 30.

30. Melinda Lundquist and Christian Smith, "Religion and Women's Work Force Participation" (Society for the Scientific Study of Religion, Boston, 1999).

31. R. Albert Mohler, Jr., "Against an Immoral Tide," *New York Times*, June 19, 2000, A19.

32. Ibid.

33. Wilcox, *Soft Patriarchs and New Men*, 60.

34. James Coleman, *Foundations of Social Theory* (Cambridge: Harvard University Press, 1990).

35. Donald Capps, Religion and Child Abuse: Perfect Together," *Journal for the Scientific Study of Religion* 31 (1992): 1–14.

36. John M. Gottman, "Toward a Process Model of Men in Marriages and Families," in Alan Booth and Ann Crouter, eds., *Men and Families: When Do They Get Involved? What Difference Does It Make?* (Mahwah, NJ: Lawrence Erlbaum Associates, 1998), 183.

37. Christopher Ellison, John Bartowski, and Michelle Segal, "Conservative Protestantism and the Parental Use of Corporal Punishment," *Social Forces* 74 (1996): 1003–29.

38. John P. Bartowski and W. Bradford Wilcox, "Conservative Protestant Child Discipline: The Case of Parental Yelling," *Social Forces* 79 (2000): 265–90.

39. W. Bradford Wilcox, "Religious Identity and Parenting" (paper given at conference "The Ties that Bind: Religion and Family in Contemporary America," Princeton University, 2001).

40. Wilcox, "Conservative Protestant Childrearing."

41. Wilcox, "Religious Identity and Parenting."

42. My analyses of the General Social Survey and the National Survey of Families and Households both indicate that members of conservative Protestant denominations are more likely to be divorced and to divorce than other Americans.

43. Julia McQuillan and Myra Marx Ferre, "The Importance of Variation Among Men and the Benefits of Feminism for Families," in Booth and Crouter, *Men and Families*.

44. Lundquist and Smith, "Religion and Women's Work Force Participation."

45. Wilcox, *Soft Patriarchs and New Men*.

46. Michael Hout, Andrew Greeley, and Melissa J. Wilde, "The Demographic Imperative in Religious Change in the United States," *American Journal of Sociology* 107 (2001): 468–500.

47. Lundquist and Smith, "Religion and Women's Work Force Participation."

48. Melinda Lundquist and Christian Smith, "The Triumph of Ambivalence: American Evangelicals on Sex-Roles and Marital Decision-Making" (Society for the Scientific Study of Religion, Montreal, 1998).

49. Wilcox, *Soft Patriarchs and New Men*.

50. John P. Bartowski and Xiaohe Xu, "Distant Patriarchs or Expressive Dads? The

Discourse and Practice of Fathering in Conservative Protestant Families," *Sociological Quarterly* 41 (2000): 465–85.

51. Wilcox, *Soft Patriarchs and New Men*.

52. Smith and Lundquist, "Male Headship and Gender Equality."

53. Current Population Survey 2001, http://stats.bls.gov/cps; Lundquist and Smith, "Religion and Women's Work Force Participation."

54. Hout, Greeley, and Wilde, "The Demographic Imperative."

55. Robert Wuthnow, *After Heaven: Spirituality in America Since the 1950s* (Berkeley: University of California Press, 1998), 67.

56. Robert Wuthnow, "Mobilizing Civic Engagement: The Changing Impact of Religious Involvement," in Theda Skocpol and Morris Fiorina, eds., *Civic Engagement in American Democracy* (Washington, DC: Brookings Institution, 1999).

57. Leora E. Lawton and Regina Bures, "Parental Divorce and the 'Switching' of Religious Identity," *Journal for the Scientific Study of Religion* 40 (2001): 99–111.

58. My analyses of the General Social Survey (GSS) indicate that the percentage of Americans affiliating with the Southern Baptist Convention (SBC) declined from 5.9 in 1996 to 5.8 in 1999. For most of the last century, the SBC grew at a higher rate than the population at large. The GSS also indicates that fertility has declined and divorce has increased in the SBC since at least the early 1980s (when the GSS started tracking the denomination).

Chapter 4: THE EVANGELICAL RESPONSE TO HOMOSEXUALITY
Jeffrey Satinover

1. Dennis Prager, "Judaism, Homosexuality, and Civilization," *Ultimate Issues* 6, no. 2 (1990): 2.

2. It should be understood that metaphysical claims per se are not subject to evidentiary assessment.

3. E. M. Pattison and M. L. Pattison, " 'Ex-Gays': Religiously Mediated Change in Homosexuals," *American Journal of Psychiatry* 137, no. 12 (1980): 1553-62.

4. Robert Spitzer, "200 Subjects Who Claim to Have Changed Their Sexual Orientation from Homosexual to Heterosexual" (paper presented at the American Psychiatric Association Annual Convention, New Orleans, May 9, 2001).

5. This number was told to me by a former member of the NGLTF. A similar number was arrived at through independent investigations by the chief of staff of a prominent former congressman.

6. Joseph Nicolosi, A. Dean Byrd, and Richard Potts, "Retrospective Self-Reports of Change in Homosexual Orientation: A Consumer Survey on Conversion Therapy Clients" (*Psychological Reports,* June 2000). Data analysis performed by statisticians at Brigham Young University.

7. Mario Bergner, *Setting Love in Order* (Grand Rapids: Baker Books, 1993).

8. Andrew Comiskey, *Pursuing Sexual Wholeness: How Jesus Heals the Homosexual* (Lake Mary, FL: Creation House, 1989).

9. Ibid., 192.

10. Bergner, *Setting Love in Order*.

Chapter 5: THE SAME-SEX "MARRIAGE" DEBATE
David Orgon Coolidge

1. I put "marriage" in quotation marks because I do not believe that same-sex unions can be marriages. So as not to try the reader's patience, I will give up this irritating habit for the rest of the essay.

2. Perry's famous book was *The Lord Is My Shepherd and He Knows I'm Gay* (1972). He continues to serve as the leader of the MCC, although it has become considerably more militant. White's poignant story is told in *Stranger at the Gate* (1994). He has brought a mixture of openness and evangelistic fervor to the cause, because he can relate to people who have not taken the step that he has. For this reason, he has been instrumental in some of the highly visible meetings that have taken place in recent years with, e.g., Jerry Falwell. For this same reason, he remains an outsider to many gay circles.

3. The organization Call to Renewal is hard to place on this spectrum. Of the evangelical participants, Ron Sider and Richard Mouw are orthodox, but Jim Wallis and Tony Campolo are ambiguous on key issues, as are many other participants.

4. The fifteen states that have not passed a defense-of-marriage statute or constitutional amendment, as of the summer of 2001, are Connecticut, Maryland, Massachusetts, Nevada (although a constitutional amendment will be on the ballot in 2002), New Hampshire, New Jersey, New Mexico, New York, Ohio, Oregon, Rhode Island, Texas, Vermont, Wisconsin, and Wyoming.

5. See Chris Bull and John Gallagher, *Perfect Enemies: The Religious Right, The Gay Movement, and the Politics of the 1990s* (1996); also Donald Haider-Markel and Alesha Doan, "Bonfire of the Righteous: Geographically Expanding the Scope of the Conflict over Same-Sex Marriage" (unpublished ms., 1998). Two more general studies done before the widening of the same-sex marriage debate are Didi Herman, *The Antigay Agenda: Orthodox Vision and the Christian Right* (1997), and James W. Button, Barbara A. Rienzo, and Kenneth D. Wald, *Private Lives, Public Conflicts: Battles over Gay Rights in American Communities* (1997). All these studies take for granted the truth of the "gay side" and assume that the "evangelical side" is the problem that needs to be explained. On the battle over Colorado's Amendment 2 and the *Romer v. Evans* decision of the U.S. Supreme Court, there is a wider literature. For starkly contrasting perspectives written by activists on either side of the debate, see Stephen Bransford, *Gay Politics v. Colorado: The Inside Story of Amendment 2* (1994), and Lisa Keen and Suzanne Goldberg, *Strangers to the Law* (1998).

6. On organizational players in Hawaii and Vermont, see David Orgon Coolidge, "The Hawaii Marriage Amendment: Its Origins, Meaning and Fate," *U. of Hawaii L. Rev.* (2001), and David Orgon Coolidge and William C. Duncan, "Beyond *Baker*: The Case for a Vermont Marriage Amendment," 25 *Vermont L. Rev.* 61 (2000).

7. For the story of the Alaska same-sex marriage debate, including the *Brause* case and the Marriage Amendment, see Kevin Clarkson, David Orgon Coolidge, and William C. Duncan, "The Alaska Marriage Amendment: The People's Choice on the Last Frontier," 16 *Alaska L. Rev.* 213 (1999).

Chapter 6: EVANGELICALS AND ABORTION
Clyde Wilcox

1. Sidney Verba, Kay Lehman Schlozman, and Henry Brady, *Voice and Equality: Civic Voluntarism in American Politics* (Cambridge: Harvard University Press, 1995); Carol Maxwell, *Moral Mosaic: Meaning and Motivation in American Pro-Life Direct Action* (Cambridge University Press, forthcoming).

2. Greg D. Adams, "Abortion: Evidence of Issue Evolution," *American Journal of Political Science* 41 (1997): 718–37.

3. Elizabeth Adell Cook, Ted G. Jelen, and Clyde Wilcox, *Between Two Absolutes: Public Opinion and the Politics of Abortion* (Boulder, CO: Westview Press, 1992).

4. Lawrence H. Tribe, *The Clash of Absolutes* (New York: Norton, 1990).

5. Julia Riches and Clyde Wilcox, "Pills in the Public Mind: RU 486 and the Framing of the Abortion Issue," *Women & Politics* (forthcoming) .

6. Cook, Jelen, and Wilcox, *Between Two Absolutes*.

7. R. Michael Alvarez and John Brehm, "American Ambivalence Towards Abortion Policy: Development of a Heteroskedastic Probit Model of Competing Values," *American Journal of Political Science* 39 (1995): 1055–82.

8. Paul B. Fowler, *Abortion: Toward an Evangelical Consensus* (Portland, OR: Multnomah Press, 1987).

9. Mainline Protestant churches interpret this passage quite differently. For many, it is irrelevant since it implies the termination of a pregnancy against the will of the mother and father. For others, the term "mischief" is thought to mean the death of the mother; thus if the pregnancy is terminated there is a cash payment, but if the mother dies the event is treated as murder.

10. The Methodist statement can be found at http://www.umc.org/genconf/pets/ BD92/TEXT/d0071.html.

11. See page 102. Since none of the groups on average approves as many as five of the circumstances making abortion permissible, the scale goes only to five.

12. Charles H. Franklin, and Liane C. Kosaki, "Republican Schoolmaster: The U.S. Supreme Court, Public Opinion, and Abortion," *American Political Science Review* 83 (1989): 751–71.

13. Although evangelicals have less education on average than mainline Protestants, these differences are not large and have been declining over time. In the GSS from 1989 to 2000, the average educational level for white evangelical respondents was more than twelve years and the average for mainline Protestants was more than thirteen years.

14. Documentation of the results summarized in the following paragraphs is available from the author; contact him at wilcoxc@erols.com.

15. Of course it is impossible to support abortion for two-thirds of a condition. More intuitively, this might be interpreted to mean that two out of three evangelicals support abortion for one fewer condition on average than do mainline Protestants.

16. In this second part of the research Catholics are *more* distinctive than in the first part. This is because we have controlled for the source of Protestant opposition

to abortion—belief in an inerrant Bible—but not for Catholic belief in natural law or the teachings of the Pope. Catholics do not generally believe that the Bible is inerrant; yet many oppose abortion for other reasons.

17. For a more general argument see Ted G. Jelen, *The Political World of the Clergy* (New York: Praeger, 1993).

18. There were several attitudes in the GSS that might measure a pro-life sentiment, but euthanasia would seem to be the best for this purpose. Unlike the death penalty, in euthanasia the person who dies is not in any way guilty or "deserving" of death. Unlike abortion, however, in euthanasia the person who dies has generally chosen that course.

19. Of course, for Catholics this commitment is to the entire faith tradition, whereas for evangelicals or mainline Protestants it is for one denomination within a faith tradition. A growing minority of evangelicals attend nondenominational churches, and for these generally very orthodox Christians there can be no commitment to a denomination.

20. Adams, "Abortion: Evidence of Issue Evolution."

Chapter 7: EVANGELICALS AND BIOETHICS
Nigel M. de S. Cameron

1. D. A. Carson and John D. Woodbridge, eds., *God and Culture* (Grand Rapids: Eerdmans, 1992). The substantive fruit of Henry's university vision was the Institute for Advanced Christian Studies (IFACS), which has sought in a modest manner to stimulate leading evangelical thinkers in the research universities through publishing, conferences, and other projects, and has had significant indirect effects. It was at a conference convened by IFACS that the Council for Christian Colleges and Universities (originally the Christian College Coalition) was born. I served as president of IFACS in the mid-1990s, during which period the Council for Christian Scholarly Societies was launched as an IFACS affiliate to link the various Christian disciplinary organizations.

2. Earlier surveys of the bioethics agenda that have touched on the theme of this chapter include my essays "Bioethics: The Twilight of Christian Hippocratism," in Carson and Woodbridge, *God and Culture*; "Bioethics and the Challenge of the Post-Consensus Society," essay with responses, *Christian Scholar's Review* 23, no. 4 (1994); and "The Christian Stake in Bioethics: The State of the Question," in John F. Kilner, Nigel M. de S. Cameron, and David L. Schiedermayer, eds., *Bioethics and the Future of Medicine* (Grand Rapids: Eerdmans, 1995).

3. The representative "bioethics" organization is still called the European Association of Centres of Medical Ethics. The term "biomedicine" also has considerable currency, as in the European Convention on Biomedicine and Human Rights.

4. Joseph Fletcher, *Morals and Medicine* (Princeton: Princeton University Press, 1954).

5. Paul Ramsey, *The Patient as Person: Explorations in Medical Ethics* (New Haven: Yale University Press, 2d ed. 2002; first published in 1970).

6. The French philosopher and theologian's many books include *The Technological Society*, *What I Believe*, and *Reason for Being*.

7. Verhey edited with Stephen E. Lammers the compendium *On Moral Medicine* (Grand Rapids: Eerdmans, 1987, 1998). The contributors' list makes instructive reading. While it includes essays by a number of evangelicals, only one or two of them beside Verhey (John F. Kilner and perhaps Gilbert Meilaender) are known primarily for their work in bioethics. The volume edited by Verhey et al. entitled *Christian Faith, Healing, and Medical Practice* (Eerdmans, 1989) was for several years unique as an evangelical project. Verhey and Lammers's *Theological Voices in Medical Ethics* (Eerdmans, 1993) is useful, not least as a lament over the absence of the evangelical voice.

8. Nigel M. de S. Cameron, *The New Medicine: Life and Death after Hippocrates* (London: Hodder and Stoughton, 1991; Wheaton, IL: Crossway Books, 1992; new ed. Chicago: The Bioethics Press, 2001).

9. John F. Kilner, *Who Lives? Who Dies? Ethical Criteria in Patient Selection* (New Haven: Yale University Press, 1990).

10. Wesley J. Smith, *Forced Exit* (New York: Random House, 1997). Smith has co-authored several books on consumer rights with Nader. Smith generally writes in "secular" terms.

11. Wesley J. Smith, *Culture of Death: The Assault on Medical Ethics in America* (San Francisco: Encounter Books, 2000).

12. Calvin College sponsored the Verhey volume *Christian Faith, Healing, and Medical Practice*, but apparently not as part of a continuing project in the field.

13. This was brought home to me forcefully in 1992 when I quietly surveyed the curricular offerings of the member schools of the (then) Christian College Coalition (now Council for Christian Colleges and Universities) and discovered that their pre-med programs were largely unaffected by the development of bioethics; that, in essence, the core curriculum of the schools, with its Bible/religion and other components, was intended to serve the needs of pre-meds without any special focus beyond their chemistry or biology majors. One fruit of that research was a joint presentation in 1993 to the annual conference of Christian college presidents by C. Everett Koop, M.D., former surgeon-general, and me, to urge them to develop programs in bioethics for their undergraduates.

14. I was the convener of the meeting. Among the participants were John F. Kilner, then at the Park Ridge Center in Chicago (a multi-faith bioethics project), and C. Ben Mitchell, then with the Christian Life Commission (now the Ethics and Religious Liberty Commission) of the Southern Baptist Convention. There was representation from the Christian Medical–Dental Society (now the Christian Medical and Dental Association) and from Focus on the Family (through its medical-issues advisor, Reed Bell). The most striking discovery of the meeting was that none of the participants had met more than three or four of the others.

15. It should be noted that Loma Linda University (Loma Linda, CA), which houses a major medical school, offers an M.A. that is focused on clinical ethics. Loma Linda is affiliated with the Seventh-Day Adventist Church. The program was for some years directed by evangelical physician Robert Orr.

16. One recent response has been the establishment by the Wilberforce Forum of the Council for Biotechnology Policy as a focus for conservative Christian opinion (biotechpolicy.com).

17. James Peterson, *Genetic Turning Points* (Grand Rapids: Eerdmans, 2001). The logic of Peterson's argument is to commend both germline interventions—even for purposes of enhancement—and "reproductive" cloning.

18. An illustration and firstfruit of this process is the op-ed I co-wrote with law professor Lori Andrews, a leading biotech critic and a renowned pro-choice feminist, in the *Chicago Tribune* (August 8, 2001) under the title "Cloning and the Debate about Abortion." This piece used the cloning debate to demonstrate how protagonists from pro-choice and pro-life camps could make common cause.

19. The Lindeboom Instituut, Ede, Netherlands; the Centre for Bioethics and Public Policy, London, U.K. (www.bioethics.ac.uk); and the Center for Bioethics and Human Dignity, Bannockburn, Illinois.

20. The Eerdmans "Horizons in Bioethics" series began with *Bioethics and the Future of Medicine: A Christian Appraisal* (1995), of which I am co-editor with John F. Kilner and David L. Schiedermeyer; other volumes have addressed *Genetic Ethics, The Changing Face of Health Care, Dignity and Dying,* and *The Reproduction Revolution.* An associated volume by Scott B. Rae and Paul M. Cox, *Bioethics: A Christian Approach in a Pluralist Age* (Eerdmans, 1999) offers a survey of approaches to the discipline.

21. Fellows—both evangelicals and Roman Catholics—include C. Ben Mitchell, Christopher Hook (Mayo Clinic), Robert P. George (Princeton University), Paige Comstock Cunningham (Americans United for Life), Samuel B. Casey (Christian Legal Society), David Stevens (Christian Medical and Dental Association), and William Saunders (Family Research Council). See biotechpolicy.com for details.

22. Christopher Hook, M.D., director of ethics education at the Mayo Clinic, testified before a House committee on stem-cell research. I myself testified before a House committee on human cloning and before a Senate committee on stem-cell research. For details see biotechpolicy.com.

Chapter 8: WELFARE REFORM, CARE FOR THE POOR
Kurt Schaefer

1. Marvin Olasky, *The Tragedy of American Compassion* (Wheaton, IL: Crossway Books, 1992). This book appears to represent the opinion of many evangelicals and also seems to have had considerable influence in secular political circles.

2. Ronald J. Sider, *Just Generosity: A New Vision for Overcoming Poverty in America* (Grand Rapids: Baker Books, 1999). Sider's thinking appears to represent the views of most evangelicals who are not represented by Olasky. He has considerable public prominence as a spokesperson for evangelicalism.

3. John Schneider, *Godly Materialism: Rethinking Money and Possessions* (Downers Grove, IL: InterVarsity Press, 1994). This book is more a study of the biblical theology relevant to thinking about poverty policy than a handbook on such policy. Schneider is, like Sider, a theologian, and some sections of his book appear to criticize Sider's positions.

4. Amy L. Sherman, *Restorers of Hope: Reaching the Poor in Your Community with Church-Based Ministries that Work* (Wheaton, IL: Crossway Books, 1997). Sherman's visibility as an articulate evangelical from the political mainstream, with

both scholarly credentials (Ph.D. in government) and practical experience (as a large evangelical congregation's minister of social ministry), makes this book a reasonable choice as representative of evangelical books on the sticky topic of congregations' responses to welfare reform.

Chapter 9: EVANGELICALS AND CHARITABLE CHOICE
Amy L. Sherman

1. Joe Klein, "In God They Trust," *The New Yorker,* June 16, 1997.
2. "In God's Name: Michigan Now Relies on Churches to Help People Leave Welfare," *Wall Street Journal,* March 17, 1997.
3. Jim VandeHei, "Some Texas Prisoners Get Religion—16 Hours a Day, 7 Days a Week," *Wall Street Journal,* January 26, 2001.
4. Marvin Olasky and Roy Maynard, "The Empire Strikes Back," *World,* July 29/ August 5, 1995.
5. For the full text of the FBO Code of Conduct, see Amy L. Sherman, *The Charitable Choice Handbook for Ministry Leaders* (Washington, DC: Hudson Institute and the Center for Public Justice, 2001).
6. "Charitable Choice," National Association of Evangelicals, March 2001.
7. Charles W. Colson, "America's Way Is to Help Thy Neighbor," *Los Angeles Times,* January 31, 2001.
8. Terry Eastland, "Is Charitable Choice Unconstitutional?" *Washington Times,* February 5, 2001.
9. Susan Orr, Family Research Council, letter to author, April 18, 2001.
10. Laura Meckler, "Conservatives Rally Around Bush Plan," Associated Press, April 11, 2001.
11. Ronald J. Sider and Heidi Rolland Unruh, "No Aid to Religion?" in E. J. Dionne Jr., and John J. DiIulio Jr., eds., *What's God Got to Do with the American Experiment?* (Washington, DC: Brookings Institution Press, 2000), 131.
12. Jim Wallis, "Eyes on the Prize," *Sojourners,* May-June 2001.
13. Transcript, "Talk of the Nation," National Public Radio, March 15, 2001, 1.
14. Ibid., 2.
15. Ibid., 8.
16. Ibid., 4.
17. "Beating the Bearhug," *World,* October 7, 2000.
18. Ibid.
19. Franklin Graham, "We Appreciate the Help, but We Remain Christian," *Raleigh News and Observer,* April 8, 2001.
20. Ibid.
21. Quoted in Stacy Mattingly, "Policy Makers Struggle with Compassionate Conservatism," *Newsroom-Online,* March 26, 2001.
22. "Pat Robertson Expresses Concern with Bush Religion Plan," Associated Press, February 21, 2001.
23. Quoted in Roy Maynard, "Fighting Poverty in Jesus' Name and with Taxpayer Funds?" *World,* August 15, 1998.
24. Joseph Loconte, *Seducing the Samaritan: How Government Contracts Are*

Reshaping Social Services (Boston: Pioneer Institute for Public Policy Research, 1997).

25. J. Brent Walker, testimony before the Subcommittee on the Constitution, Committee on the Judiciary, U.S. House of Representatives, April 24, 2001.

26. For a lucid discussion of the shift from strict separationism to neutrality theory, see Carl H. Esbeck, "A Constitutional Case for Governmental Cooperation with Faith-Based Social Service Providers," *Emory Law Journal,* Winter 1997.

27. Dietrich Gruen, "President-Elect Bush Encourages 'Faith-Based' Groups," *Middleton* (WI) *Times Tribune,* January 11, 2001.

28. "There's still concern that this takes away our freedom to present the gospel. Basically, I'd say most of our missions aren't taking any government money." Quoted in Diane Winston, "Strings Attached?" *Dallas Morning News,* March 4, 2000.

29. Quoted in Carla Crowder, "LoDo Rebirth Disrupts Street Life Rhythms," *Rocky Mountain News,* November 21, 1999.

30. Under the heading "Conservative/Evangelical Protestant," Chaves included the Southern Baptist Convention, the three main black Baptist denominations, other Baptists, and Pentecostals. African-American congregations were more enthusiastic about applying for government funds than were predominantly white congregations. Mark Chaves, "Religious Congregations and Welfare Reform: Who Will Take Advantage of 'Charitable Choice'?" The Aspen Institute, Nonprofit Sector Research Fund, Working Paper Series (Spring 1999), 9.

31. Amy L. Sherman, *The Growing Impact of Charitable Choice* (Washington, DC: Center for Public Justice, 2000). The nine states were California, Illinois, Massachusetts, Michigan, Mississippi, New York, Texas, Virginia, and Wisconsin.

32. Telephone interview, January 18, 2001.

33. Gruen, "President-Elect Bush Encourages 'Faith-Based' Groups."

Chapter 10: THE LOYAL OPPOSITION
David Sikkink

1. In this paper, I use "evangelical" to refer to the movement that began to separate from fundamentalism in the 1940s. Evangelicals attempted to oppose fundamentalist separatism by moving conservative religious traditions into contact with the surrounding culture and society. (See two works by George M. Marsden, both published by Eerdmans: *Reforming Fundamentalism: Fuller Seminary and the New Evangelicalism,* 1987, and *Understanding Fundamentalism and Evangelicalism,* 1991.) One of the distinctive traits of evangelicals has been their emphasis on the importance on religious presence in public institutions—a strategy of engaged orthodoxy. See, e.g., Mark D. Regnerus and Christian Smith, "Selective Deprivation among American Religious Traditions: The Reversal of the Great Reversal," *Social Forces* 76 (4): 1347–72. The evangelical sense of a custodial relationship of religion in relation to public life—in which religious believers are obligated to participate in public life to help preserve it from ruin—may increase the extent to which evangelicals see interaction with a diverse and secular world as a religious calling. On the custodial relationship see Grant Wacker, "Uneasy in Zion," in George M. Marsden, ed., *Evangelicalism and Modern America* (Eerdmans, 1984).

2. Robert Wuthnow, "Mobilizing Civic Engagement: The Changing Impact of

Religious Involvement," in Theda Skocpol and Morris P. Fiorina, eds., *Civic Engagement in American Democracy* (Washington, DC: Brookings Institution Press, 1999).

3. See Robert D. Putnam, *Bowling Alone: The Collapse and Revival of American Community* (NewYork: Simon & Schuster, 2000).

4. Michael R. Welch, David Sikkink, and Carolyn Bond, "Religion and General Trust," 2001 (unpublished).

5. The dataset is the 2000 General Social Survey, conducted by the National Opinion Research Center. Evangelicals are defined as those who meet three conditions: they self-identify as "evangelical," do not view the Bible as a "book of fables," and attend church services at least several times a year. (In addition, to reduce measurement error, self-identified evangelicals in the Evangelical Lutheran Church in America were considered "evangelical" only if they reported attending church at least every week.) Like evangelicals, Pentecostal respondents are self-identified, do not view the Bible as fables, and attend church at least several times a year. Mainline respondents are also self-identified.

6. General Social Survey (see note 5). The results on confidence in schools and funding of education hold up after statistical controls are applied for age, education, sex, race, marital status, children under six, region, and urban/rural residence.

7. These results are based on data from the 1996 Religious Identity and Influence Survey. Religious categories are based on self-identity, though Pentecostals are identified through denomination. These results are net of a standard set of demographic control variables, including measures of school quality and crime rates.

8. David Sikkink, "The Social Sources of Alienation from Public Schools," *Social Forces* 78 (1): 51–86.

9. See Stephen Arons, *Compelling Belief: The Culture of American Schooling* (New York: McGraw-Hill, 1983).

10. This survey did not ask whether respondents considered themselves evangelical. Thus this analysis is based on responses to a question about the denomination of the church the respondent attends. The responses are classified into mainline, evangelical, and black Protestant categories according to the scheme of Brian Steensland et al., "The Measure of American Religion: Toward Improving the State of the Art," *Social Forces* 79 (1): 291–318. The data are from the National Election Study, conducted by the University of Michigan. The results reported are net of controls for age, education, sex, race, marital status, and children under 18 in household.

11. 1996 Religious Identity and Influence Survey (see note 7).

12. Sikkink, "Social Sources of Alienation."

13. 1996 Religious Identity and Influence Survey (see note 7).

14. General Social Survey (see note 5). Fundamentalists are self-identified and pass the same screens as evangelicals.

15. Again, these results are net of the standard control variables; see note 6.

16. David Sikkink and Andrea Mihut, "Religion and the Politics of Multiculturalism," *Religion and Education* 27 (2001): 30–46.

17. 1996 Religious Identity and Influence Survey (see note 7).

18. See Christian Smith, *Christian America? What Evangelicals Really Want* (Berkeley: University of California Press, 2000).

19. These interviews were conducted as part of a larger project on evangelicals and public life. A total of 187 evangelicals were interviewed from several areas of the country. For details on the sampling strategy, see Christian Smith et al., *American Evangelicalism: Embattled and Thriving* (Chicago: University of Chicago Press, 1998).

20. Again, this survey did not ask a religious identity question. This analysis is based on the denomination of the respondent, which is recoded according to the scheme of Steensland et al. (see note 10). The data are from the Social Capital Benchmark Survey. The results are net of age, sex, race, education, income, children under six, region, and urban/rural residence.

21. General Social Survey (see note 5).

22. This estimate is based on data from the National Center for Education Statistics, which is part of the U.S. Department of Education. See also David Sikkink, "Speaking in Many Tongues: Diversity Among Christian Schools," *Education Matters* 1 (2001): 36–45

23. See Alan Peshkin, *God's Choice: The Total World of a Fundamentalist Christian School* (Chicago: University of Chicago Press, 1986); and Susan D. Rose, *Keeping Them Out of the Hands of Satan: Evangelical Schooling in America* (New York: Routledge, 1988).

24. The dataset is the National Household Education Survey. I use the parent file, which includes interviews with 9,900 parents with children in the sixth through twelfth grade. The results are net of age, highest education in household, income, home ownership, race, work hours per week, family structure, region, urban/rural residence, political knowledge, attention to the news, political efficacy, church attendance, and extent of parental involvement in child's school.

25. Sikkink, "Social Sources of Alienation."

26. See Anthony S. Bryk, Valerie E. Lee, and Peter B. Holland, *Catholic Schools and the Common Good* (Cambridge: Harvard University Press, 1993).

27. Sikkink, "Speaking in Many Tongues."

28. See Melinda Bollar Wagner, *God's Schools: Choice and Compromise in American Society* (New Brunswick, NJ: Rutgers University Press, 1990).

29. See Sidney Verba, Kay Lehman Schlozman, and Henry E. Brady, *Voice and Equality: Civic Voluntarism in American Politics* (Cambridge: Harvard University Press, 1995).

30. Wuthnow, "Mobilizing Civic Engagement."

31. National Household Education Survey. Results are net of highest education in household, family income, sex of respondent, family structure, children under six in household, age of child, region, urban/rural residence, work hours per week, and church attendance.

Chapter II: FAITH THAT SEPARATES
Michael Emerson

1. Michael O. Emerson and Christian Smith, *Divided by Faith: Evangelical Religion and the Problem of Race in America* (New York: Oxford University Press, 2000).

2. Charles Jaret, *Contemporary Racial and Ethnic Relations* (New York: Harper Collins College Publishers, 1995), 394.

3. This information is available in data from the Bureau of Labor Statistics.

4. Charles E. Hurst, *Social Inequality: Forms, Causes and Consequences* (Boston: Allyn & Bacon, 1998), 147.

5. This information is available in poverty data at www.census.gov.

6. Melvin L. Oliver and Thomas M. Shapiro, *Black Wealth/White Wealth: A New Perspective on Racial Inequality* (New York: Routledge, 1995).

7. Douglas S. Massey and Nancy A. Denton, *American Apartheid: Segregation and the Making of the Underclass* (Cambridge: Harvard University Press, 1993).

8. Richard Williams, Reynold Nesiba, and Eileen McConnell, "The Changing Face of Inequality in Home Mortgage Lending," May 2001, at http://www.nd.edu/~rwilliam/research/cfi2000.html.

9. May 2001, at http://www.witi.com/center/researchstatist/glassceilingrep/executivesummar.pdf.

10. Bureau of the Census, *Statistical Abstract of the United States, 1998* (Washington, DC: U.S. Government Printing Office).

11. Emerson and Smith, *Divided by Faith*, chap. 1.

12. Most criminology textbooks discuss this fact in more detail.

13. Bill McCartney, with David Halbrook, *Sold Out: Becoming Man Enough to Make a Difference* (Waco, TX: Word Publishing, 1997).

14. Ann Swidler, "Culture in Action: Symbols and Strategies," *American Sociological Review* 51 (1986): 273–86.

15. William H. Sewell, "A Theory of Structure: Duality, Agency, and Transformation," *American Sociological Review* 57 (1992): 1–29.

16. General Social Survey, 1996.

17. Michael O. Emerson, Christian Smith, and David Sikkink, "The Religious Factor in Explanations of Black-White Inequality: A Quantitative and Qualitative Analysis of White Conservative Protestants," *Social Problems* 46 (1999): 398–417.

18. Rodney Stark, *Wayward Shepherds: Prejudice and the Protestant Clergy* (New York: Harper & Row, 1971), 102–3; John Woodbridge, Mark A. Noll, and Nathan O. Hatch, *The Gospel in America: Themes in the Story of America's Evangelicals* (Grand Rapids: Zondervan, 1979), 246.

19. Stephen Hart, *What Does the Lord Require? How American Christians Think about Economic Justice* (New York: Oxford University Press, 1992), 50–52.

20. Lyman A. Kellstedt and Corwin Smidt, "Measuring Fundamentalism: An Analysis of Different Operational Strategies," *Journal for the Scientific Study of Religion* 30 (1991): 259–78.

21. Richard A. Apostle et al., *The Anatomy of Racial Attitudes* (Berkeley: University of California Press, 1983).

22. James R. Kluegel, "Trends in White Explanations of the Black-White Gap in Socioeconomic Status, 1977–1989," *American Sociological Review* 55 (1990): 512–25.

23. Martin Gilens, "Racial Attitudes and Opposition to Welfare," *Journal of Politics* 57 (1995): 994–1014.

24. Cornel West, *Race Matters* (Boston: Beacon Press, 1993), 13.

25. Ibid., 95.

26. Ibid., 12.

27. Mary R. Jackman and Marie Crane, "'Some of My Best Friends Are Black':

Interracial Friendship and Whites' Racial Attitudes" (*Public Opinion Quarterly* 50 (1986): 459–86.
   28. *Christianity Today*, October 2, 2000, 34–49.
   29. Ibid., November 13, 2000, Letters to the Editor.

Chapter 12: CREATING A DIVERSE URBAN EVANGELICALISM
Rhys H. Williams and R. Stephen Warner

   1. See, e.g., Michael J. Donohue and Peter L. Benson, "Religion and the Well-Being of Adolescents," *Journal of Social Issues* 51 (1995): 145–60.
   2. See, e.g., Christian Smith et al., *American Evangelicals: Embattled and Thriving* (Chicago: University of Chicago Press, 1998).
   3. Leaders from one church estimated that 60 percent of their senior high group come to church with their parents.
   4. Some sociological scholarship is beginning to explore the effects of these "virginity pledges." Bearman and Bruckner report that pledge signers (e.g., those participating in the "True Love Waits" campaign) are significantly more likely to delay intercourse than non-pledgers. Peter S. Bearman and Hannah Bruckner, "Promising the Future: Virginity Pledges and First Intercourse," *American Journal of Sociology* 106, no. 4 (2001): 859–912. Interestingly, and in keeping with our idea that the urban ministry programs we have observed work in part because they seem "edgy" and somewhat countercultural, Bearman and Bruckner report that the "pledge effect" on delaying sexual activity is much more likely if there are some but not too many other pledgers around. It must seem non-normative, almost as a sign of rebellion, and mark the young people off with a special collective identity. Significantly, when those who pledge do in fact engage in first intercourse, they are much less likely than non-pledgers to use contraception.
   5. H. Wesley Perkins, "The Contextual Effect of Secular Norms on Religiosity as a Moderator of Student Alcohol and Other Drug Use," in D. Moberg, ed., *Research in the Social Scientific Study of Religion* (Greenwich, CT: JAI Press, 1994), 187–208.
   6. See, e.g., Rodney Stark and Roger Finke, *Acts of Faith: Explaining the Human Side of Religion* (Berkeley: University of California Press, 2000); and Laurence R. Iannaccone, "Why Strict Churches Are Strong," in N. J. Demerath et al., eds., *Sacred Companies* (New York: Oxford University Press, 1998), 269–91.
   7. Latinos have higher rates of cross-cultural or cross-ethnic marriage than either blacks or whites. In particular, the rate of black-white intermarriage is much lower than either the black-Hispanic or the Hispanic-Anglo rate.
   8. See, e.g., Michelle Lamont and Marcel Fournier, eds., *Cultivating Differences* (Chicago: University of Chicago Press, 1992).

Chapter 13: INTERNATIONAL ENGAGEMENT
Allen D. Hertzke

   1. "Relief Operations Endangered," *Christianity Today*, April 24, 2000.
   2. Gilles Kepel, *The Revenge of God: The Resurgence of Islam, Christianity, and Judaism in the Modern World*, trans. Alan Braley (University Park: Pennsylva-

nia State University Press, 1994); first published as *La Ravanche de Dieu*, 1991.

3. Paul E. Pierson, "The Rise of Christian Mission and Relief Agencies," in Elliott Abrams, ed., *The Influence of Faith: Religious Groups and U.S. Foreign Policy* (Lanham, MD: Ethics and Public Policy Center/Rowman & Littlefield, 2001).

4. Samuel P. Huntington, *The Clash of Civilizations and the Remaking of the World Order* (New York: Simon & Schuster, 1998).

5. 1999 figures are from *2000 Britannica Book of the Year;* 1950 figures are from *Britannica Book of the Year 1950.*

6. David B. Barrett, "Annual Statistical Table on Global Mission, 1996," *International Bulletin of Missionary Research,* January 1996; and "A Century of Growth," *Christianity Today,* November 16, 1998.

7. Ann Motley Hallum, *Beyond Missionaries: Toward an Understanding of the Protestant Movement in Central America* (Lanham, MD: Rowman & Littlefield, 1996).

8. Huntington, *Clash of Civilizations,* 99.

9. This is a point made by Paul Marshall, *Their Blood Cries Out* (Dallas: Word, 1997).

10. Samuel Huntington, *The Third Wave: Democratization in the Late Twentieth Century* (Norman: University of Oklahoma Press, 1991).

11. Laurie Goodstein, "Christians Gain Support in Fight on Persecution," *New York Times,* November 9, 1998.

12. Ibid.

13. Robert Putnam, *Bowling Alone: The Collapse and Revival of American Community* (New York: Simon & Schuster, 2000).

14. Christian Smith, *Christian America? What Evangelicals Really Want* (Berkeley: University of California Press, 2000).

15. Cal Thomas and Ed Dobson, *Blinded by Might* (Grand Rapids: Zondervan, 1999).

16. Duane Oldfield, "Resisting the New World Order: The Emerging Foreign Policy Agenda of the Christian Right" (paper delivered at the annual meeting of the American Political Science Association, Atlanta, September 2–5, 1999).

17. Interview with Sam Ericsson, April 2000. Numerous publications and tapes of Advocates International echo these sentiments.

18. Ericsson interview. The quote from Tom White is from the March 2000 issue of the Voice of the Martyrs publication.

19. Testimony of Robert Seiple before the House subcommittee on International Operations and Human Rights, October 6, 1999.

20. Saperstein was elected the first chair of the Commission and Abrams the second.

21. Speech to the National Campaign of Conscience on Sudan symposium, November 6, 1998.

22. This assessment is based on interviews conducted from summer 1999 through summer 2000 with numerous congressional staff and key members of Congress, such as Chris Smith, Frank Wolf, and Sam Brownback, all of whom confirm a steady constituent concern about international human rights that seems deep and heartfelt.

23. This comment, from a meeting on September 15, 1999, between Secretary Albright and NGO representatives, has circulated widely in advocacy letters to Congress and the president.

24. Betty M. Cooney, "Hunger Strike by Elmhurst Pastor Urges Vallone to Keep Promise," *Queens Chronicle*, September 9, 1999.

25. Several of the advocacy groups were, in fact, consulted by the producers of "Touched by an Angel." The plot line involved a member of Congress pressed by her son to go to Sudan to see slave redemption taking place, against the wishes of a lobbyist concerned about the loss of gum arabic imported from Sudan.

26. Holly Lebowitz, "A Resurrection of Campus Activism," *Sojourners*, September-October 1999.

27. Gary A. Haugen, *Good News about Injustice* (Downers Grove, IL: InterVarsity Press, 1999).

28. Peter Benson and Dorothy Williams, *Religion on Capitol Hill* (New York: Oxford University Press, 1986).

29. Lori Montgomery, "Party Lines Blur for Area Lawmakers," *Washington Post*, May 24, 2000, A15.

30. Brownback staff member Sharon Payt, who worked for religious freedom in Eastern Europe and the former Soviet Union, recounted repeated instances of meeting religious leaders who faithfully carried with them letters written by Congressman Wolf as a shield against harassment.

31. A fuller discussion of Tony Hall's work is provided by Robert Booth Fowler, Allen D. Hertzke, and Laura Olson, *Religion and Politics in America*, 2d ed. (Boulder, CO: Westview Press, 1999), 130–31.

32. Ibid., 129.

Index of Names

Vanderbijl, Andrew, 234
Vang, Dr., 221
Van Leeuwen, Mary Stewart, 94
VAT proposals, 140
Verba, Sidney, 183
Verhey, Allen, 120, 122
Vermont, 94
Vietnam, 40, 221
Virginia, 41–43
Vogel, Barbara, 228
Voice of the Martyrs, 220, 224–25, 228, 235

Walker, J. Brent, 167
Wallis, Jim, 104, 163
Wall Street Journal, 157, 187
Wally, Pastor, 221
War on Poverty, 133
Washington Post, 157, 231
Washington Times, 163
Watts, J. C., 157, 163
Webster v. Reproductive Health Services, 107, 113–14
Wei Jingsheng, 233
West, Cornell, 201
Weyrich, Paul, viii
Wheaton College, 91, 162, 228
White House Office of Faith-Based

and Community Initiatives, 158, 161, 165, 168
White, Mel, 82, 93
White, Tom, 224, 235
Wilberforce Forum, 117, 123
Wilberforce, William, 230
Wilcox, Clyde, 47
Willett, Don, 158
Williams, Juan, 165
Wolf, Frank, 227, 229, 231, 233
Works Progress Administration, 133
World Evangelical Alliance, 216, 221, 235
World Magazine, 158, 161, 165, 224
World Relief, 217, 235
World Vision, 216–17, 224–25, 232, 235
World Vision Today, 224
World War I, 218
World War II, 12, 173
Wurmbrand, Richard and Sabina, 235
Wuthnow, Robert, 65, 173, 184

Yeshiva University, 89–90
Ye Xiaowen, 223–24
Youth and Religion Project, 207–8

Zogby poll, 43

ABOUT THE
ETHICS AND PUBLIC POLICY CENTER

The moral issues that shape foreign and domestic policy are central to the work of the Ethics and Public Policy Center. The Center is a non-profit institution established in Washington in 1976 to clarify and reinforce the role of the Judeo-Christian moral tradition in the American public-policy debate. The president is Hillel Fradkin; his predecessors were Elliott Abrams, George Weigel, and founder Ernest W. Lefever. Primary activities are research, writing, publications, and conferences. The Center has four main program areas:

Religion and Society works with Protestant, Catholic, Orthodox, Jewish, and Islamic scholars and religious leaders to create a more thoughtful encounter between religiously grounded moral values and the American public-policy agenda. The *Evangelical Studies* project is playing a major role in the development of evangelical Protestant social ethics and civic engagement. *Catholic Studies* help to clarify and deepen the understanding of modern Catholic social thought. The *Jewish Studies* project seeks to affect the debate over secularism, spirituality, and public policy within the Jewish community. The *Islamic Studies* project aims to nurture a productive discussion about the future relationship of Islam and American democracy. *Religion and the Media* seeks to improve religion reporting through seminars for reporters, editors, and producers.

Law, Culture, and Society assesses legal, moral, and cultural trends that affect society by altering its politics, institutions, arts, and beliefs. Among the areas of interest are Supreme Court decisions affecting freedom of speech and freedom of religion, the Constitution, and the state of American representative democracy.

Biotechnology and Society examines moral and religious problems presented by innovations in medical science and technology such as stem-cell research and cloning.

Foreign Policy addresses issues of America's political, economic, military, and human-rights responsibilities in the world; it seeks to clarify how America's religious traditions should affect its foreign policy.

The Center's website, www.eppc.org, offers extensive information about the work of the Center, and the quarterly Newsletter gives substantive reports on recent projects and activities. For a copy of the Center brochure and the Newsletter, please contact us online or by telephone, fax, or mail.

ETHICS AND PUBLIC POLICY CENTER
1015 Fifteenth Street NW ♦ Washington, D.C. 20005
202-682-1200 ♦ *fax* 202-408-0632 ♦ www.eppc.org

269